First World War
and Army of Occupation
War Diary
France, Belgium and Germany

5 CAVALRY DIVISION
Ambala Cavalry Brigade
Headquarters,
8th (King's Royal Irish) Hussars,
9 Hodson's Horse,
18 Lancers and 14 Cavalry Machine Gun Squadron
1 January 1917 - 27 February 1918

WO95/1164

The Naval & Military Press Ltd
www.nmarchive.com
Published in association with The National Archives

Published by

The Naval & Military Press Ltd

Unit 10 Ridgewood Industrial Park,

Uckfield, East Sussex,

TN22 5QE England

Tel: +44 (0) 1825 749494

www.naval-military-press.com

www.nmarchive.com

Contents

Document type	Place/Title	Date From	Date To
Heading	##		
Heading	5th Cavalry Division Ambala Cavalry Bde. Bde Headquarters Jan 1917-Feb 1918		
Heading	War Diary of Headquarters, Ambala Cavalry Brigade. From 1st January 1917 To 31st January 1917		
War Diary		01/01/1917	11/03/1917
Miscellaneous	Appendix "A"-Attached to Ambala Cavalry Brigade. War Diary for Month of March 1917.		
War Diary		13/03/1917	31/03/1917
Operation(al) Order(s)	5th. Cavalry Division. Operation Order No. 23.		
Operation(al) Order(s)	Ambala Cavalry Brigade Operation Order. No. 5		
War Diary		01/04/1917	30/06/1917
Miscellaneous	App. A		
Operation(al) Order(s)	Ambala Brigade Operation Order No. 12	03/06/1917	03/06/1917
Miscellaneous	March Table issued in conjunction with Ambala Brigade Operation Order No. 12.		
Miscellaneous	Administrative Instructions.	03/06/1917	03/06/1917
Miscellaneous	App. B		
Miscellaneous	Account of the Preparation for a Raid, and the actual Operation itself, carried out by the 9th. H. Horse, Ambala Cavalry Brigade on the night 18th/19th. June 1917.		
Operation(al) Order(s)	Ambala Brigade Operation Order No. 14	14/06/1917	14/06/1917
Miscellaneous	Table of Details Issued with Ambala Cavalry Brigade Operation Order No. 14.		
Miscellaneous	Headquarters Ambala Cavalry Brigade.		
Miscellaneous	Guns.		
Miscellaneous	Case No. 271		
Miscellaneous	Map Showing		
War Diary		18/07/1917	29/10/1917
Miscellaneous	Training Programme for the Week Ending 27th. October 1917.		
Miscellaneous	Training Programme for the Week Ending 3rd, November 1917		
War Diary		01/11/1917	31/12/1917
Miscellaneous	Ambala Cavalry Brigade. Appendix "A"		
Miscellaneous	Training Programme for the Week Ending November 10th, 1917. Appendix A		
Miscellaneous	Training Programme for the Week Ending 3rd, November 1917.		
War Diary		01/01/1918	28/02/1918
Operation(al) Order(s)	Ambala Cavalry Brigade Operation Order. No. 35	25/02/1918	25/02/1918
Miscellaneous	March Table for 26th, and 27th, February issued with Operation Order No. 35.		
Heading	5th Cavalry Division Ambala Cavalry Bde 8th (K.R.I.) Hussars Jan 1917-Feb 1918.		
Heading	War Diary of 8th (K.R.I). Hussars. From 1st January 1917 To 31st January 1917		
War Diary	Gamaches (Somme)	01/01/1917	28/02/1917

Heading	War Diary of VIII (King's Royal Irish) Hussars From 1st March to 31st March 1917 Vol 31.		
War Diary	Gamaches	01/03/1917	20/03/1917
War Diary	Hornoy	20/03/1917	20/03/1917
War Diary	Hornoy Wailly	21/03/1917	21/03/1917
War Diary	Wailly Cayeux	22/03/1917	22/03/1917
War Diary	Cayeux Bois de Mereaucourt	23/03/1917	23/03/1917
War Diary	Bois de Mereaucourt Devise	24/03/1917	24/03/1917
War Diary	Devise	25/03/1917	27/03/1917
War Diary	Villers Fancon	27/03/1917	29/03/1917
War Diary	Devise	28/03/1917	28/03/1917
War Diary	Devise Bois de Mereaucourt	29/03/1917	29/03/1917
War Diary	Bois de Mereaucourt Warfusee	30/03/1917	30/03/1917
War Diary	Warfusee	31/03/1917	31/03/1917
Heading	War Diary of VIII (King's Royal Irish) Hussars From 1st April to 30th April 1917 Vol 32		
War Diary	Warfusee-Abancourt	01/04/1917	14/04/1917
War Diary	Caulaincourt Wood.	14/04/1917	30/04/1917
Heading	War Diary of VIII (Kings Royal Irish) Hussars From 1st May 1917 to 31st May 1917 Vol 33		
War Diary	Caulaincourt Wood.	01/05/1917	14/05/1917
War Diary	Vermand & Bihecourt	15/05/1917	15/05/1917
War Diary	Bihecourt	16/05/1917	19/05/1917
War Diary	Pontru (M & A to St Helene-Bihecourt Rd) (Sheet 62c 1/40,000)	20/05/1917	20/05/1917
War Diary	Pontru Sector	21/05/1917	25/05/1917
War Diary	Bihecourt	26/05/1917	29/05/1917
War Diary	Caulaincourt Wood.	30/05/1917	31/05/1917
Heading	War Diary of VIII (Kings Royal Irish) Hussars From 1st June to 30th June 1917 Vol 34		
War Diary	Caulaincourt Wood	01/06/1917	05/06/1917
War Diary	Vadencourt R.17 a.1.9. Sheet 62C 1/40,000	05/06/1917	05/06/1917
War Diary	Vadencourt.	06/06/1917	23/06/1917
War Diary	Caulaincourt	24/06/1917	26/06/1917
War Diary	Caulaincourt Wood.	27/06/1917	30/06/1917
Heading	War Diary of VIII (Kings Royal Irish) Hussars From 1st July to 31st July 1917 Vol 35.		
War Diary	Caulaincourt Wood.	01/07/1917	07/07/1917
War Diary	Bivouac N of Tertry.	08/07/1917	12/07/1917
War Diary	Bivouac N. of Tertry Buire.	13/07/1917	13/07/1917
War Diary	Buire. Suzanne	14/07/1917	14/07/1917
War Diary	Suzanne Ville Sour Corbie	15/07/1917	15/07/1917
War Diary	Ville Sous Corbie Sarton	16/07/1917	16/07/1917
War Diary	Sarton St. Michel	17/07/1917	17/07/1917
War Diary	St. Michel	18/07/1917	31/07/1917
Heading	War Diary of VIII (King's Royal Irish) Hussars From 1st August to 31st August 1917 Vol 36		
War Diary	St. Michel Sur Ternoise (Pas De Calais)	01/08/1917	09/08/1917
War Diary	St. Michel Sur Ternoise	10/08/1917	31/08/1917
Heading	War Diary of VIII (King's Royal Irish) Hussars From 1st September to 30th September 1917 Vol 37		
War Diary	St. Michel Sur Ternoise P d. C	01/09/1917	30/09/1917
Heading	War Diary of VIII (King's Royal Irish) Hussars From 1st October to 31st October 1917 Vol 38		
War Diary	St Michel Sur Ternoise	01/10/1917	08/10/1917
War Diary	Steenbecque	09/10/1917	11/10/1917

War Diary	Watou Area	11/10/1917	14/10/1917
War Diary	Campagne	14/10/1917	15/10/1917
War Diary	Campagne Fauquembergues	15/10/1917	15/10/1917
War Diary	Fauquembergues Maresquel	16/10/1917	16/10/1917
War Diary	Maresquel	16/10/1917	19/10/1917
War Diary	Beaurainville	20/10/1917	31/10/1917
Heading	War Diary of VIII (King's Royal Irish) Hussars From 1st February to 28th February 1918 Vol 42		
War Diary	Sector A.1.	01/02/1918	01/02/1918
War Diary	Berteaucourt Ailly Le Haut Clocher	01/02/1918	01/02/1918
War Diary	Sector A.I	02/02/1918	03/02/1918
War Diary	Le Verguier	04/02/1918	15/02/1918
War Diary	Vermand	16/02/1918	18/02/1918
War Diary	Roisel Lihons	19/02/1918	20/02/1918
War Diary	Lihons	21/02/1918	22/02/1918
War Diary	Ailly Le Haut Clocher	23/02/1918	23/02/1918
War Diary	Ailly Le Ht Clocher	24/02/1918	28/02/1918
Heading	War Diary of VIII (King's Royal Irish) Hussars From 1st November to 30th November 1917 Vol 39		
War Diary	Beaurainville	01/11/1917	08/11/1917
War Diary	Beaurainville Longuevillette	09/11/1917	09/11/1917
War Diary	Longuevillette Bavelincourt	10/11/1917	10/11/1917
War Diary	Bavelincourt Suzanne	11/11/1917	11/11/1917
War Diary	Suzanne Cartigny	12/11/1917	12/11/1917
War Diary	Cartigny	12/11/1917	19/11/1917
War Diary	N.W. of Fins S of Marcoing	20/11/1917	20/11/1917
War Diary	S of Marcoing Ribecourt	21/11/1917	21/11/1917
War Diary	Ribecourt Equancourt	22/11/1917	22/11/1917
War Diary	Equancourt Bray	23/11/1917	23/11/1917
War Diary	Bray	24/11/1917	26/11/1917
War Diary	Bray Cauvigny Farm	27/11/1917	29/11/1917
War Diary	Cauvigny Farm Villers Faucon	30/11/1917	30/11/1917
War Diary	W. 6 Sheet 62	30/11/1917	30/11/1917
Heading	8th (K.R.I.) Hussars War Diary Vol 40 December 1917		
War Diary	Revelon Farm Heudicourt	01/12/1917	03/12/1917
War Diary	Villers Faucon Revelun Fm	04/12/1917	05/12/1917
War Diary	Villers Faucon	06/12/1917	07/12/1917
War Diary	Cartigny	08/12/1917	28/12/1917
War Diary	Tertry	29/12/1917	25/01/1918
War Diary	Sector A.I.	26/01/1918	26/01/1918
War Diary	Sector A.I. Tertry	29/01/1918	30/01/1918
War Diary	Sector A.I. Marcelcave	31/01/1918	31/01/1918
Heading	9th Hodson's Horse Jan 1917-Mar 1918 To Egypt. 5 Mtd Bde. Aus Mtd Div		
Heading	War Diary of 9th Hodson's Horse. From 1st January 1917 To 31st January 1917		
War Diary	Montieres	01/01/1917	30/03/1917
War Diary	Warfusee	01/04/1917	30/06/1917
War Diary	Field	04/07/1917	26/07/1917
War Diary	Ostreville and Marquay	01/08/1917	31/08/1917
War Diary	Ostreville	01/09/1917	31/10/1917
War Diary	Tennay	07/10/1917	07/10/1917
War Diary	Cavron St Martin	24/10/1917	09/11/1917
War Diary	Outre Bois	09/11/1917	09/11/1917
War Diary	Franvillers	10/11/1917	10/11/1917
War Diary	Bray	11/11/1917	11/11/1917

War Diary	Brusle	12/11/1917	21/11/1917
War Diary	Equancourt	22/11/1917	22/11/1917
War Diary	Etinehen	23/11/1917	25/11/1917
War Diary	Tertry	27/11/1917	30/11/1917
Miscellaneous	Appendix "B".		
War Diary	Janken road 1 mile S. of Gouzeaucourt	30/11/1917	04/12/1917
War Diary	Vauchelette Farm	05/12/1917	05/12/1917
War Diary	Villers Faucon	08/12/1917	08/12/1917
War Diary	Brusle	21/12/1917	21/12/1917
War Diary	Tertry Area	21/12/1917	31/12/1917
War Diary	Harbonnieres	30/01/1918	30/01/1918
War Diary	Flesselles	31/01/1918	31/01/1918
War Diary	Tertry	19/00/1918	19/00/1918
War Diary	Mouflers	01/02/1918	01/02/1918
War Diary	Vadencourt area	01/02/1918	15/02/1918
War Diary	Roisel	16/02/1918	16/02/1918
War Diary	Saleux	16/02/1918	16/02/1918
War Diary	Mouflers	26/02/1918	01/03/1918
War Diary	Marseilles	02/03/1918	06/03/1918
War Diary	Alexandria	15/03/1918	16/03/1918
War Diary	Tel El Kebir	17/03/1918	31/03/1918
Heading	18th K.G.O. Lancers Jan 1917-Mar 1918		
Heading	War Diary of 18th Lancers From 1st January 1917 To 31st January 1917		
War Diary	Bazinval	01/01/1917	01/01/1917
War Diary	Longroy-Gamaches	02/01/1917	02/01/1917
War Diary	St Adelaide	02/01/1917	02/01/1917
War Diary	Gousse Auville	06/01/1917	06/01/1917
War Diary	Le Lieu Dieu	08/01/1917	28/01/1917
War Diary	Bazinval	28/01/1917	28/01/1917
War Diary	Longroy	28/01/1917	28/01/1917
War Diary	St Adelaide	28/01/1917	28/01/1917
War Diary	Gousse Auville	28/01/1917	28/01/1917
War Diary	Le Lieu Dieu	28/01/1917	31/01/1917
War Diary	Bazinval Longroy-Gamaches St Adelaide Fousseauville Le Lieu-Dieu	01/02/1917	26/02/1917
War Diary	Bazinval Longriy St Adelaide Gousseauville Lieu-Dieu	01/03/1917	19/03/1917
War Diary	Villers Campsart Drosmesnil	20/03/1917	20/03/1917
War Diary	Fremontiers	21/03/1917	21/03/1917
War Diary	Velennes	21/03/1917	21/03/1917
War Diary	Uzenneville	21/03/1917	24/03/1917
War Diary	Hancourt Bernes Flechin Marquaix Hamelet	24/03/1917	31/03/1917
War Diary	Warfusee-Abancourt	01/04/1917	20/04/1917
War Diary	Caulaincourt Tertry area.	20/04/1917	30/04/1917
War Diary	Tertry Caulaincourt	11/04/1917	25/04/1917
War Diary	Tertry Caulaincourt area.	01/05/1917	15/05/1917
War Diary	Le Verguier	15/05/1917	28/05/1917
War Diary	Tertry-Caulaincourt	28/05/1917	05/06/1917
War Diary	Pontru	05/06/1917	20/06/1917
War Diary	Vadencourt	20/06/1917	23/06/1917
War Diary	Caulaincourt	23/06/1917	30/06/1917
War Diary	Tertry-Caulaincourt	01/07/1917	17/07/1917
War Diary	Roellecourt	18/07/1917	29/09/1917
War Diary	D.A.G. 3rd Echelon		
War Diary	C. G. S. Simla		
War Diary	Depot 18 L.		

War Diary	Roellecourt	01/10/1917	01/10/1917
War Diary	Thiennes	07/10/1917	11/10/1917
War Diary	Watou (Belgium)	12/10/1917	13/10/1917
War Diary	Heuringhen	14/10/1917	14/10/1917
War Diary	Fauquembergues	15/10/1917	15/10/1917
War Diary	Aubin St Vaast Bouin	16/10/1917	17/10/1917
War Diary	Aubin St Vaast Bouin and Ecquemicourt	17/10/1917	08/11/1917
War Diary	Barly	09/11/1917	09/11/1917
War Diary	Frechencourt	10/11/1917	10/11/1917
War Diary	Suzanne	11/11/1917	11/11/1917
War Diary	Brusle	12/11/1917	20/11/1917
War Diary	E of Bois Couillet	20/11/1917	21/11/1917
War Diary	Ribecourt	21/11/1917	23/11/1917
War Diary	Chipilly	24/11/1917	30/11/1917
War Diary	Sunken Road near V of Villers Guislain	30/11/1917	30/11/1917
War Diary	Sunken Road W 6 c	30/12/1917	30/12/1917
War Diary		01/12/1917	01/12/1917
War Diary	Abriel	01/12/1917	03/12/1917
War Diary	Lessons	03/12/1917	03/12/1917
War Diary	Villers Faucon area	04/12/1917	04/12/1917
War Diary	S.W of Goureaucourt	04/12/1917	08/12/1917
War Diary	Brusle	09/12/1917	21/12/1917
War Diary	Tertry	22/12/1917	18/01/1918
War Diary	E of Vadencourt & Tertry	28/01/1918	31/01/1918
War Diary	Tertry	18/01/1918	26/01/1918
War Diary	A.1 Sector E of Vadencourt	27/01/1918	27/01/1918
War Diary	Long	01/02/1918	01/02/1918
War Diary	Bellenglise & Vadencourt Neighbourhood	29/01/1918	31/01/1918
War Diary	Vadencourt Vicinity	01/02/1918	12/02/1918
War Diary	Vadencourt	12/02/1918	28/02/1918
War Diary	Guisemicourt	01/03/1918	05/03/1918
War Diary	Marseilles	05/03/1918	07/03/1918
War Diary	Malta	10/03/1918	10/03/1918
War Diary	Alexandria	15/03/1918	30/03/1918
Heading	Machine Gun Squadron Jan 1917-Feb 1918		
Heading	War Diary of Machine Gun Squadron. Ambala Cavalry Brigade. From 1st January 1917 To 31st January 1917		
War Diary	Tilloy.	01/01/1917	31/01/1917
War Diary	Tilloy Floriville	01/02/1917	28/02/1917
War Diary	Field	01/03/1917	31/03/1917
Operation(al) Order(s)	Ambala Brigade Operation Order No. 1.	19/03/1917	19/03/1917
Operation(al) Order(s)	Ambala Brigade Operation Order No. 2.	20/03/1917	20/03/1917
Operation(al) Order(s)	Ambala Brigade Operation Order No. 3.	21/03/1917	21/03/1917
Operation(al) Order(s)	Ambala Brigade Operation Order No. 4.		
Operation(al) Order(s)	Ambala Brigade Operation Order No. 5.		
Operation(al) Order(s)	Ambala Brigade Operation Order No. 6.	28/03/1917	28/03/1917
Miscellaneous	The Brigade will move to Warfusee-Abbincourt today as follows	30/03/1917	30/03/1917
War Diary	La Motte	01/04/1917	03/04/1917
War Diary	Bois D'Arquaire.	04/04/1917	14/04/1917
War Diary	Caulaincourt	15/04/1917	27/04/1917
Operation(al) Order(s)	Operation Orders No. 8.	13/04/1917	13/04/1917
War Diary	Caulaincourt.	01/05/1917	31/05/1917
Miscellaneous	Plan of Defence.	01/06/1917	01/06/1917
Operation(al) Order(s)	Ambala Cavalry Brigade Operation Order No. 11.	27/05/1917	27/05/1917
Operation(al) Order(s)	Secunderabad Cav. Bde. Operation Order No. 37.	14/05/1917	14/05/1917

War Diary		01/06/1917	30/06/1917
Operation(al) Order(s)	Ambala Brigade Operation Order No. 12.	03/06/1917	03/06/1917
Operation(al) Order(s)	Ambala Brigade Operation Order No. 24.	14/06/1917	14/06/1917
Miscellaneous	Table of Details, Issued with Ambala Cavalry Brigade Operation Order No. 24.		
Miscellaneous	Machine Gun Barrage and Fire Table.		
War Diary	Forward Party at Vadencourt and Back Party on Caulincourt	01/07/1917	01/07/1917
War Diary	On Omignon River	02/07/1917	07/07/1917
War Diary	Vadencourt forward Party	08/07/1917	08/07/1917
War Diary	Back Party	08/07/1917	08/07/1917
War Diary	Tertry	09/07/1917	31/07/1917
War Diary	Roellecourt.	01/08/1917	16/10/1917
War Diary	Wambercourt.	29/10/1917	31/12/1917
War Diary	Tertry	01/01/1918	30/01/1918
War Diary	Lamotte en Santerre	30/01/1918	31/01/1918
War Diary	Naours	31/01/1918	31/01/1918
War Diary	Cauvigny Farm	01/02/1918	16/02/1918
War Diary	Epagne	24/02/1918	27/02/1918

B.E.F. FRANCE & FLANDERS.

FITH CAVALRY DIVISION.

AMBALA CAV BDE H.Q.

1917 JAN TO 1918 FEB.

8 HUSSARS.

1917 JAN TO 1918 FEB.

9 HODSONS HORSE.

1917 JAN TO 1918 MAR.

18 LANCERS.

1917 JAN TO 1918 MAR.

AMBALA (14 CAVALRY)
MACHINE GUN SQUADRON
1917 JAN TO 1918 FEB.

1164

B.E.F. FRANCE & FLANDERS

FITH CAVALRY DIVISION.

AMBALA CAV BDE H.Q.

1917 JAN TO 1918 FEB.

8 HUSSARS.

1917 JAN TO 1918 FEB.

9 HODSONS HORSE.

1917 JAN TO 1918 MAR.

18 LANCERS.

1917 JAN TO 1918 MAR.

AMBALA (14 CAVALRY)

MACHINE GUN SQUADRON

1917 JAN TO 1918 FEB.

1164

1917-1918

5TH CAVALRY DIVISION

AMBALA CAVALRY BDE.

BDE HEADQUARTERS

JAN 1917-FEB 1918

SERIAL NO. 108.

Confidential

War Diary

of

HEADQUARTERS, AMBALA CAVALRY BRIGADE.

FROM 1st January 1917 191(TO 31st January 1917 191

Army Form C. 2118.

Vol VII

Instructions regarding War Diaries and Intelligence Summaries are contained in F. S. Regs., Part II, and the Staff Manual respectively. Title pages will be prepared in manuscript.

WAR DIARY
of
INTELLIGENCE SUMMARY.
AMBALA CAVALRY BRIGADE.
(Erase heading not required.)

Hour, Date, Place.	Summary of Events and Information.	Remarks and references to Appendices.
1st. January 1917.	New Year's Day. 3 Officers Corps Cav: attd. 8th. Hrs. for Instruction	(14 days)
2nd. " "	Ambala Pioneer Batt. entrained for duty with XV Corps.) Strength — Offcrs. / Men.: 6 / 240. 8 Hrs. ; 11. ø / 259. 9. H. H. ; 11. ø / 256. 18. Lcrs.	ø Includes 5 I. O. ø " 5 I. O.
4th. " "	Brigade Tactical Exercise. BOUILLANCOURT. C. O's and Corps Cav: Officers attended.	
5th. " "	Brigadier attended 18th. Lcrs. Tactical Exercise at MELLEVILLE.	
6th. " "	Brigadier inspected M. G. Sqdn. in marching Order.	
8th. " "	" attended 8th. Hussars Tactical Exercise.	
9th. " "	Pioneer Batt. transferred to Third Army, VI Corps for duty.	
11th. " "	Conference at B. H. Qrs. of C. O's and "X" Battery Commander reference Divisional Winter Scheme.	
12th. " "	Staff Ride with attached Corps Cavalry Officers. Inspection of Sig. Troop and B. H. Qrs. Transport by G. O. C.	
13th. " "	Conference at Div. H. Qrs. of Brigade Majors and Staff Captains. Capt. Gwatkin 18th. Lcrs. assumed temporarily duties of Staff Captain.	
15th. " "	Two Corps Cav: C. O's joined for a week's instruction.	
16th. " "	Capt. H. COLMORE A. D. C. to G. O. C. left Brigade on re-appointment to R. F. C.	
19th. " "	Brigade Tactical Exercise.	

...lab Singh & Sons, Calcutta—No. 34 Army C.—26-8-14—1,07,000.

Army Form C. 2118.

WAR DIARY
or
~~INTELLIGENCE SUMMARY~~.

AMBALA CAVALRY BRIGADE.
(Erase heading not required.)

Instructions regarding War Diaries and Intelligence Summaries are contained in F. S. Regs., Part II, and the Staff Manual respectively. Title pages will be prepared in manuscript.

Hour, Date, Place.	Summary of Events and Information.	Remarks and references to Appendices.
20th. January 1917.	Brig. GenL: Rankin CMG, DSO. proceed on Leave in France. Lt. Col. Mussenden, 8th. Hussars rejoined Brigade from the Curragh and assumed duties of GOC. (Temporarily)	
22nd. " "	Corps Cav: Officers left the Brigade.	
25th. " "	Brigade Conference on Divisional Winter Scheme.	
29th. " "	G.O.C. rejoined from leave in France.	
30th. " "	Major Dyce/9th. H.H took over Command of Pioneer Batt. from Major Rowcroft. 9th. H.H.	
31st. " "	Major Rowcroft/9th. H.H. proceeded with party of 5 Indian Officers and 1. Indian Orderly to England to form part of Imperial escort for opening of Parliament.	

T. W. Corbett Captain.
Acting Brigade Major, Ambala Cavalry Brigade.

Army Form C. 2118.

Vol VIII

WAR DIARY
or
~~INTELLIGENCE SUMMARY.~~

AMBALA CAVALRY BRIGADE.

(Erase heading not required.)

Instructions regarding War Diaries and Intelligence Summaries are contained in F. S. Regs., Part II, and the Staff Manual respectively. Title pages will be prepared in manuscript.

Hour, Date, Place.	Summary of Events and Information.	Remarks and references to Appendices.
1st. February 1917.	G.O.C. attended a Bombing Demonstration by 9th. H.H. Four Officers per Unit were present.	
3rd. " "	G.O.C. inspected horses of 8th. Hussars after exercise. Lt. V.C.Alcock R.of O. assumed duties of A.D.C. to G.O.C.	
6th. " "	G.O.C. inspected horses and billets of M.G.Squadron.	
7th. " "	Captain A.Graham MC. Brigade Major rejoined from Junior Staff School. Captain F.Gwatkin 18th. Lancers, attached to Divisional Staff. Captain T.W.Corbett re assumed duties of Staff Captain.	
8th. " "	Brigade Tactical Exercise conducted by G.O.C. on Sand Table.	
14th. " "	Captain R.Dening 18th. Lancers, was attached to Brigade Staff.	
15th. " "	Lt.Col. F.W.Mussenden conducted a Brigade Exercise. at the Headquarters of the 9th. H.Horse.	
20th. " "	The Major General inspected the horses of the three Regiments at exercise.	
22nd. " "	Lt. Col.F.W.Mussenden conducted a Brigade Tactical Exercise at TRANSLAY.	AG.

Army Form C. 2118.

Instructions regarding War Diaries and Intelligence Summaries are contained in F. S. Regs., Part II, and the Staff Manual respectively. Title pages will be prepared in manuscript.

WAR DIARY

or

~~INTELLIGENCE SUMMARY~~.

AMBALA CAVALRY BRIGADE.

(Erase heading not required.)

Hour, Date, Place.	Summary of Events and Information.	Remarks and references to Appendices.
24th. February 1917	The Brigadier visited the Pioneer Battalion in the 3rd. Army Area.	
26th. " "	The Brigadier attended a Tactical Exercise carried out by the 8th. Hussars.	
28th. " "	Captain G.B.Reeves, 9th. H.Horse, was accidently killed on a Musketry Inspection.	
	Captain R.Dening 18th. Lancers, terminated his attachment to Brigade Headquarters.	

[signature]

Captain,

Brigade Major, Ambala Cavalry Brigade.

Instructions regarding War Diaries and Intelligence Summaries are contained in F. S. Regs., Part II, and the Staff Manual respectively. Title pages will be prepared in manuscript.

WAR DIARY
or
~~INTELLIGENCE SUMMARY~~.

AMBALA CAVALRY BRIGADE.
(Erase heading not required.)

Army Form C. 2118.

Vol IX

Hour, Date, Place.	Summary of Events and Information.	Remarks and references to Appendices.
2nd. March 1917.	Funeral of Capt. G. B. Reeves 9th. Hodson's Horse took place at FRESSENNEVILLE. The Major General and Brigadier attended.	
3rd. March 1917	The Brigadier inspected the horses of the 8th. Hussars, 18th. Lancers and 9th. Hodson's Horse at GUERVILLE. A party of 9 Indian personnel (4 from 9th. H. H. and 5 from 18th. Lcrs) proceeded to EGYPT to be used as M. G. instructors in the HEDJAZ.	
5th. March 1917	Brigadier attended at Tactical Exercise carried out by 8th. Hussars under Lt. Col. F. W. Mussenden.	
6th. March 1917.	Brigadier attended Field Practices carried out by 14th. M. G. Sqdn.	
7th. March 1917.	The Brigadier (in place of G. O. C. Division) presented ~~xxx fxxxxxxxx~~ medal ribbons to individuals, for Distinguished Service in the Field.	
8th. March 1917.	Brigade Tactical Exercise had to be posponed owing to the weather. The Brigadier conducted a Conference at Brigade Hd. Qrs. on the 1st. phase of the Exercise.	
9th. March 1917.	14th. M. G. Sqdn. inspected by Corps M. G. Officer. The Brigadier attended the inspection.	
10th. March 1917.	Brigadier attended a demonstration by the 8th. Hussars of Hotchkiss Gun versus Rifle. 15 rifles proved equivalent in accuracy ~~xx~~ and rate of fire to 1 Hotchkiss Gun at 200 yards range.	
11th. March 1917.	Brig. Genl. Wardrop ~~xx~~ commanding 14th. Corps Artillery delivered a lecture at the School at GAMACHES. 37 Officers of the Brigade attended.	HH

APPENDIX "A" - Attached to AMBALA CAVALRY BRIGADE.

WAR DIARY for Month of MARCH 1917.

---------oOo--------------

<u>CONTENTS.</u>

(1) 1/100,000 Map.

(2) 5th. Cavalry Division Operation Order No. 23.

(3) Ambala Cavalry Brigade Operation Order No. 5.

Army Form C. 2118.

WAR DIARY

or

~~INTELLIGENCE~~ SUMMARY.

AMBALA CAVALRY BRIGADE.
(Erase heading not required.)

Instructions regarding War Diaries and Intelligence Summaries are contained in F. S. Regs., Part II, and the Staff Manual respectively. Title pages will be prepared in manuscript.

Hour, Date, Place.	Summary of Events and Information.	Remarks and references to Appendices.
13th. March 1917.	The Brigade was warned by wire to be prepared to move at 48 hours notice .	
15th. March 1917.	Brigade Tactical Exercise in the neighbourhood of HELICOURT and AIGNEVILLE . "The Pursuit" . Directed by the Brigadier and attended by Officers Commanding Units.	
16th. March 1917.	Pioneer Battalion started from ARRAS Neighbourhood to rejoin the Brigade	
17th. March 1917.	Brigadier attended a Rifle versus Hotchkiss Gun display by the 9th. H. H. Pioneer Battalion rejoined. Mounted sports 8th. Hussars GAMACHES.	
19th. March 1917.	Warning received that the Division would move Eastwards on the 20th. continuing the March on the following day.	
20th. March 1917.	The Brigade moved to the area round HORNOY . The horses all got under cover.	1/100,000 Map att Appendix (a).
21st. March 1917.	The march was continued to the area round CONTY. It snowed during most of the march. Conference at Divisional Headquarters PONT DE METZ.	
22nd. March 1917.	Move to CAIX area . Occasional snow storms. This was the last occasion when the horses and men all got under cover.	
23rd. March 1917.	The Brigade moved to bivouacs in BOIS DE MERTAUCOURT West of PERONNE. (a) Brigadier attended a conference at Division in PERONNE at 5 pm. 5th. Cav. Divn. Operation Order No. 23 was issued and discussed. The following Troops came under the Order of the Brigadier 1 Fld. Tp. 5th. Fld. Sqdn. RE. ,Mhow Cav. Fld. Amb.	

Instructions regarding War Diaries and Intelligence Summaries are contained in F. S. Regs., Part II, and the Staff Manual respectively. Title pages will be prepared in manuscript.

WAR DIARY
or
~~INTELLIGENCE SUMMARY.~~
AMBALA CAVALRY BRIGADE.
(Erase heading not required.)

Army Form C. 2118.

Hour, Date, Place.	Summary of Events and Information.	Remarks and references to Appendices.
24th. March 1917.	The Brigade moved into the line in relief of the 4th. and 3rd. Corps Cavalry. 9th. H. Horse on the right took over the line at ETREILLERS VAUX BEAVVOIS CAULAINCOURT POEUILLY XXXXXX XXXXXXXX. 18th. Lcrs. on the left relieved the 3rd. Corps Cavalry in the line FLECHIN BERNES Point 114 MARQUAIX. Touch was gained with the enemy practically all along the line. Brigade Operation Order No. 5 attached.	Appendix (a)
25th. March 1917.	Obtained touch with enemy all along the line. 9th. H. H. occupied VILLEVEQUE 3 am without resistance. A certain number of Infantry detachments both fom General Warde's Column and from 61st. Division came under commandx of Brigadier in the line. 1 Squadron 8th. Hussars wnnt to VAUX insupport of Major Fraser's Squadron at ETREILLERS. The Field Troop started on repairs to the ESTREES - BEAUVOIS Road through TERTRY and the Bridges there.	
26th. March 1917.	2 Squadrons 18th. Lancers and 3 Cars 9th. L. A. C. Battery co-operated with 1 Company 48th. Division in an attack on ROISEL. The attack proved successful, though the garrison of the village succeeded in getting away. Armoured cars dispersed about 40 Germans but did not cause much damage. 1 Prisoner reported taken. The Canadian Brigade on the left took EQUANCOURT and LONGUAVESNES.	
27th. March 1917.	The Canadian Brigade on the left occupied LIERAMONT in the early morning. The Canadian and Ambala Brigades were ordered to attack the villages on the line VILLERSFANCON SAULCOURT GUYENCOURT. The first named being the objective of the Ambala Brigade. "A" Battery RHA. 1 18pdr. Battery, 1 4.5. How Battery and 1 Sect. 60 pdr. Battery were put at the disposal of the Brigadier. There was to be a 40 minutes bombardment of the village commencing at 4.30 pm. after which 8th. Hussars were to attack the village by means of an enveloping movement round the Southern flank while two L. A. Cars were to approach the village along the MARQUAIX VILLERSFANCON Road and occupy its attention in front. The attack was entirely successful, 2 Sqdns. under Major Van der Byl having occupied the village by 5.25 pm.	

HG

Army Form C. 2118.

WAR DIARY
or
~~INTELLIGENCE SUMMARY~~.
AMBALA CAVALRY BRIGADE.
(Erase heading not required.)

Instructions regarding War Diaries and Intelligence Summaries are contained in F. S. Regs., Part II, and the Staff Manual respectively. Title pages will be prepared in manuscript.

Hour, Date, Place.	Summary of Events and Information.	Remarks and references to Appendices.
27th. March 1917. (contd)	Casualties to the 8th. Hussars in the actual attack on the village was 2 other ranks wounded. The prisoners and booty taken was 1 Officer and 10 men, 2 machine guns. The 2 L. A. Cars however suffered severely they were both put out of action by hostile machine gun fire within a quarter mile of the village, the whole teams of both Cars with the exception of one Officer were killed or wounded. The village was held that night by 3 Squadrons of the 8th. Hussars with one in support.	
28th. March 1917.	The Infantry and Corps Cavalry of the 3rd. and 4th. Corps took over the line and by seven pm. the Brigade was concentrated at follows :- Brigade Headquarters, ESTREES EN CHAUSSEE, 8th. Hussars, "X" Battery RHA. ,5th. Field Sqdn. RE. (less 1 Troop) DEVISE, 9th. H. Horse, MONCHY LAGACHE ,18th. Lancers, (less one Squadron left VILLERSFANCON) HANCOURT Orders were received at 7 pm. that the Division was being withdrawn West on the next day.	
29th. March 1917.	Brigade moved to their original bivouacs in MEREAUCOURT WOOD. It rained all day, and that night over half the men of the Brigade were out.	
30th. March 1917.	Brigade continued the march West to WARFUSEE ABANCOURT where the whole Brigade once again got under cover.	
31st. March 1917.	In billets. Conference was held at Brigade Headquarters to discuss any points relating to tactics, organisation, equipment which had been notived during the recent fighting.	

C. Graham Capt. — Bde Major — [illegible]

SECRET. 5TH. Cavalry Division. Copy No....3....

OPERATION ORDER No. 23.

Reference map.
1/100,000.

1. Information as already circulated.

2. The tasks of the Division are :-

(a) To ascertain the dispositions of the advanced hostile detachments.

(b) To ascertain the enemy's defences and strength.

(c) To picket the enemy so as to prevent his advancing and so as to give instant information of any withdrawal.

(d) To be ready to follow up the enemy if he withdraws.

Brig.Genl. Rankin.

Ambala Cav. Bde.
& attached troops
100 IX Corps Cyclists.
2 platoons III Corps
Cyclists.

3(a) AMBALA CAVALRY BRIGADE. (Strength as per margin) will be responsible for carrying out the above task between the lines VIEFVILLE (inclusive)-VILLERS ST. CHRISTOPHE -DOUCHY-ROUPY-ST. QUENTIN (all exc) and AIZECOURT LE HAUT -TEMPLEUX-LONGAVESNES-EPEHY- HONNECOURT (all exclusive)

Advanced detachments will be on the line GERMAINE-BERNES-MARQUAIX by 11. 30 am. The Brigade will advance via BIACHES-HALLE-PERONNE.

Touch to be established with the advanced detachments of the French.

BrigGenl. SEELY.

Canadian Cav. Bde.
and attached troops
XIV Corps Cav.Regt.
& Cyclist Bn. (Temporarily only)

(b) Canadian Cav. Bde(Strength as in margin)will be responsible for carrying out the above tasks between the lines AIZECOURT LE HAUT-TEMPLEUX-LONGAVESNES-EPEHY-HONNECOURT (all inclusive) and LE TRANSLOY- BARASTRE-BERTINCOURT-HAVRINCOURT (all inclusive)

Advanced detachments will be on the line TEMPEUX-AIZECOURT-LE BAS-NURLU-BUS-BERTINCOURT by 11. 30 am.

Touch to be established with the advanced detachments of Fifth Army (Anzac Corps) 'c) Divisional Headquarters and signal Squadron do not move.

(d) No. 9 LA.C. Battery will move at 9 am to FOUCAUCOURT and will there wait further orders.

Brig. Genl. GREGORY.

Sec'bad Cav. Bde.
& attached troops
Main Ammu. Column.
Field Squadron
(less 2 troops)
Sec'bad Field Amb.
A. H. T. Coy.

(e) Remainder of Division as in margin will march under orders of G. O. C. Sec'bad Cav. Bde.
Starting point X roads CHUIGNOLLES 10 am .
Route - CAPPY - S of FRISE.
Destination BOIS DE MEREAUCOURT.

"B" Echelons will however move to HERBECOURT and come under the orders of the senior Officer there.

Attachment of Corps mounted troops.

4(a) 1 Company of IV Corps Cyclists and 2 platoons III Corps Cyclists come under orders of G. O. C. Ambala Cav. Bde. at 11 am at ATHIES and ESTREES EN CHAUSSEE respectively. They will used principally for establishing relay posts between the Brigade and Divisional Headquarters and within the Brigade. The Wireless detachment of III Corps Cavalry at the same time and place.

(b) XIV Corps Cavalry Regiment and cyclist Battalion come under orders of G. O. C. Canadian Bde. at 10 am at MOISLAINS. He will report assuming command. A portion of the Cyclists may be used for relay posts as in (a) above. The rest will not be moved without reference to Divisional Headquarters.

Intercommunication

5(a) Brigades will communicate direct with Corps on whose front they are operating . For this purpose Liaison Officers of Corps Cavalry will report as follows :-

To Ambala Cavalry Brigade from III Corps
ESTREES EN CHAUSSEE - 11 am.

To Ambala Cavalry Brigade from IV Corps
ATHIES - 11 am.

To Canadian Cavalry Brigade from XIV & XV Corps
MOISLAINS - 10 am.

(b) Liaison Officers and Gallopers will report at Divisional Headquarters at 9 am (Ambala & Canadian) and noon (Sec'bad)

Aeroplanes.

6. R. F. C. Liaison Officer will arrange for two machines to be continuously on contact patrol from 11.30 am to 2 pm. and from 4.30 pm. to 6 pm.
And for as much of the rest of the day as is possible. The machines should between them work over the whole front of the Division.

Line of resistance.

7. The Line of Resistance in case of attack will be GERMAINE -BEAUVOIS-POEUILLY-BERNES-MARQUAIX-LONGAVESNES-LIERAMONT-NURLU thence EQUANCOURT-YTRES-BERTINCOURT, if in our possession, otherwise the line at present held by xxx infantry.

Instructions as regards holding and strengthening the above line will be issued later. Brigades will reconnoitre it and submit proposals as early as possible

8. Situation reports are required to reach Divisional Headquarters by 5 am and 5 pm.

9. Reports to PERONNE.

10. Acknowledge.

(Sgd) R. G. HOWARD VYSE.

Lt. Col. G. S.
5th. Cavalry Division.

Copies to :-1-21 Normal Distribution.
22 Cavalry Corps
23 Fourth Army
24 III Corps
25 IX Corps
26 XIV Corps
27 XV Corps
28 Anzac Corps
29 RFC. Liaison Officer.
30 O. C. "B" Echelon.

Issued by DR. at 5 pm.

AMBALA CAVALRY BRIGADE OPERATION ORDER. Copy No........

No.....5..........

Ref. map 1/100,000
Sheets 12,17 & 18.

1. Information is already given verbally.

2. The task of the 5th. Cavalry Division is
(a) To ascertain the dispositions of the advanced hostile detachments.
(b) To ascertain the enemy's defences and strength.
(c) To picket, the enemy so as to prevent his advancing and so to give instant information of any withdrawal.
(d) To be ready to follow up the enemy if he withdraws.

(3) The Ambala Brigade (and attached troops) in conjunction with XIV French Corps Cavalry on its right and Canadian Bde. on its left will carry out the above task as follows commencing tomorrow.

Commander Lt. Col. Beatty 9th. H. H. 9th. H. Horse. 1 Sect. 14th. M. G. Sqdn. 2 platoons 4th. Corps Cyclists. "A" Echelon.	(a) Right Sector Detachment. (Strength as per margin) will cross the SOMME River at ST. CHRIST BRIOST and will reach the line approx. LANCHY- TERTRY with detachments on the line GERMAINE-BEAUVOIS-POEUILLY 11.15 am.
Commander. Lt Col. Muspratt 18th. Lcrs. 1 Sect. 14th. MG. Sqdn. 2 platoons 3rd. Corps Cyclists.	(b) Left Sector detachment (Strength as per margin) will march at 8.15 am from bivouac via BIACHES-FAUBOURG DE PARIS - PERONNE-PERONNE Stn - Cross roads 1 mile SW. of CARTIGNY to reach the line ∅ with detachments on the line FLECHIN-BERNES-MARQUAIX by 11.15 am. Small detachments can cross the SOMME River at ETERPIGNY. ∅ HANCOURT - BOUCLY.
B. H. Q. Fld. Tp. RE. 14th. MG. Sqdn. (Sections 2) 8th. Hussars "X" Battery L. S. Ammu. Col. Mhow F. A. M. V. S. "A" Echelon.	(c) Remainder of the Brigade order as per margin will pass road Junction North of FLAUCOURT at 8.45 am and will move in rear of Col. Muspratt's detachment to MONS-EN-CHAUSSEE. (Less "A" Echelon Left Sector detachment) will be brigaded under Captain Houston 8th. Hussars at cross roads North of T of HERBECOURT at 8.45 am.

"B" Echelon will move under orders of Staff Captain.

4. Boundary lines between sectors.
(a) Between Right Sector and XIV French Corps
BIEFVILLE (inc)-VILLERS ST. CHRISTOPHE-DOUCHY-ROUPY-ST. QUENTIN (exc. to right Sector)
(b) Between right and left Sectors.
BRIE -VERMAND (inc. to right Sector)
(c) Between Left Sector and Canadian Brigade.
AIZECOURT LE HAUT -TEMPLEUX-LONGAVESNES-EPEHY-HONNECOURT-(all exc. to left Sector)

5. Touch will be obtained as early as possible between Sectors and between sectors and advanced detachments of formations on either flank. Touch gained will be reported to Brigade Report Centre.

6. In the event of our detachments being driven in by a strong hostile force the main line of resistance will be GERMAINE-BEAUVOIS-POEUILLY-BERNES-MARQUAIX-LONGAVESNES-LIERAMONT-NURLU.

7. Mhow Field Ambulance will form a dresing station at the P of PRUSLE.

The Tent Section will be at FALVY.

8. Further instructions later.

9. Brigade Report Centre closes at BOIS DE MEREAUCOURT 8.30 am and opens MONS EN CHAUSSEE at 11 am.

10. Acknowledge.

Captain.

Brigade Major, Ambala Cavalry Brigade.

Issued at 11 pm.

Copy No. 1 8th. Hussars.
2 9th. H. H.
3 18th. Lcrs.
4 M. G. Sqdn.
5 . "X" Battery
6 Mhow F. A.
7 Fld. Troop RE.
8 5th. Cav. Divn.
9 4th. Corps
10. 3rd. Corps
11 War Diary
12. Office.
13. Can. Bde.

Seen

Instructions regarding War Diaries and Intelligence Summaries are contained in F. S. Regs., Part II, and the Staff Manual respectively. Title pages will be prepared in manuscript.

WAR DIARY

or

~~INTELLIGENCE SUMMARY.~~

AMBALA CAVALRY BRIGADE.
(Erase heading not required.)

5 DIV

Army Form C. 2118.

Hour, Date, Place.	Summary of Events and Information.	Remarks and references to Appendices.
1st. April 1917.	In billets at WARFUSEE ABANCOURT . Cleaning up and refitting.	
4th. " "	Dismounted party arrived from GAMACHES.	
5th. " "	Intercommunication Scheme between Aircraft and Signal Units of the Brigade.	
6th. " "	Dismounted Party 9th. H.Horse and 18th. Lancers left for attachment to 3rd. Corps, to build roads, erect huts etc. They were billeted at MARLY Camp 500x N.E. of CHUIGNOLLES. 8th. Hussars Dismounted party left at HAMEL.	
7th. " "	Brigade warned to be ready to move at 8 hours notice from midnight 8th/9th.	
8th. " "	9th. H.Horse and 18th. Lancers Dismounted parties ordered to concentrate at FOUCAUCOURT on the 9th. for road repair duties under 3rd. Corps. Major V.A.S.Keighley, 18th. Lancers ordered to be prepared to proceed to MARSEILLES.	Appendix 'A' Map 1/100,000 Amiens
9th. " "	Major V.A.S.Keighley 18th. Lancers ordered to proceed to MARSEILLES in relief of Capt. Henry 18th. Lancers Brigade Route March had to be postponed on account of snow and rain in the morning. 1st., 3rd., and 5th. Armies started the offensive against the German Trench system.	

Army Form C. 2118.

WAR DIARY

or

~~INTELLIGENCE/SUMMARY~~.

AMBALA CAVALRY BRIGADE.

(*Erase heading not required.*)

Instructions regarding War Diaries and Intelligence Summaries are contained in F. S. Regs., Part II, and the Staff Manual respectively. Title pages will be prepared in manuscript.

Hour, Date, Place.	Summary of Events and Information.	Remarks and references to Appendices.
11th. April 1917.	Scheme for intercommunication with aircraft had to be postponed owing to the inclemency of the weather. Brigade received orders at 5.30 pm. to move East on the morrow. This order was cancelled at 9 pm.	
12th. " "	Brigade Route March.	
13th. " "	Brigadier inspected transport horses with Units. Brigade received orders at 7 pm. to move East on the morrow.	
14th. " "	Brigade moved East at 9.30 am. and was bivouacked as follows :-	
	Brigade H.Qrs., 8th. Hussars, M.V. Section - Wood East of CAULAINCOURT Village. 9th. H. Horse, 18th. Lancers, 14th. M.G. Sqdn., "X" Battery RHA. Woods West of CAULAINCOURT about ST.MARTIN des PRES - Mhow F.A. CAULAINCOURT.	See map Appendix A. 1/10000 ST. QUENTIN -
16th. " "	In Bivouac - Weather cold and raining.	
17th. " "	The Brigade provided permanent working parties of 200 men for the improvement of roads and approaches.	
18th. " "	Troop and Squadron Training begun.	
19th. " "	The Brigadier inspected "X" Battery, R.H.A. and 14th. M.G. Sqdn, in marching order on the road.	

Army Form C. 2118.

WAR DIARY
or
~~INTELLIGENCE~~ SUMMARY.
AMBALA CAVALRY BRIGADE.
(*Erase heading not required.*)

Instructions regarding War Diaries and Intelligence Summaries are contained in F. S. Regs., Part II. and the Staff Manual respectively. Title pages will be prepared in manuscript.

Place	Date	Hour	Summary of Events and Information	Remarks and references to Appendices
	1917			
	20/4		Brigadier attended Squadron Training of Units.	
	21/4		Brigade Range for Hotchkiss and Machine Guns established.	
	23/4		The Major General inspected "X" Battery RHA, Light Section Ammunition Column and 14th. M.G.Sqdn.	
	24/4		Brigade Tactical Exercise with Troops. Aircraft took part in the Exercise.	
	27/4		Brigadier inspected the troops at Training.	
	28/4		Tactical Exercise carried out by 9th.H.Horse and attended by the Brigadier.	
			Working Parties from the Brigade commenced the digging and wiring of M.G. emplacements on the POEUILLY - CAULAINCOURT Line.	
	29/4		Sunday - Holiday for all ranks.	
	30/4		Brigadier inspected Working Parties and 9th.H.Horse and 18th. Lancers Drilling.	

T.W. Corbett. Captain.
for Brigade Major, Ambala Cavalry Brigade.

2353 Wt. W2544/1454 700,000 5/15 D. D. & L. A.D.S.S./Forms/C. 2118.

Army Form C. 2118.

Instructions regarding War Diaries and Intelligence Summaries are contained in F. S. Regs., Part II, and the Staff Manual respectively. Title pages will be prepared in manuscript.

WAR DIARY

or

~~INTELLIGENCE SUMMARY.~~

AMBALA CAVALRY BRIGADE. HQRS. VOL XI

(Erase heading not required.)

Hour, Date, Place.	Summary of Events and Information.	Remarks and references to Appendices.
1st. May 1917.	Tactical Exercise, carried out by the 8th.Hussars, was attended by the Brigadier.	
2nd. " "	Echelon "A" and "B" of the Brigade was inspected by the Major General.	
4th. " "	Brigade Tactical Exercise, directed by the Brigadier.	
5th. " "	Brigadier attended Regimental Drill carried out by the 18th.Lancers.	
7th. " "	Inspection of "B" Squadron(Major Dyce) 9th.H.Horse and of "A" Sqdn. (Major Ryder) 8th.Hussars by the Major General. Sports held in billets by the 20th. Deccan Horse.	
8th. " "	"X" Battery R.H.A. came under orders of III Corps and moved North.	
10th. " "	Inspection of Squadron (Capt.Lorimer) 18th.Lancers by the Major General. "X" Battery R.H.A. returned to bivouac from the COLOGNE River.	
11th. " "	Dismounted Reinforcements 8th.Hussars, joined up. Army Commander inspected Sec'bad Brigade and all who had been recently rewarded for gallantry. A tactical Exercise ensued between Sec'bad Bde. and ~~Ambala~~ Canadian Cav. Bde.	
13th. " "	Brigadier inspected Dismounted parties of 8th.Hussars and 14th.M.G.S. Dismounted Reinforcements of the 9th.H.Horse and 18th.Lcrs. returned to their Units.	
14th. " "	Brigadier inspected the Dismounted Trench Parties of the 9th.H.H. and 18th.Lcrs. 8th.Hussars Trench Party moved into Divisional Reserve.at SOYECOURT and came under orders of G.O.C. Canadian Bde. (Cav).	H.G.

Army Form C. 2118.

WAR DIARY

or

~~INTELLIGENCE/SUMMARY~~.

AMBALA CAVALRY BRIGADE.

(Erase heading not required.)

Instructions regarding War Diaries and Intelligence Summaries are contained in F. S. Regs., Part II, and the Staff Manual respectively. Title pages will be prepared in manuscript.

Hour, Date, Place.	Summary of Events and Information.	Remarks and references to Appendices.
15th. May 1917.	9th.H.Horse Trench Party moved up to the main line in Support of the 7th.D.G's. 18th.Lancers Trench Party moved into Sec'bad Brigade Reserve. 14th. M.G.Sqdn. and above parties came under orders of G.O.C. Sec'bad Brigade.	
16th. " "	The Brigadier took over command of the "Led Horses" and Back Area Details.	
17th. " "	"X" Battery R.H.A. moved up to LE VERGUIER under orders C.R.H.A.	
18th. " "	Brigadier inspected horses of F.G.H. & 5th.Cav.Div. A.H.T.Col.	
19th. " "	Brigadier inspected horses of 5th. Field Squadron and 5th.Divisional Ammunition Col., ...	
21st. " "	Brigadier inspected horses of "N" and "X" Batteries R.H.A.	
23rd. " "	Conference at Divl.H.Qrs. on the Defence of the line.	
24th. " "	Brigadier inspected horses of the R.C.Dragoons and of the 5th.Res.Park.	
25th. " "	Brigadier inspected the horses of the Poona Horse and Deccan Horse. Also 2 Sqdns. of 7th.D.G's.	
26th. " "	Major General inspected the horses of the 5th.Res.Park, Ammu.Col. and A.H.T. Col.	
28th. " "	Major General inspected the horses of the Canadian Cav.Brigade. 9th.H.H.,& 18th.Lcrs. Trench Parties (less 100 O.R's and 2 Officers each, Dismounted Reinforcements) rejoined the Brigade.	

Gulab Singh & Sons, Calcutta—No. 34 Army C.—26-8-14—1,07,000.

Army Form C. 2118.

WAR DIARY

or

~~INTELLIGENCE/SUMMARY.~~

AMBALA CAVALRY BRIGADE.

(*Erase heading not required.*)

Instructions regarding War Diaries and Intelligence Summaries are contained in F. S. Regs., Part II, and the Staff Manual respectively. Title pages will be prepared in manuscript.

Hour, Date, Place.	Summary of Events and Information.	Remarks and references to Appendices.
29th. May 1917 .	8th. Hussars Trench Party (less 100 O.R's and 2 Officers) Rejoined the Brigade.	
30th " "	Bde. (less dismounted Reinforcements) commenced Mounted Training – in original back area –	
31st. " "	Brigadier inspected Units of the Brigade at Mounted Training.	

[signature] Captain.

Brigade Major, Ambala Cavalry Brigade.

Gulab Singh & Sons, Calcutta—No. 34 Army C.—26-8-14—1,07,000.

5 DIV

Instructions regarding War Diaries and Intelligence Summaries are contained in F. S. Regs., Part II, and the Staff Manual respectively. Title pages will be prepared in manuscript.

WAR DIARY
or
~~INTELLIGENCE SUMMARY.~~
AMBALA CAVALRY BRIGADE.
(Erase heading not required.)

Army Form C. 2118.

Case No 271

Hour, Date, Place.	Summary of Events and Information.	Remarks and references to Appendices.
June 4th. 1917.	Brigadier attended Squadron Drill of Units Major General inspected the Horse-lines of the Ammu.Col. and "X" and "N" Batteries, R.H.A. 1 Section 14th.M.G.Sqdn. relieved 1 Section Canadian M.G.Sqdn. at VADENCOURT.	
" 5th. "	The Dismounted Trench Parties of the Brigade relieved the Canadian Trench Parties in the A.1.Sector as follows :- 8th. Hussars..........Right Sub-Sector 18th.Lancers..........Left " 9th.H.Horse...........Bde. Reserve , VADENCOURT. The relief was carried out without trouble.	See Appx."A" O.O. No. 12.
" 6th. "	Work in the Front and Support Lines. A quiet day.	
" 8th. "	Capt. T.W.CORBETT, Staff Captain, left for 1st.Cav. Bde., 1st. Cav. Divn. to which he had been appointed Brigade Major.	
" 9th. "	Situation Normal. French Division on the Right of the Brigade was relieved.	
" 10th. "	Capt. Gwatkin, 18th.Lancers took up the position of Staff Captain to the Brigade. At 11 pm. during the relief of Capt. Gwatkin's Squadron by Capt. Dening's Squadron (18th.Lcrs) the Germans attempted a raid on SOMERVILLE WOOD. The raid proved abortive, but Lt. PRINSEP, 18th.Lcrs., was wounded.	

Army Form C. 2118.

Instructions regarding War Diaries and Intelligence Summaries are contained in F. S. Regs., Part II, and the Staff Manual respectively. Title pages will be prepared in manuscript.

WAR DIARY

or

INTELLIGENCE SUMMARY.

AMBALA CAVALRY BRIGADE.

(Erase heading not required.)

Hour, Date, Place.	Summary of Events and Information.	Remarks and references to Appendices.
June 11th. 1917.	The Germans were reported massing for an attack on SOMERVILLE WOOD, our artillery dispersed them.	
" 12th. "	Normal. Sec'bad Bde. carried out a raid.	
" 13th. "	Between 11 pm. and 9.30 a.m. 14th., German Artillery activity increased. Retaliation by our Batteries was given.	
" 14th. "	Quiet day.	
" 15th. "	Between 1 and 2.30 a.m. Fairly heavy hostile shelling of N.end of SOMERVILLE WOOD and DRAGOON POST. Retaliation given.	
" 16th. "	Early in the morning, before dawn, patrol of 8th. Hussars, which was reconnoitring the enemy's wire, ran into a hostile listening post. They got one wounded prisoner, who died on the way back. Day and night abnormally quiet.	
" 17th. "	Quiet Day. SOMERVILLE WOOD was evacuated during night 17th/18th, without the enemy knowing.	
" 18th. "	A successful raid was carried out against a Sector of the German outpost Line. 9th.H.Horse, supported by 2 half Squadrons from 8th. Hussars and 18th.Lcrs entered German system, killed 15 enemy and brought back 3 prisoners, two of whom had the Iron Cross. Our casualties in the Brigade including raiding and covering parties, 4 slightly wounded. for details see Appx. "B".	See Appx. "B"

Army Form C. 2118.

Instructions regarding War Diaries and Intelligence Summaries are contained in F. S. Regs., Part II, and the Staff Manual respectively. Title pages will be prepared in manuscript.

WAR DIARY

or

INTELLIGENCE SUMMARY.

AMBALA CAVALRY BRIGADE.

(Erase heading not required.)

Hour, Date, Place.	Summary of Events and Information.	Remarks and references to Appendices.
June 19th. 1917.	Hostile Artillery Activity NIL. In the evening, abnormal movement seen in German Lines, probably due to a premature relief, necessitated by our raid. By 11.30 p.m. 9th.H.Horse had relieved 18th Lcrs., in the front Line and 18th.Lancers had become Bde. Reserve.	
" 20 - 21st. "	Situation Normal. On the evening of the 21st. the artillery carried out a short intense bombardments of the enemy's approaches, as it was reported that a relief was in progress of being carried out.	
" 22nd. "	A party of the 18th. Lancers went out to deal with an enemy listening Post in the ST.HELENE Road, but the occupants fled and would not be caught.	
" 23 - 24th "	The Brigade was relieved in the line by the Sec'bad Brigade as follows:- 8th. Hussars..........by ....7th. D.Guards. 9th. H.Horse..........by.....34th. Poona Horse. 18th. Lancers.........by.....20th. Deccan Horse. 14th. M.G.Sqdn..(less.1 Sect).remained in the line, and came under orders of G.O.C. Sec'bad Brigade.	
" 25 - 30th."	Brigade as Divl. Reserve carried out training in its original Back Area. Horses were hardened up and 3 hours grazing per day was given. [signature] Captain. Brigade Major, Ambala Cavalry Brigade.	

App. A

SECRET

Copy No 18

AMBALA BRIGADE OPERATION ORDER No.12

Ref: Map 62-C
1:40,000

3rd June 1917

1. The Ambala Cavalry Brigade will take over the line from the Canadian Cavalry Brigade in Sub Sector A.1, on the 5th inst and night 5th/6th in accordance with the attached table. Relief to be completed by 3-0 a.m. 6th inst.

2. (a) 8th Hussars and 18th Lancers will relieve L.S.H. and F.G.Horse respectively, after dusk, dividing line between the regiments being the VADENCOURT-SOMERVILLE WOOD Road to where the road crosses SALT TRENCH, and thence to M.2.b.10.10.

Dispositions as follows:-

Right Sector. H.Qrs VADENCOURT Chau.
1 Sqdn CRESSY TRENCH.
1 " SALT TRENCH.
1 " PONTRU-Twin Crater Road
1 " INTERMEDIATE LINE.

Left Sector. H.Qrs COKER QUARRY.
1 Sqdn (2 Troops SOMERVILLE WOOD.
(2 Troops BONE TREE POST

1 Sqdn. (1 Troop DRAGOON POST.
(2Troops FORT GARRY.
(1 Troop RED WOOD POST.

1 Sqdn. HODSONS POST.

1 Sqdn INTERMEDIATE LINE.

9th H.H. will relieve R.C.D. at 3 p.m., in Brigade Reserve VADENCOURT CHATEAU.
1. Section 14th M.G.Sqdn will relieve 1 Section Canadian Brigade Machine Gun Sqdn before the 5th under arrangements to be made between Officers Commanding Canadian and 14th Machine Gun Sqdns.

3. All details of relief and guides will be arranged directly between C.O's concerned.

4. Horses will not be taken East of VERMAND in daylight or East of VADENCOURT by night.

5. (a) All Maps, Air Photographs, Trench Stores, Ammunition and Shelters will be taken over, and receipts given.
(b) All B.A.B. Trench Code Books will be taken over.

6. Commands pass on completion of reliefs which will be reported by the Code Word "DELHI".

7. ADMINISTRATIVE Instructions attached.

8. Brigade Report Centre will close at CAULINCOURT at 9-0 p.m., and will open at Chateau De VADENCOURT at 10-0 p.m.

9. ACKNOWLEDGE.

Issued at 10.0 p.m.

CAPTAIN.
BRIGADE MAJOR AMBALA BRIGADE.

Copy No.1-7 Normal Distribution.
8 Can Cav Bde.
9 Sec'bad "
10 5th Cav Divn
11 91st French Regt
12 87th French Ifty Bde.
13 C.R.H.A., 5th Cav Dn.
14 Lt Col F.W.Mussenden Comdg Back Area Dtls.

MARCH TABLE issued in conjunction with

AMBALA BRIGADE OPERATION ORDER No. 12.

Relieving Force.	From.	To.	Route.	Formation to be relieved.	Frontage.	Remarks.
(1) 9th. H.H.	Bivouac.	VADENCOURT.	VERMAND.	R. C. D.	Bde. Reserve.	1. Will reach VERMAND at 2.45 p.m. 2. 10 minutes Interval between Squadrons.
(2) 18th.Lcrs.	"	R.21.b.	Cross country to VERMAND or BIHECOURT Stn. (R.26.b)	F. G. H.	Lt. Sector. SOMERVILLE WOOD - VADENCOURT Track to G.31.b.7.3.	1. Will reach BIHECOURT Stn. R.26.b. at 8.45 p.m. 2. Will maintain 5 minutes interval between Sqdns.
(3) 8th. Hussars	"	R.21.b.	- do -	L. S. H.	Rt. Sector. from R. OMIGNON to SOMERVILLE WOOD - VADENCOURT TRACK.	1. Will reach BIHECOURT Stn. R.26.b. at 9.15 pm. 2. Will maintain 5 minutes interval between Sqdns.

B.H.Q. will move under orders of C.C. to VADENCOURT Chateau arriving there at 2 am 6th.
Signal Troop will move under orders of Lt. STANILAND to VADENCOURT Chateau and will have completed taking over from O.C. Signal Troop Canadian Cav. Bde. by 2 am 6th.

NOTES.
(1) Regiments will reconnoitre routes to BIHECOURT Stn.
(2) Led Horses will return North of the VERMAND-VADENCOURT Road.
(3) The Transport of the Dismounted Brigade will concentrate at the Road Junction in W. 35.c. at 9 pm. and will proceed to bivouac in VERMAND under orders of Lt. WILLIAMS, 8th. Hussars.

ADMINISTRATIVE INSTRUCTIONS.

Ref.Map 62.c.
1/40,000

3rd. June 1917.

SUPPLIES. 1.(a) All troops will take with them rations for the 6th. June.

(b) All ranks must be in possession of one Iron Ration and Water Bottles should be filled before leaving present bivouacs.

(c) On the night of the 6th/7th June and subsequent nights rations will be brought up by the Limbered Train under Lt.CUSSELL B.T.O. from the Refilling Point at Cross Roads in W.11.c. to the Cross Roads at BIHECOURT where Units will have guides waiting at 830pm. nightly.

(d) Regiments and 14th.M.G.Sqdn., will each detail an N.C.O. and other Units each a man to load up rations at Refilling Point at Cross Roads W.11.c. and to march with Limbered Train under the B.T.O. These details will be bivouaced at the Refilling Point at Cross Roads W.11.c. under the orders of Capt.HUNT ,B.S.O. and must report to him there at noon on the 5th.
9th.H.H. will provide a Trench Cover for the Indian and 14th.M.G.Sqdn., one for the British representatives

(e) Units in forward Area must submit their own A.B.55 to include extra Trench Ration.

(f) RESERVE RATIONS. Two days full Indian Rations or two days British Rations, special scale, xxx xx xx fxkx as follows as the case may be:-

Biscuit........ ¾ lb.
Preserved
Meat....... "
Tea.......... 5/8 oz.
Sugar........ 3 oz.
Milk......... 1 oz.
Jam.......... 3 oz.

are maintained at the following advanced Posts.

Sub.Sector A/1.

POST.	No.of men to be rationed for 2 days.	REMARKS.
SOMERVILLE WOOD G.32.c.6.6.	20	
RED WOOD POST. G.31.c.3.9.	20	(In addition 500 British rations are dumped at Advanced BHQ. VADENCOURT)
LONE TREE G.32.c.3.1.	30	
HODSON's POST. R.6.a.8.7.	40	
SALT TRENCH M.1.d.5.7.	40	
CRESSY TRENCH M.7.a.9.6.	40	
TWIN CRATER R.6.c.6.1.	40	

TRANSPORT.2.(a) The Brigade Transport for the Forward Area will be parked at VERMAND under orders of Lt. WILLIAMS, 8th.Hussars.
All Vehicles will be for internal use in the Bde. and will not be required for carrying rations
(b) 8th.Hussars, 9th.H.H., 18th.Lcrs., will each detail two pack horses to march and park with the Brigade Transport. They will take empty tool packs and will be used for carrying water and rations to Advanced Posts where required.

WATER.3. (a) The following Water Carts will be taken up:-
Mhow F.A.........1.
18th.Lcrs........1.
8th.Hussars......1.
The Water carts of the two latter will remain at VERMAND with the transport and proceed filled each night with the Ration limbers.
Mhow F.A. Water Cart will remain with the Advanced Dressing Station and supply the Regiment in Reserve and B.H.Q.Units.
(b) Units will take over all petrol tins for water from the respective Units of Canadian Bde. which they relieve.
(c) Particulars regarding wells in the area and the amount chlorination necessary are being issued separately to all concerned.
(d) Two days reserve of water in petrol tins are stored at the posts mentioned in para 1.(f)
The Water in these tins must be changed every three days.

AMMUNITION 4.(a) All S.A.A. will be taken over by Units from the Units of Canadian Bde. they relieve.
(b) 9th.H.H. will find a guard of one N.C.O. and 2 men for the Brigade Ammunition Dump in R.10.d.9.6. This guard will always be found by the Regiment in Brigade Reserve.

R.E.STORES 5. The Advanced Divisional R.E.Dump is at VERMAND. The Brigade Dump is at R.10.d.9.6.

RETURNS 6. The following Returns must be sent in punctually by all concerned :-
(1) Daily Casualty Return (12 noon to 12 noon)
(2) Daily expenditure of S.A.A.
(3) Fighting Strength.

The above to be submitted to B.H.Q. by 2 pm.

(4) The following Returns will be submitted to Staff Captain by Mid-day on the 7th. inst.
(1) S.A.A. and Grenades after taken over in the line.
(2) - do - the Bdc.Dump. by 9th.H.Horse.
(3) Reserve Rations taken over.
(4) Trench Stores taken over.
(5) Tents and Trench Covers taken over.
(6) The number of Petrol Tins taken over.
(All Tins in possession of Can.Bdc. must be handed over)

POSTAL 7. No. 7 Field Post Office will not move.
Units will arrange to send their Mails back by cycle orderly to reach Post Office in CAULAINCOURT by 12.30 pm. Daily.
The same orderly will bring back letters after they have been sorted at Units'Back Area Quarters.
Parcels must be sent up with the ration limbers and Units in Back Area will arrange accordingly.

MEDICAL 8. (a) The following Medical personnel, Transport and Equipment will be detailed by Units concerned.

Medical Officers. (Capt. J.J.MAGNER RAMC. 8th.Hrs.
(Lieut. S.DUTT I.M.S. 9th.H.H.

Orderlies ~~xxxx~~ for duty with M.O's.

1 from 8th. Hussars, 1 from 9th. H.Horse.

R.A.M.C. for Water Duties 2 O.R.s. from 8th.Hussars
Sub. Asst Surgeon. from 18th. Lancers.
Ward Orderlies. 1 from 9th.H.Horse.
1 from 18th.Lcrs.
Stretcher Bearers:- 24
8 from 8th. Hussars.
8 from 9th.H.Horse.
8 from 18th.Lancers.

Sanitary Duties. 2 O.R.B. from 8th. Hussars.
2 O.R.I. from Sanitary Section.
for each Indian Regiment.
Batmen for M.O's. 2

TRANSPORT.

2 Half Limbered G.S. Wagons for Medical Equipment.
1 from 8th. Hussars, 1 from 9th.H.Horse.
Water Carts. See para 3.

EQUIPMENT.

2 Pairs Field Medical Panniers. 1 Pr. from MO.8th.Hrs
1 " " " 9th.H.H
2 Field Surgical Haversacks. - do -
2 Field Medical Companions. - do -
2 Haversacks Shell Dressing - do -
12 Field Stretchers from Mhow F.A.
50 Ammonia Capsules from Mhow F.A.
The Lance Pattern Regimental Stretcher will not be taken into the line.

(2) The Advanced Dressing Station of Mhow I.C.F.A. will take over the Advanced Dressing Station at VADENCOURT (R.18.a.9.4) afternoon of June 5th.
Regimental Aid Post (for both Regiments in line) will be at COOKERS QUARRY (R.11.a. 8.4.)
An Advanced Regimental Aid Post can be established at TWIN CRATERS (R.6.c.6.1.) when required. Mhow F.A. will keep two wheeled stretchers there but no personnel.

(3) The Transport of all wounded unable to walk is by handunder Regimental arrangements from the line to Regimental Aid Post. Thence by Bearer Party with wheeled carriers or horsed ambulance after dusk to the Advanced Dressing Station.

TENTS &
TRENCH COVERS. Will be taken over by units from the respective
9. Units they relieve.

POLICE. 10. (a) 9th.H.H. will establish a post on Road R.10.b.3.0 to prevent any vehicles or horses proceeding beyond this point.
(b) 9th.H.H. will put up a board at Cross Roads BIHECOURT with following Notice "MOTORS ,MOTOR CYCLES and HORSEMEN Dead Slow" facing towards VERMAND.
(c) The Road running N.E. beyond the Road Junction at R.11.c.0.6. will not be used in daylight by any but single men , who must keep close to the hedge on the Southern Side.

CEMETERIES.11. British.......R.16.b.3.4.

Indian....... Notified later.

ORDNANCE 12. Stores are sent up with the supplies from the Refilling point.

BATHS 13. Brigade Baths are at VERMAND. Application for use will be made through Staff Captain.

LAUNDRY 14. Underclothing is sent to the Back Area for disinfection at the Mhow and Canadian Field Ambulances and then taken in lorries to the Fourth Army Laundry where they are exchanged for clean underclothing.

T.W. Corbett Captain.
Staff Captain, Ambala Cavalry Brigade.

Case No 271

34

App. B.

No.........

Headquarters Ambala Cavalry Brigade.
Field.......19th. June......1917.

Account of the Preparation for a Raid, and the actual operation itself, carried out by the 9th.H.Horse,Ambala Cavalry Brigade on the night 18th/19th. JUNE 1917.

--------oOo-----------

Reference Maps attached, 1:20,000 BELLENGLISE.

OBJECT. 1. The raid was to be made against the enemy's front line trench and roads in the vicinity of ST.HELENE , with the object of cleaning out that Sector and securing identifications.

PLAN OF OPERATION. 2. Surprise was to be the main factor to attain this Object.
The hostile wire was to be destroyed by means of Bangalore Torpedoes (in M.3.a.8.6) and at the moment that this gap was created, a Box Barrage was to be put down round the Sector of Operations and two raiding parties were to enter the enemy's system.
One party was to work down the BUISSON GAULAINE FM. - PONTRUET Road, the other down the front line trench, and both to meet eventually about M.3.d.3.6., where an exit had been prepared to come away.
Raiding parties were to leave the hostile lines within 45 minutes of the explosion of the Bangalore Torpedoes (which denoted ZERO hour); the barrages also were to cease at ZERO hour plus 45 minutes.

PREPARATION. 3. The plan was discussed with all concerned, and the following preparations made, commencing 6 days before the actual raid took place.

(a) Training.

(i) The raiding parties were told off and consisted of two columns each of 2 B.O's, 2 I.O's, 60 rifles, 4 stretcher bearers.
These were put into training and ran 2 miles per day.

(ii) The facsimile of the hostile trench system was traced out with help of aerial photographs and wire erected 25 feet wide
Every evening and every night the raiding parties went through the actual manouvres which they were to perform on the night of the raid.

(iii) Experiments were carried out with Bangalore Torpedoes and in wire cutting.

(iv) The men were practised in the special use of "P" bombs, and hand grenades. Flares and rockets were also used.

(b)........../.

36 Pinch

(b) Reconnaissances.

(i) All Officers and N.C.O's of the raiding party studied their objectives in the hostile lines from Intelligence O.P's South of BERTHAUCOURT and at LONE TREE POST.
Reconnaissances were made daily and as often as possible.

(ii) Special information was required and obtained from Regimental Intelligence Personnel in the various Intelligence O.P's.
Hostile movements and work were so closely studied that the fullest possible knowledge was gained of the objective and its defenders.
The French Regiment on the Right very kindly provided a reconnaissance report of the area.
Air photographs were obtained both under Divisional arrangements and from the French on our Right, and a stereoscope was lent which proved most valuable.

(iii) Both Regiments in the Line succeeded, by means of continual offensive patrols in establishing the mastery over "No Man's Land".
During the last 4 nights before the raid not a single enemy patrol was met West of the German Front Line.

(iv) Artillery Officers who were going to support the raid carried out careful, reconnaissances to enable them to completely understand the operation in view.

(v) Machine Gun Officers did the same and paid special attention to the siting of Machine Gun positions for the purpose of assisting with an enfilade Barrage.

(c)

The time allowed in which to prepare the plan of operations was sufficiently long to enable all the main points to be decided upon long before the actual night of the raid, and for Operation Orders to be issued to all concerned 4 days before the operatiðn came off.

ORDERS & INSTRUCTIONS. 4. Attached. (a) Operation Order No. 14 and Instructions.
(b) Map of Barrages.
(c) Map of Machine Gun Babrages.

FURTHER DETAILS. 5.(a) Dress.

Boots (Torpedo carrying parties wore rope soled shoes) Puttees, Coats, Lungis, P.H.Helmets.

(b) Distinctive Marks.
No Identity discs. White band 12 inches wide on each arm.

(c) Arms & Equipment.
(1) Rifle, magazines charged, 2 chargers in the pocket, chamber empty, Fixed bayonet, 1 pr. wire cutters (Torpedo carrying party were armed with revolvers)
No bayonet scabbards or bandoliers.
(2) 30 % carried five Mills No.5 Hand Grenades in haversack.
(3) 20 % carried "P" Bombs in haversack.

ACCOUNT OF THE OPERATION.......

ACCOUNT OF THE OPERATION.

6. (a) Raiding party reached Sunken Road in H.3.a.0.5. in good time, and started off to the "Jumping off" point at 11.20 pm.

NOTE. (1) The Machine Gun firing intermittently from SOMERVILLE WOOD served the purpose of making a very good covering noise.

(2) 2 H.E. shells on H.3.b.3.7. at 11.30 pm. which had been asked for to show the O.C. Raiding parties the Southern limit of the barrage proved useful and made him alter his course slightly South (2 shells were arranged for "in case one should be dud", which in fact one was).

(b) The party reached the wire undiscovered 11.40 pm., the head was withdrawn and the torpedoes placed and fired at 11.46 pm. (2 minutes before it was calculated possible)

(c) Officers commanding Column firing their "VERY" Lights together and the TUMULUS rocket went off 10 seconds afterwards.

NOTE. (1) Two rockets, each in charge of a specially detailed Officer were placed at the TUMULUS and the first one failed to go off.

(2) Owing to the fact that there was more than one Signal for ZERO hour (i.e. Explosion of Torpedoes VERY Flares, a Green Rocket) one battery opened on the explosion of the torpedoes, followed by the whole of the French Artillery.
The remainder opened up when the TUMULUS rocket appeared, followed by the Heavy Artillery.

(d) The parties worked through their respective areas without opposition.
They arrived practically simultaneously at the exit gap which had been made, and was being lit up according to plan. A gap had also been made by the trench party North of the Road.
Both columns were clear of the hostile trenches by 12.20 a.m., and made their way back to PONTRU through a thin Barrage arriving there at 12.30am. just after the signal to come in (Green Rocket) had gone up from the TUMULUS.
All artillery except a few heavy Batteries had ceased fire 5 minutes later.

RESULT OF THE RAID.

7. Of the Garrison of the Sector, 5 were bayoneted or bombed in the open.
One was killed trying to escape through our barrage.
Nine were bombed in the various dug-outs.
3 prisoners were brought in.
16 dug-outs were bombed of which 11 were set on fire and burnt out.

Captain.
Brigade Major, Ambala Cavalry Brigade.

Copy No.........

SECRET.

AMBALA BRIGADE OPERATION ORDER No. 14.

Ref. Map 1:20,000
BELLENGLISE.

14th. June 1917.

1. At ZERO hour on the night 18th/19th June 1917, a raid will be carried out against the enemy's front Line trench and roads, in the vicinity of ST.HELENE, with the Object of cleaning out that Sector, and securing identifications.

2. ZERO hour will be signalled by the explosion of 2 Bangalore torpedoes in M 3.a.8.6; the firing of a red and green Very light at the same point, and by the appearance of a green rocket at the TUMULUS.

3. The raid will be carried out by 2 Squadrons of the 9th.H.Horse, strength each, 2 B.O's, 2 I.O's 60 other ranks.

Times and dispositions of these, of subsidiary patrol (x) and of covering parties of 8th.Hussars and 18th.Lcrs., as per attached Table of Details.

4. The raiding parties will leave the hostile trenches at ZERO hour plus 45 minutes.

At ZERO hour plus 40 minutes a green rocket will be fired from the TUMULUS to warn the raiding party that the barrage will cease in 5 minutes time.

5. Machine Gun shoots will be carried out as per attached Table.

6. Artillery co-operation will be given for 45 minutes as per attached barrage Table.

7. Watches will be synchronised at B.H.Q. at 6 p.m. 18th. inst by the following.

Representatives of
- 9th.H.Horse.
- 18th.Lancers.
- 8th.Hussars
- 14th.M.G.Squadron.
- 17th.Bde. R.H.A.
- Cam. Cav. Bde.
- French Artillery co-operating.

8. Acknowledge.

[illegible] Captain.
Brigade Major, Ambala Cavalry Brigade.

Despatched by D.R.
Distribution.

Copy No. 1. 8th.Hussars
2. 9th.H.Horse.
3. 18th.Lancers.
4. 14th.M.G.Sqdn.
5. C.R.H.A.
6. 5th.Cav.Divn.
7. Cam.Cav.Bde.
8. French Mission.
9. O.C. 128th. Divl Artillery (Translation)
10. 85th. French Regt. "
11. 128th.I.D.French Bde. "

59

Table of Details Issued with Ambala Cavalry Brigade Operation Order No. 14.

1. Times and Dispositions of Raiding Parties.

TIME.	UNIT.	PLACE.	REMARKS.
10.10 p.m.	"A" Col. "B" Col.	W. of TUMULUS	
11.10 p.m.	"A" Col. "B" Col.	Sunken road in M.3.a.0.5.	
11.30 p.m.	"A" Col. "B" Col.	100 yards West of wire in M.3.a.8.6.	"Jumping off" Point Torpedo-carrying parties work forward to, place and fire torpedoes.
12. 0 m.n.	"A" Col. "B" Col.	About to pass through hostile wire.	ZERO hour will be taken from explosion of torpedoes and firing of flares and rocket asper Operation Order. It should be any time after 11.50 p.m.
Between ZERO hour and ZERO plus 45 minutes.	"A" Col.	Crosses hostile trench in M.3.a.9.6. and works down BUISSON GAULAINE FM PONTRUET Road, to Junction of road and trench in M.3.d.7.6. Thence West along trench to M.3.d.2.5. to prepare exit gap in wire, if not already done by X patrol. Thence cleans up trench to FISHER CRATER - BELLENGLISE Road.	
	"B" Col.	Enters hostile trench in M.3.a.9.6. and works down South to FISHER CRATER - BELLENGLISE Road, where it prepares a gap.	

2. X patrol strength 1, IO. 5 O.R. will proceed with the third torpedo from ROBINSON'S REDOUBT to cut an exit for the raiding party in the hostile wire at about M.3.d.2.5.
It will be within 200 yards of above point at 11.50 p.m. and will place and fire torpedo, as soon as possible after ZERO hour plus 30 minutes.
It will await the raiding party at the gap, and will attract its attention by blowing a whistle.

3. From 10.30 p.m. till ZERO plus 60 minutes.
(a) MAX WOOD will be occupied by half Squadron 18th. Lcrs.
(b) FISHER CRATER " " " " 9th. Hussars.

No. 2234   SECRET.   Headquarters Ambala Cavalry Brigade.

Field.......17th. June......1917.

40

To. 8th. Hussars
9th. H.H.
18th. Lancers.
M.G. Sqdn.
Mhow F.A.

The following Instructions are issued in confirmation of the directions given at the Brigade Conference today.

1. PASWORD. The Pass Word of the Brigade and of the French, from 12 noon 18th. inst. to 12 noon 19th. inst. will be "THIAUMONT" All ranks of the raiding party will be practised in this [illegible]

2. FLANK GUARDS will be in position from 10.30 p.m. till ZERO hour plus 60 minutes as per O.O. No. 24.
The object of the Flank Guard is to prevent any enemy patrols moving
   (a) North of the Line FISHERS CRATER - BELLENGLISE Road
   (b) South of the Line M.3.a.30.65 and the German wire in M.3.a.80.65.
Between the hours of 10.30 pm. and ZERO.
Their main weapon of offence to this end will be the bayonet.
Right Flank Guard will carry two green rockets, one of which will be fired in an Easterly direction at ZERO plus 40 minutes, and one spare.

3. ROCKETS AND FLARES. In addition to the above and those laid down in O.O. No. 24
   (a) "X" Patrol will fire a white Very light from time to time after ZERO hour plus 30 mins. towards the exit gap in the wire.
   (b) 8th. Hussars will fire once every 20 minutes (commencing at ZERO hour plus 60 minutes) a green Very light from CRESSY TRENCH to guide in stragglers. Personnel of the raiding party will be warned of this.

4. TIME LIMITS OF RAID.
   (a) If, from any reason whatever, the raiding party having been discovered before an entry gap has been blown in the wire, the O.C. decides that he will not be able to create this gap before 12.30 a.m. 19th., the raiding party will withdraw.
   (b) The raiding parties will leave the hostile trenches whenever their tasks have been fulfilled regardless of time, provided that ZERO hour plus 45 minutes has not been past.

5. TROPHIES. Special parties will be detailed for the collection of hostile documents, and for the carrying in of hostile M.G's.

6. ROUTE TO OUR LINES. On leaving the hostile trenches Officers commanding columns will decide according to circumstances the best way to regain our line.

7. MEDICAL ARRANGEMENTS. 8th. Hussars will have 8 stretcher bearers and [illegible] stretchers at FISHERS CRATER. An Aid Post will be established inside the garden at M.7.b.6.0. (PONTRU)
All further details will be settled direct with those concerned by [illegible] MATTHEWS, R.A.M.C.

[signature]
Captain,
Brigade Major, Ambala Cavalry Brigade.

41

GUNS.

No's. 1. 2. 3. 4.	Barrages as per Map. From ZERO hour till ZERO plus 45 minutes.	
5. 6.	1st. Phase.	Junction of Trench and Road in M.3.d.8.6. ZERO hour to ZERO plus 10 minutes.
5. 6.	2nd. Phase.	BELLENGLISE Road M.4.a.4.0. - M.4.a.9.9. ZERO plus 10 minutes to ZERO plus 95 minutes.
7.	1st. Phase.	XI Trees G.33.c.7.8. - G.33.d.0.8. ZERO — 40 minutes to ZERO hour (to make a covering noise)
7. 8.	2nd. Phase.	INK ALLEY. G.33.d.5.0 - G.33.d.9½.2. ZERO hour to ZERO plus 45 minutes.

Case No 271

Maps Showing

1. Route taken by Raiding Party
2. Gaps in Wire
3. Artillery Barrage
4. Position of covering parties

Army Form C. 2118.

Instructions regarding War Diaries and Intelligence Summaries are contained in F. S. Regs., Part II, and the Staff Manual respectively. Title pages will be prepared in manuscript.

~~WAR DIARY~~
or
INTELLIGENCE SUMMARY.
AMBALA CAVALRY BRIGADE.
(Erase heading not required.)

Hour, Date, Place.	Summary of Events and Information.	Remarks and references to Appendices.
18th. to 23rd. July 1917.	Training in Back Area.	
23rd. " "	Brigadier inspected horses of R.C.H.A. and Res. Park as G.O.C. Division.	
24th. " "	Tactical Exercise carried out by the 8th. Hussars.	
25th. " "	Inter- communication Scheme carried out by the Brigade and Co-operation with Aeroplane.	
26th. " "	Tactical Exercise by 18th. Lancers.	
27th. " "	" " " 9th.H.Horse.	

A Graham [signature]

Captain.
Brigade Major, Ambala Cavalry Brigade.

Instructions regarding War Diaries and Intelligence Summaries are contained in F. S. Regs., Part II, and the Staff Manual respectively. Title pages will be prepared in manuscript.

WAR DIARY
or
INTELLIGENCE SUMMARY.

Army Form C. 2118.

AMBALA CAVALRY BRIGADE.
(Erase heading not required.)

Hour, Date, Place.	Summary of Events and Information.	Remarks and references to Appendices.
1st. to 5th. August 1917.	Continuous rain.	
6th. August 1917.	Inter-communication Scheme with Aircraft , stopped by mist. The Major-General attended.	
	Officers Signalling Class commenced at Brigade Headquarters.	
	A party of Officers and N.C.O's proceeded to AIRE to witness the construction of a special pontoon bridge, rapidly erected for the crossing of dykes and small waterways.	
7th. " "	8th. Hussars carried out Tactical Exercise in the neighbourhood of BRYAS. A party of Officers (1 per Squadron) were instructed in the firing of the Lewis Gun at Brigade Headquarters.	
8th. " "	9th.Hodson's Horse carried out Tactical Exercise.	
9th. " "	Lt. Col. F.W.MUSSENDEN, 8th.Hussars, departed for ROUEN to take over command of the training of Reinforcements . Major G.MORT took over command of the 8th. Hussars.	
10th. " "	Tactical Exercise carried out with Aeroplanes, Armoured Cars and all Troops.	
12th. " "	Brigade Horse Show.	
14th. " "	Brigadier attended Squadron Training of the 13th. Lancers.	AK.

... Sons, Calcutta—No. 34 Army C.—26-8-14—1,07,000.

Army Form C. 2118.

Instructions regarding War Diaries and Intelligence Summaries are contained in F. S. Regs., Part II, and the Staff Manual respectively. Title pages will be prepared in manuscript.

WAR DIARY
or
INTELLIGENCE SUMMARY.

AMBALA CAVALRY BRIGADE.
(Erase heading not required.)

Hour, Date, Place.	Summary of Events and Information.	Remarks and references to Appendices.
15th. August 1917.	8th. Cavalry Division Horse Show BRYAS Chateau.	
16th. " "	Tactical Exercise by 9th. Hodsons Horse.	
17th. " "	" " " 18th. Lancers.	
18th. " "	Inspection of Arms, Equipment, and Saddlery.	
19th. " "	Sunday.	
20th. " "	Staff Ride. 8th. Hussars.	
21st. " "	Brigade inspected by G.O.C. Division in Marching Order.	
22nd. " "	Tactical Exercise 9th. Hodsons Horse.	
23rd. " "	" " 18th. Lancers.	
24th. " "	Squadron Training.	
25th. " "	Squadron Training.	
26th. " "	Sunday.	
27th. " "	Staff Ride Junior Officers. 8th. Hussars.	

Instructions regarding War Diaries and Intelligence Summaries are contained in F. S. Regs., Part II, and the Staff Manual respectively. Title pages will be prepared in manuscript.

WAR DIARY

or

INTELLIGENCE SUMMARY.

AMBALA CAVALRY BRIGADE.

(Erase heading not required.)

Army Form C. 2118.

Hour, Date, Place.	Summary of Events and Information.	Remarks and references to Appendices.
28th. August 1917.	Rain.	
29th. " "	Rain.	
30th. " "	One Squadron 9th. Hodsons Horse inspected Field Firing by G.O.C. Division.	
31st.v " "	Brigade Tactical Exercise postponed owing to bad weather.	

A.Jackson

Captain.

~~Ag.~~ Brigade Major, Ambala Cavalry Brigade.

Serial No: 108.

Army Form C. 2118.

WAR DIARY
or
INTELLIGENCE SUMMARY.

AMBALA CAVALRY BRIGADE.
(Erase heading not required.)

Instructions regarding War Diaries and Intelligence Summaries are contained in F. S. Regs., Part II, and the Staff Manual respectively. Title pages will be prepared in manuscript.

Hour, Date, Place.	Summary of Events and Information.	Remarks and references to Appendices.
1st. September 1917	Cavalry Corps Horse Show in the neighbourhood of ST POL. The Brigade had 132 entries.	
3rd.-6th " "	Squadron and Regimental Training.	
7th. " "	Brigade Intercommunication Scheme. 9th.H.Horse Rifle Meeting at MONCHY BRETON.	
8th. " "	9th.H.Horse ,18th.Lancers, & Mhow F.A. together with the Indian Units of the Sec'bad Cav.Bde. were inspected by Lt.Gen.Sir H.Cox, K.C.M.G, C.B., C.S.I. in the neighbourhood of BETHONUAL. After the inspection 9th.H.Horse gave a display.	
9th. " "	"X" Battery returned to the Brigade from attachment to the 1st. Army.	
10 - 13th " "	Squadron Training and Musketry.	
14th. " "	Brigade Route March.	
15th. " "	Brigadier inspected 9th.H.Horse at Foot Drill and manual exercises in billets.	
18th. " "	Brigadier attended Tactical Exercise by 8th.Hussars.Attack on Convoy.	
20th. " "	Brigade Gymkhana .	
22nd. " "	Brigadier inspected 8th.Hussars at Foot drill and manual exercises in billets.	

Army Form C. 2118.

Instructions regarding War Diaries and Intelligence Summaries are contained in F. S. Regs., Part II, and the Staff Manual respectively. Title pages will be prepared in manuscript.

WAR DIARY
or
INTELLIGENCE SUMMARY.

AMBALA CAVALRY BRIGADE.
(*Erase heading not required.*)

Hour, Date, Place.	Summary of Events and Information.	Remarks and references to Appendices
25th. September 1917	Brigadier attended a Tactical Exercise by the 8th. Hussars.	
28th. " "	Brigade Route March.	
29th. " "	Brigadier inspected 18th. Lancers at Foot drill and Manual Exercises.	

Captain.

for Brigade Major, Ambala Cavalry Brigade.

Army Form C. 2118.

108.

Instructions regarding War Diaries and Intelligence Summaries are contained in F. S. Regs., Part II, and the Staff Manual respectively. Title pages will be prepared in manuscript.

WAR DIARY
or
~~INTELLIGENCE~~ SUMMARY.
AMBALA CAVALRY BRIGADE.
(Erase heading not required.)

Hour, Date, Place.			Summary of Events and Information.	Remarks and references to Appendices
2nd.	October	1917.	Col. Hardin D.D.R inspected Horses for Casting. Tactical Exercise 8th. Hussars.	
3rd.	"	"	Marching Order Parade 9th. Hodson's Horse.	
4th.	"	"	Marching Order Route March 18th. Lancers.	
5th.	"	"	Brigade Tactical Exercise.	
6th.	"	"	Orders received to march North.	
7th.	"	"	Brigade marched to STEENBECQUE Area. 7.30 am. Rain in afternoon. Arrived 5.15 pm.	See Map Appx. "A"
8th.	"	"	Orders received to halt until further orders. Rain in afternoon.	
9th.	"	"	Brigade remained in STEENBECQUE Area.	"
10th.	"	"	- do -	
11th.	"	"	Brigade marched to WATOU Area .	"
12th.	"	"	~~- do -~~ WATOU Area.	
13th.	"	"	WATOU Area.	

Army Form C. 2118.

Instructions regarding War Diaries and Intelligence Summaries are contained in F. S. Regs., Part II, and the Staff Manual respectively. Title pages will be prepared in manuscript.

WAR DIARY
or
~~INTELLIGENCE SUMMARY.~~
AMBALA CAVALRY BRIGADE.
(Erase heading not required.)

Hour, Date, Place.	Summary of Events and Information.	Remarks and references to Appendices
14th. October 1917.	Brigade Marched to ST.OMER Area.	See Map Appx."B"
15th. " "	Brigade marched to FAUQUEMBERGUES Area.	"
16th. " "	Brigade went into billets in MARESQUEL Area.	"
18th. " "	Nucleus for Pioneer Battalion sent to BAILLEUL.	
21st. - 29th. Oct.	Squadron, Regimental and Brigade Training.	See Appx. "C".

[signature]

Captain.

Brigade Major, Ambala Cavalry Brigade.

App. C.

TRAINING PROGRAMME for the Week Ending 27th. OCTOBER 1917.

BRIGADE. Location.	UNIT. Location of H.Q.	Description of Training.	REMARKS.
AMBALA - MARESQUEL.	8th. Hussars. BEAURAINVILLE.	Equitation, Sqdn. Training, Officers Staff Rides. Map-Reading, Training of Signallers Footdrill, Respirator Drill.	Sqdn. Training, Equitation, Footdrill in Regtl. Training Area, 22nd., 23rd., 25th. Regtl. Scheme Rendezvous BRICKWORKS. S. of CAMPAGNE LEZ HESDIN. 10 am. 26th. Inspections. 27th.
	9th. H. Horse. CAVRON St. MARTIN.	Equitation, Sqdn. Training, Officers Staff Rides, Map reading, Training of Signallers Footdrill, Respirator Drill.	Sqdn. Training, Equitation, Footdrill in Regtl. Training Area. 22nd, 23rd, 25th. 26th. Inspections 27th.
	18th. Lancers. AUBIN St. VAAST.	Equitation, Sqdn. Training, Officers Staff Rides. Map reading, Training of Signallers Footdrill, Respirator Drill.	Sqdn. Training, Equitation, Footdrill, in Regtl. Training Area. 22nd., 25th., 26th. Regtl. Scheme in Brigade Training Area Rendezvous, AUBIN St. VAAST 9 am. 23rd. Inspections 27th.
	14th. M.G. Sqdn. WAMBERCOURT.	Equitation, Gundrill, Firing, Range Finding, Respirator Drill.	In Squadron Area, 22nd., 23rd., 25th., 26th. Inspections 27th.
	Brigade.	Tactical Exercise.	Rendezvous. GOUY St. ANDRE. 8.30 am. 24th.

Headquarters Ambala Cavalry Brigade.
Field.........21st. October 1917.

To. General Staff,
5th. Cavalry Division.

Forwarded.

Captain.
Brigade Major, Ambala Cavalry Brigade.

To. 8th. Hrs., 9th. H.H,
18th. Lcrs., M.G. Sqdm.

War Diary

App. C.

TRAINING PROGRAMME for the Week Ending 3rd. NOVEMBER 1917.

BRIGADE. Location of H.Q.	UNIT. Location of H.Q.	Description of Training.	Remarks.
AMBALA MARESQUEL.	8th.Hussars BEAURAINVILLE	Sqdn.Training & Equitation. Officer's Staff Rides.,Map reading. Training of Signallers, Foot Drill. Respirator Drill.	Regtl.Area .9.30 am. 29th.,30th.Oct. Officers Staff Ride 1st.Nov. C.O.inspects 3 Sqdns. of Regt. 9.30 am. on 29th.,30th. Oct. 1st.Nov Regtl.Drill. 9.30am. 2nd. Nov.
	9th.H.Horse. CAVRON St. MARTIN.	Sqdn.Training. & Equitation. Officers Staff Rides. Map reading. Training of Signallers. Foot Drill. Respirator Drill.	Regtl.Area 9 am. 29th.Oct. 1st. 2nd. ov Officers Staff Ride.Regtl.Area 10 am. 30th. Oct.
	18th.Lancers. AUBIN St. VAAST.	Sqdn.Training & Equitation. Officers Staff Rides. Map reading. Training of Signallers. Foot Drill. Respirator Drill.	Regtl.Area 9 am.29th., 30th. Oct. 1st., 2nd. Nov.
	14th. M.G.Sqdn. WAMBERCOURT.	Sqdn.Training.,Range Finding, Indication and recognition of targets. Respirator Drill.	Squadron Area.
	Ambala Brigade.	Inter-Regimental Exercise.	Rendezvous. 9.30 am. 31st. Oct. St.ANDRE AU BOIS.

Headquarters Ambala Cavalry Brigade.
Field..........24th. October 1917.

To. General Staff,
5th. Cavalry Division.

Forwarded.

208/29

A. P. ...
Captain.
Brigade Major, Ambala Cavalry Brigade.

Copy to. 8th.Hrs, 9th.H.H.
18th.Lcrs., M.G.Sqdn.

Army Form C. 2118.

108

WAR DIARY
or
INTELLIGENCE SUMMARY.
AMBALA CAVALRY BRIGADE.
(Erase heading not required.)

Instructions regarding War Diaries and Intelligence Summaries are contained in F. S. Regs., Part II, and the Staff Manual respectively. Title pages will be prepared in manuscript.

Hour, Date, Place.	Summary of Events and Information.	Remarks and references to Appendices
1st. - 8th. Nov. 1917.	See Appendix "A"	
8th. November 1917.	Capt. W.E.P. CAIRNES, 8th. Hrs., proceeded to England. Instructor Reserve Cavalry.	
9th. " "	Brigade moved to OUTREBOIS Area, OCCOCHES.	See Map No. 1.
10th. " "	" " " CONTAY " , BEHENCOURT.	" " "
11/12th. " "	" " " SUZANNE.	
13th. " "	" " " CARTIGNY.	
14th.-19th. Nov. "	Brigade remained in CARTIGNY Area.	
20th. November 1917.	Brigade moved at 1 am. to BOIS DE DESSART. Advanced concentration Point. Thence to R.9.a., where it passed the night in the open	See App. "B" & Map No. 2
21st. " "	Brigade moved to the support of the 1st. Cavalry Division at 3 pm. but was not required. It spent the night at about R.30.c.	- do -
22nd. "	8 am. Brigade marched to EQUANCOURT, where it spent the night.	- do -
23rd. " "	6.30 am. Brigade marched to BRAY Area.	See Map No. 1.
24th. " "	Brigade was at ½ hours notice to move. Horses were rested and kits and saddlery cleaned.	"

Army Form C. 2118.

WAR DIARY

or

INTELLIGENCE SUMMARY.

AMBALA CAVALRY BRIGADE.

(Erase heading not required.)

Instructions regarding War Diaries and Intelligence Summaries are contained in F. S. Regs., Part II, and the Staff Manual respectively. Title pages will be prepared in manuscript.

Hour, Date, Place.	Summary of Events and Information.	Remarks and references to Appendices
25th.-26th Nov. 1917.	Brigade remained in BRAY Area.	See Map No. 1.
27th. November "	9 am. Brigade moved to TERTRY Area.	
28th. " "	Brigade remained in TERTRY Area. Received warning that a Dismounted body would shortly be required to take over the line.	

[signature]

Captain.

Brigade Major, Ambala Cavalry Brigade.

Army Form C. 2118.

108.

Instructions regarding War Diaries and Intelligence Summaries are contained in F. S. Regs., Part II, and the Staff Manual respectively. Title pages will be prepared in manuscript.

WAR DIARY
or
~~INTELLIGENCE~~ SUMMARY.
AMBALA CAVALRY BRIGADE.
(Erase heading not required.)

December 1917

Hour, Date, Place.	Summary of Events and Information.	Remarks and references to Appendices
30th. November 1917.	Brigade called out at 9.15 am. proceeded via VILLERS FAUCON into action in the neighbourhood of GAUCHE WOOD. Majors FRASER and ATKINSON . 9th.Horse and Major RYDER 8th.Hussars killed.	See Appdx."A" and Map "A".
1st. December 1917.	18th.Lancers attacked and captured GAUCHE WOOD. Lt.Col. E.C.CORBYN, 18th.Lancers killed. Lt. KERNICK 14th.M.G.Sqdn. seriously wounded, subsequently died.	
Night Dec.1/2nd.1917.	Sec'bad Bde. relieved Ambala Cavalry Brigade, in the line. Brigade remained in the Valley South West of GENIN WELL Copse No.2.	
December 3rd. 1917.	Brigade returned to VILLERS FAUCON. Brigade was warned that it would have to produce a Dismounted Party to mann and work on the support line on the evening of the 4th. till further orders, in support of the 2nd. Cavalry Division.	
4th. December 1917.	A Dismounted Party 560 rifles moved up to the Sup ort line and occupied it as follows :- Right Sector.....9th.Hodson's Horse.W.18.d.Cent.- W.12.c.0.0. Centre Sector....8th.Hussars. W.12.c.0.0. - W.11.Cent. Left Sector...... 18th.Lancers. W.11.Cent. - W.5 Cent. Brigade Report Centre .W.28.b.8.8.	
Night 5/6th.Dec.1917.	Brigade relieved in the support line by elements of the 9th. and 21st. Infantry Divisions . Brigade returned to VILLERS FAUCON.	
6/7th. December 1917.	Brigade remained at VILLERS FAUCON.	
8th. December 1917.	Brigade moved to the CARTIGNY Area .	
9th. December 1917.	CARTIGNY Area. Parties went up to reconnoitre the Corps Line between TEMPLEUX le GUERARD and JEANCOURT. This line was to be occupied by the Brigade in case of alarm.	

Army Form C. 2118.

Instructions regarding War Diaries and Intelligence Summaries are contained in F. S. Regs., Part II, and the Staff Manual respectively. Title pages will be prepared in manuscript.

WAR DIARY

or

INTELLIGENCE SUMMARY.

AMBALA CAVALRY BRIGADE.
(Erase heading not required.)

Hour, Date, Place.	Summary of Events and Information.	Remarks and references to Appendices
10th. December 1917.	CARTIGNY AREA. The Brigade was warned to be at short notice to proceed to the Corps or intermediate line in support of 24th Division. Conference of Commanding Officers, at Brigade Headquarters	
11th. December 1917.	14th. M.G.Squadron left CARTIGNY to be attached to 6th. Corps at GOMIECOURT,	
12th. to 15th. "	CARTIGNY AREA.	
16th. "	Brigade came off short notice and ceased to be Mounted Reserve to the 24th. Division. A working party, 300 strong, was detailed by the Brigade nightly for work on the 2nd. Line under C.R.E. 24th Division.	
17th. "	The Brigadier proceeded to England on four weeks leave. Lt.Col G.A.Beatty, D.S.O., 9th. H. Horse, appointed to command the Lucknow Cavalry Brigade, proceeded the following morning to the 4th. Cavalry Division Headquarters. Lt.Col. G.Mort, 8th. Hussars assumed command of the Brigade. Major C.H.Rowcroft assumed command of the 9th. H. Horse.	
20th. "	Brigade ceased to detail Digging Parties, 300 strong. 14th. M.G. Squadron returned from attachment to 40th. Division, 6th. Corps.	
21st. "	9th. H. Horse and 14th. M.G.Squadron moved into billets in the TERTRY AREA.	
22nd. "	13th. Lancers and Mhow F. Amb. moved into billets at TERTRY.	
23rd. "	Brigade H.Q. and M.V.S. moved in TERTRY area.	
24th. "	From this day onwards a Digging Party had to be detailed nightly, 300 strong, for work under C.R.E., 24th. Division in the 2nd. Line.	
29th. "	8th. Hussars joined Brigade in TERTRY area.	
31st. "	Brigade ceased to provide Digging Parties to C.R.E., 24th. Division.	

Captain,
Brigade Major, Ambala Cavalry Brigade.

AMBALA CAVALRY BRIGADE.

APPENDIX "A"

Short account of the Operations carried out by the Ambala Cavalry Brigade between Midnight 30th. xxxxxxxx xxx November and 3rd. December 1917.

8.45 am. A telephone message from Division warned the Brigade to be prepared to move at short notice.

9.15 am. Another message ordered the Brigade to turn out at once and rendezvous at Cross road 1,000 yards East of ESTREES en Chaussee.

11.30 am. Brigade was concentrated at above Starting Point.

12.15 pm. Brigade less Echelon "B" arrived on the North Eastern outskirts of VILLERS FAUCON .

1.30 pm. Following orders were received from 5th. Cavalry Division .

"1 (a) The enemy has attacked on a front GUILLEMONT FARM - HONNECOURT and is now reported to be holding a line LE PETIT PRIEL FARM - VAUCELLETTE FARM - GHAUZEAUCOURT - LE VACQUERIE

(b) 1 Battalion of the "Queens" is at X.14 a.
1 Battalion of the Middlesex W. 5.d.
5th. Cavalry Brigade Q.35.b.
1 Sqdn. x.4th.Cav.Divn. Q.29.c.
2nd.Cav.Divn.H .Qrs. W.1.a.

2. The intention of the enemy appears to be to push his attack in a north westerly directon .

3. It is the intention of the G.O.C. to move on the outer flank of the enemy's north westerly attack, and to operate so as to drive him eastward.

4. In consequence, the Division will march on the FM. de BOIS at once as follows ,
Advanced Guard. Ambala Cavalry Brigade.
Main Body. Remainder of Division.

etc. etc.

The Brigadier decided to advance on GAUCHE WOOD AT once and seize it, and to discover the situation between GHAUZEAUCOURT and VILLERS GUISLAIN .
The Brigade advanced as follows :-
Advanced Guard. 8th.Hussars.
Main Body. B.H.Qrs., 9th.Horse, 14th.M.G.Sqdn.18th.Lcrs. Chow F.A., in that order.

x2.30 pm. Brigade Headquarters arrived at W.24.c.9.9.
It was discovered that VAUCELLETTE FARM was held by our Infantry and 2 Squadrons of Northumberland Hussars (Corps Cavalry) were xxxxxxx (advanced) by the Brigadier to support them.
Brigade got into touch with Headquarters West Surrey Regiment Point 143 (W.18.b) .

3. pm. 8th.Hussars held up by Machine gun fire ½ mile south of GOUZEAUCOURT, and reported enemy holding the ridge East of GOUCHE WOOD in X. 1.a. and c. and X.7.a. and c.
9th.Horse sent forward to support 8th.Hussars,the latter being ordered to make a dismounted attack on GAUCHE WOOD .
Main body moved to GENIN WELL Copse No. 2.

Operations were cheked for a short time for the following reasons 8th.Hussars in their advance came upon a band of wire entrenched line roughly between W.18.a.9.7. and W.1.a.7.3.
Whilst they were trying to find a passage through it they came under fairly heavy shell fire and so left their horses in the valley W.17.b.
The 9th. Horse passed through the wire East of REVELON FARM and also came under shell fire. They therefore dismounted in the valley W.11.b. (whence their horses were afterwards recalled to W.17.c.) and proceeded on foot .

<u>3.50 pm.</u> 8th.Hussars and 9th.Horse arrived in the sunken road W.6.c.and W.6.d. - b. respectively. Enemy in W.6.d.central driven back.

<u>4 pm.</u> 8th.Hussars found it impossible to advance , as on leaving sunken road they were counter attacked and were not strong enough to drive this counter attack further East than the Railway It was now getting very dark.

<u>4.55 pm.</u> 9th.Horse got into touch with Squadron of 20th. Hussars (2nd.Cav.Divn) to their left rear.

<u>Situation.</u> Sunken road in W. 6.b. and d. and C. held by 9th. H.Horse and 8th.Hussars. Enemy holding railway line in X.1 and 7.
Casualties 3 Squadron Leaders (Major Ryder, 8th.Hussars,Major Fraser, and Major Atkinson, 9th.H.Horse , all killed, and about 30 other ranks per Unit .
The Brigadier decided it was impracticable to attack GAUCHE WOOD without further preparation.
By this time Sec'bad Brigade had arrived at GOUZEAUCOURT(retaken during the afternoon by the Guards) and Canadian Brigade had pushed up to VAUCELLETTE FARM.

<u>5.pm.</u> "A" Battery R.C.H.A. reported to Brigade and came into action S.W. of GENIN WELL Copse No. 2 to cover the sunken road .

<u>7 pm.</u> 18th. Lancers ordered to relieve 8th.Hussars.
18th.Lancers was ordered (a) To reconnoitre GAUCHE WOOD during the night.
(b) To occupy it if the enemy had withdrawn.
(c) If still held to make every preparation to attack it on receipt of further orders.

<u>7.45 pm.</u> 8th.Hussars patrols all returned to sunken road, on account of heavy rifle and machine gun fire from railway line. 9th.Horse gained touch through the 20th. Hussars with the Guards Division, who told them that they were not going to advance any further that night . On relief of 8th.Hussars by 18th.Lancers situation was as follows :-
18th.Lancers . Sunken road W.12.a.3.8. - W.6.c.9.6. in touch with the "Queens". which were echeloned back 200 yds. to the right rear(this gap was filled with 2 H.G's and a squadron of the 9th. Horse.)

<u>Dec.1st. 12.10 am.</u> Following order received from 5th. Cav.Divn.
"1. 8 tanks from REVELON FARM will cross the line in Squares W.12 and 18 not later than 6.30 am. tomorrow to attack BOIS GAUCHE .

2. The attack by these tanks will be supported by the Ambala Brigade and BOIS GAUCHE is to be captured and held.

3. At the same time 8 other tanks will attack VILLERS GUISLAIN supported by the Lucknow Brigade

4.

....

4. An attack is to be made by the Guards Division tomorrow morning to secure the ridge East of Gouzeaucourt in Squares R.26.,31. 22. "

etc. etc.;

2. am. 18th.Lancers ordered to capture and hold GAUCHE WOOD with the co-operation of 8 tanks.
6 tanks were to advance on VILLERS GUISLAIN from further south, and 8 more from GOUZEAUCOURT were to co-operate. The attack was to start behind the tanks at 6.30 am. and the Guards were seize the ridge east of GOUZEAUCOURT whilst the Lucknow and Canadian Brigades pushed forward to secure the high ground on the PEIZIERES - VILLERS GUISLAIN Road in Squares S.14. 9.
There was also to be artillery co-operation in which "A" Battery took part.
It was however found impossible to get the tanks up to their various Starting Points in time and they eventually collected at 6.30 am. at GENIN WELL Copse No. 2.
The tanks arrived at the Railway Line and crossed at X.1.c. at 7.15 am.

7.30 am. 18th.Lancers seen crossing the railway in X.1.

8.30 am. 18th.Lancers and Guards consolidating on the Eastern and Southern edge of GAUCHE WOOD. 50 odd prisoners were passed back. 4 Guns of 14th. M.G.Squadron were sent up to GAUCHE WOOD During the tank attack some of these machine only entered the wood and then from the North. It is believed that they lost their way as after crossing therailway they turned North, leaving GAUCHE WOOD on their right. None of them succeeded in reaching VILLERS GUISLAIN.

9.30 am. Guards held up about R.31.Central. The Brigade reinforced by 7th.D.G's (Sec'bad Bde) ordered to attack Northwards from GAUCHE WOOD along the MONT ST.QUENTIN Spur to help the Guards.

9.45 am. 7th.D.G's ordered to advance via sunken road to GAUCHE WOOD and thence to attack North. 9th.Horse ordered to co-operate.
As the attack was developing the Guards advanced to R.32.c. and from this point a line was occupied to GAUCHE WOOD by 7th.D.G's.

12.noon. Situation was as follows :- Grenadier Guards and 18th.Lancers.held East and Southern faces of GAUCHE WOOD. Grenadiers from South West corner to X.7.Central. 1 Sqdn.9th.Horse thence in a S.W. direction trying to get touch with L.B.H. on the right. 7th.D.G's as above. The line was not sufficiently strongly held to resist a determined counter attack, and this fact submitted to Division. The enemy had shelled GAUCHE WOOD and the ground between it and sunken road pretty heavily all day, and the Brigade had suffered a certain number of casualties including the loss of Lt.Col.H.C.CORBYN, 18th.Lancers.

1.15 pm. G.A.675 received from Division. It detailed an attack on VILLERS GUISLAIN at 3 pm. by the 4th. Cav.Divn. and Canadian Bde. Ambala Brigade had no active part in this attack.

6 pm. G.A.679 received from Division. Sec'bad Bde. was to relieve Ambala Brigade in the line on the night 1st/2nd.December.

Relief was completed by 5 am. 2ndDecember but 8th.Hussars and 14th. M.G.Sqdn. were left as reserve to Sec'bad Brigade.

Night 2nd/3rd. A working party of 2 Officers and 31 O.R's from each of the Indian Regiments worked on the 2nd. Line.

3rd. December. Brigade less "A" Battery R.C.H.A. was concentrated again at VILLERS FAUCON.

APPENDIX A

TRAINING PROGRAMME for the WEEK ENDING NOVEMBER 10th. 1917.

Brigade Location of H.Q.	UNIT. Location of H.Q.	Description of Training.	REMARKS.
AMBALA MARESQUEL.	8th.Hussars BEAURAINVILLE	Squadron Training, Equitation Respirator and Foot Drill.	Regtl.Training Area. 5th.,6th.,9th.
		Officers Staff Ride.	Regtl.Training Area 9 am. 8th.
	9th.H.Horse. CAVRON ST.MARTIN.	Squadron Training,	Regtl.Training Area 9 am. 5th.
		Respirator and Foot Drill.	" " "
		Regtl.Foot Route March.	From Billets 10am. 8th.
		Inter-Sqdn. Exercise.	Regtl.Training Area 9am. 9th.
		Officers Staff Ride.	" " " 10 am. 6th.
	18th. Lancers. AUBIN ST.VAAST.	Squadron Training	Regtl.Training Area 9 am. 5th.6th.8th.
		Respirator and Foot Drill.	" " "
		Officers Staff Ride.	Rendezvous AUBIN ST.VAAST 9am. 9th.
	14th.M.G.Sqdn. WAMBERCOURT.	Firing on Range and Range finding. Map reading. Barrage Drill. Respirator Drill.	Squadron Training Area.
	Ambala Bde. MARESQUEL.	Inter-Regtl.Exercise.	Rendezvous.AUBIN ST.VAAST 10am. 7th.

Headquarters Ambala Cavalry Brigade.
Field........31st. October 1917.

To. General Staff,
5th. Cavalry Division.

Forwarded.

[signature]
Captain.
Brigade Major, Ambala Cavalry Brigade.

Copies to.8th.Hrs,9th.H.H.
18th.Lcrs., M.G.Sqdn.

TRAINING PROGRAMME for the Week Ending 3rd, NOVEMBER 1917.

BRIGADE. Location of H.Q.	UNIT. Location of H.Q.	Description of Training.	Remarks.
AMBALA MARESQUEL.	8th.Hussars BEAURAINVILLE	Sqdn.Training & Equitation. Officer's Staff Rides.,Map reading. Training of Signallers, Foot Drill. Respirator Drill.	Regtl.Area .9.30 am. 29th.,30th. Officers Staff Ride 1st.Nov. C.O.inspects 3 Sqdns. of Regt. 9.30 am. on 29th.,30th. Oct. 1st,Nov Regtl.Drill. 9.30am. 2nd. Nov.
	9th.H.Horse. CAVRON St. MARTIN.	Sqdn.Training. & Equitation. Officers Staff Rides. Map reading. Training of Signallers. Foot Drill. Respirator Drill.	Regtl.Area 9 am. 29th.Oct. 1st. 2nd. ov Officers Staff Ride.Regtl.Area 10 am. 30th. Oct.
	18th.Lancers. AUBIN St. VAAST.	Sqdn.Training & Equitation. Officers Staff Rides. Map reading. Training of Signallers. Foot Drill. Respirator Drill.	Regtl.Area 9 am.29th., 30th. Oct. 1st., 2nd. Nov.
	14th. M.G.Sqdn. WAMBERCOURT.	Sqdn.Training.,Range Finding, Indication and recognition of targets. Respirator Drill.	Squadron Area.
	Ambala Brigade.	Inter-Regimental Exercise.	Rendezvous. 9.30 am. 31st. Oct. St.ANDRE AU BOIS.

Headquarters Ambala Cavalry Brigade.
Field.........24th. October 1917.

To. General Staff,
5th. Cavalry Division.

Forwarded.

208/29

A[illegible]
Captain.
Brigade Major, Ambala Cavalry Brigade.

Copy to. 8th.Hrs, 9th.H.H.
18th.Lcrs., M.G.Sqdn.

Instructions regarding War Diaries and Intelligence Summaries are contained in F. S. Regs., Part II, and the Staff Manual respectively. Title pages will be prepared in manuscript.

WAR DIARY
or
INTELLIGENCE SUMMARY.

H.Qrs. AMBALA CAVALRY BRIGADE.
(Erase heading not required.)

January 1918.

Army Form C. 2118.

108.

Hour, Date, Place.	Summary of Events and Information.	Remarks and references to Appendices
Jany.1 - 10/ 18.	TERTRY Area - Brigade was occupied in building accomodation, and constructing 3 foot walls, round hutments, and stables, to localise the effect of hostile air-raids. Training consisted of Dismounted work, round billets. During this period Brigade was mounted Reserve to Dismounted Division.	
January 11th. 1918.	Brigade received Secret Orders that it was to be at short notice to move for service overseas.	
" 13th. "	Brigade ceased to be Mounted reserve to Dismounted Division.	
" 16th. "	Col. Mort, 8th.Hussars went on leave to England, Lt.Col.Keighley 18th. Lancers took over command of the Brigade.	
" 18th. "	Brigade furnished a digging party 200 strong for cable-laying and burying under C.R.E.Corps. Corps Commander presented medals for gallantry in recent operations. 1 Sqdn. 8th.Hussars attended as escort.	
" 25th. "	Brigade received warning that it would take over the Line from the 1st. Dismounted Brigade on the night 26th/27th. All digging parties cancelled.	
" 26th. "	Brigade took over Front Line Sub-sector A.1. between River OMIGNON and No. 4 Post G.31.b.5.8. Strength of Brigade :- 8th.Hussars...205 all ranks. 9th.Horse..230 all ranks. 18th.Lancers...230 all ranks.	

(Contd)

Army Form C. 2118.

WAR DIARY
or
INTELLIGENCE SUMMARY.
AMBALA CAVALRY BRIGADE.
(Erase heading not required.)

Instructions regarding War Diaries and Intelligence Summaries are contained in F. S. Regs., Part II, and the Staff Manual respectively. Title pages will be prepared in manuscript.

Hour, Date, Place.	Summary of Events and Information.	Remarks and references to Appendices
Jany. 26th. 1918. (Continued)	Relief completed by 9.30 pm. 9th. Hussars held Line on the Right. 18th. Lancers " " " " LEFT. 9th. Horse [illegible] Regiment in Support. Intermediate Line.	See Map No. 1.
January 30th. 1918.	Led Horses under Major C.H. Rowcroft, 9th. H. Horse marched West from TERTRY to WARFUSEE - ABANCOURT Area. 9th. Horse relieved 18th. Lancers in the Left Sub-sector. 18th. Lancers became Regiment in Support, and [illegible] back to the Intermediate Line.	
January 31st. 1918.	Led Horses marched via Amiens to VIGNACOURT area.	

Captain.
Brigade Major, Ambala Cavalry Brigade.

Instructions regarding War Diaries and Intelligence Summaries are contained in F. S. Regs., Part II, and the Staff Manual respectively. Title pages will be prepared in manuscript.

WAR DIARY
or
INTELLIGENCE SUMMARY.

AMBALA CAVALRY BRIGADE.
(Erase heading not required.)

Army Form C. 2118.

(108.)

Hour, Date, Place.	Summary of Events and Information.	Remarks and references to Appendices
1st. February 1918.	Led Horses arrived in neighbourhood of ABBEVILLE, LONGWY Area. Where they remained.	
3rd. " "	Brig. Genl. C. RANKIN C.M.G., D.S.O. returned from England and assumed command of the Brigade. The Brigade was relieved in the line by Sec'bad Brigade and went into Reserve at VADENCOURT.	
4th. " "	8th. Hussars garrison forts at LE VERGUIER - 9th. H. Horse and 18th. Lancers in Reserve at VADENCOURT. Digging parties furnished by these two Units alternately.	
8th. " "	18th. Lancers patrol reconnoitred wire and trenches W. of ST. HELENE and found them held. Lieut. W. D. HENRY and 1 O.R. 8th. Hussars wounded at LE VERGUIER.	
9th. " "	18th. Lancers patrol reconnoitred wire W. of ST. HELENE switch trench. Heavily fired on by M.G's and rifles.	
10th. " "	18th. Lancers Raid rehearsed by day.	
11th. " "	18th. Lancers Raid rehearsed by day and by night.	
12th. " "	Raid carried out - A failure - No prisoners taken. 2 men slightly wounded. 14th. M.G. Squadron relieved by 7th. M.G. Squadron,	
15th. " "	Brigade relieved in the line by Units of the 1st. and 9th. Cavalry Brigades. 9th. H. Horse relieved by 15th. Hussars 3.30 pm. 18th. Lancers by 5th. D.G's 2 pm. B.H.Q. by 1st. Cav. Bde. 8th. Hussars remained in line. Code word sent 4.15 pm.	

Army Form C. 2118.

Instructions regarding War Diaries and Intelligence Summaries are contained in F. S. Regs., Part II, and the Staff Manual respectively. Title pages will be prepared in manuscript.

WAR DIARY
or
~~INTELLIGENCE~~ ~~SUMMARY~~.

AMBALA CAVALRY BRIGADE.
(Erase heading not required.)

Hour, Date, Place.	Summary of Events and Information.	Remarks and references to Appendices
16th. February 1918.	8th. Hussars relieved by 18th. Hussars.	
19th. " "	12 mules killed, 5 O.R's wounded, 8th. Hussars, VERMAND from bomb dropped by E.A.	
22nd. " "	Orders received for preliminary moves of 9th., 18th. and 14th. M.G. Sqdn.	
23rd. " "	R.H.A. Drivers attached to Indian Units despatched to ROUEN. Capt. GRAHAM, Brigade Major joined 1st. Cav. Div. as Brigade Major. Following entrained today for TORANTO, leaving SALEUX 4.20 pm. B.O's / I.O's / O.R.B. / O.R.I. 9th. H. Horse: 2 / 2 / - / 50 18th. Lancers: 3 / 2 / - / 50 14th. M.G. Sqdn.: - / - / - / -	
24th. " "	Following entrained today for TORANTO, leaving SALEUX 4.20 pm. B.O's / I.O's / O.R.B. / O.R.I. 9th. H. Horse: 7 / - / 1 / 7 18th. Lancers: 6 / - / 1 / 8 14th. M.G. Sqdn.: 1 / - / 9 / 1 Capt. LOMAS, A.V.C. transferred to M.V.S. Sec'bad Brigade.	
25th. " "	Billetting parties of 9th. H.H., 18th. Lcrs. proceeded to entraining area.	
26th. " "	9th. H.H., 18th. Lcrs., Mhow F.A. & M.V.S. (Indian Personnel) moved to entraining area around SALEUX.	Capt., S.C. for B.M. Ambala Cavalry Bde.
27th " "	Portion of 9th. H.H. and 18th. Lcrs. entrained - Mhow F.A. and M.V.S. entrained also at SALEUX.	
28th. " "	M.G's and remainder of Brigade entrained SALEUX.	

SECRET. Copy No.......13

S.6

Ambala Cavalry Brigade Operation

Order . No...35...

-----oOo--------

Ref.Maps 1:100,000 25th.February 1918.
LENS,AMIENS,ABBEVILLE.

1. 9th.H.Horse, 18th.Lancers, 14th. M.G.Squadron, remainder of Mhow F.A. and portion of M.V.Section will march to entraining area as per attached table.

2. Billoting parties except the M.G.Squadron will proceed ahead on the 25th. inst. to their respective areas.

3. Present billets will be left scrupulously clean. Rear guards to be left to see that this is done.

4. An Officer to be left behind to settle all claims. Due notice to be given to the Maire and all billeting certificates to be completed before departure.

5. Lorries for the conveyance of kit will be detailed later.

6. ACKNOWLEDGE.

Captain.

for Brigade Major, Ambala Cavalry Brigade

Distribution thro.Sigs. 11 am.

Copy No. 1. 9th.Horse.
2. 18th.Lcrs.
3. M.G.Sqdn.
4. Mhow F.A.
5. M.V.Section.
6. 5th.Cav.Divn.
7 to 9. War Diary.
10. Office.

MARCH TABLE for 26th. and 27th. February issued with Operation Order No. 35.

ORDER OF MARCH.	TIME.	STARTING POINT.	ROUTE.	DESTINATION.	REMARKS.
9th. Horse.	10.15 am. 26th. inst.	Cross Roads L'ETOILE.	N. Bank of R. SOMME via FLIXECOURT. Cross river SOMME at PICQUIGNY and thence to billeting areas.	PROUZEL - PLACHY BUYON BUYON - NAMPTY-NEUVILLE sous LOEUILLY.	
18th. Lcrs.	-do-	in rear of 9th. Horse.	-do-	SAISSEVAL-CLAIRY SAULCHOIX-GUIGNEMICOURT-BOVELLES.	
"A" Echelons.	-do-	in rear of 18th. Lcrs.	-do-		
M.V. Sect.	-do-	In rear of "A" Echelons.	-do-	With 18th. Lancers.	
Mhow F.A.	-do-	In rear of M.V. Section.	-do-	RUMIGNY.	(To cut into the column (at FLIXECOURT. (Motors to move (independently.
"B" Echelons.	-do-		-do-		
14th. M.G.S.	9.30 am. 27th. inst.	Cross Rds. EAUCOURT.	-do-	RUMIGNY.	

"A" Echelon under an Officer of 9th. H. Horse.
"B" Echelon under an Officer of 18th. Lancers.

1917-1918
5TH CAVALRY DIVISION
AMBALA CAVALRY BDE

8TH (K.R.I.) HUSSARS

JAN 1917 - FEB 1918.

FROM 2 IND CAV DIV
AMBALA BDE
BOX 1185

TO 1 CAV DIV 9 BDE
BOX 1115

1164

SERIAL NO. 110.

Confidential

War Diary

of

8th (K.R.I). HUSSARS.

FROM 1st January 1917 ... 191 TO 31st. January 1917 ... 191

Instructions regarding War Diaries and Intelligence Summaries are contained in F. S. Regs., Part II. and the Staff Manual respectively. Title Pages will be prepared in manuscript.

WAR DIARY

~~INTELLIGENCE SUMMARY~~

(Erase heading not required.)

Army Form C. 2118

Place	Date	Hour	Summary of Events and Information	Remarks and references to Appendices
GAMACHES (Somme)	1.1.17		Dull rain all day. Squadrons paraded. Orders received for Pioneer Battalion to entrain between 6.0 am and 9.0 am on the 2nd inst. Transport to be loaded at 6.0 am. 6512 Pte D. COULSON (Bronchitis) 13379 Pte HOLMES (Commotion) 6236 L/c WALE (Bronchitis) to Hospital. Major R BONSOR 3rd Corps Cav: Major W.E. ROYDS 3rd Corps Cav: and Major A MITCHELL 13th Light Horse Regt. 1st A.N.Z.A.C., reported their arrival for attachment.	G.R.A.
GAMACHES (Somme).	2.1.17		Dull warm. Some rain early. Squadrons exercised. Pioneer Bn entrained at 8.0 am. Lieut C.A. WILLES as Adjutant; Captain P.S. ALEXANDER Comdg Company and 2/Lts. A.L. WILLIAMS, R.W. KNIGHT, Hon W.M. STOURTON, H.E.A.E. BOLTON 240 other ranks 20 D.H. 1 R.H and 6 vehicles.	G.R.A.
GAMACHES (Somme).	3.1.17		Dull Drizzle – high wind. Squadrons exercised. Regimental Tactical exercise for junior officers	G.R.A.
—.—	4.1.17		Dull – rain all morning. Squadrons exercised. Brigade Tactical exercise (without troops) Casualties with sniping party to noon 30th – 2/Lt J.P. ROBINSON reported slightly wounded – at duty.	G.R.A.
—.—	5.1.17		Dull – no rain. Sniping party casualties to noon 3rd – Wounded – No 6059 Pte. T. BLACKBURN No 9006 " F. BATTERSBY.	G.R.A.

1875 Wt. W593/826 1,000,000 4/15 J.B.C. & A. A.D.S.S./Forms/C. 2118.

Army Form C. 2118

Instructions regarding War Diaries and Intelligence Summaries are contained in F. S. Regs., Part II. and the Staff Manual respectively. Title Pages will be prepared in manuscript.

WAR DIARY
or
~~INTELLIGENCE SUMMARY~~
(Erase heading not required.)

Place	Date	Hour	Summary of Events and Information	Remarks and references to Appendices
GAMACHES (Somme)	6.1.17		Dull - cold. Squadrons exercised. Inspection of "B" Squadron horses by B.V.O 2.30p.m.	G.R.A.
—"—	7.1.17		Dull - cold. Squadrons exercised. Divine Service C of E — Holy Communion 8.30am, Parade Service 10.0am. Lieut A. LADENBURG MC reported his arrival for duty from Intelligence Officer 5th Cavalry Division.	G.R.A.
—"—	8.1.17		Rain all night - High wind - showers of sleet. Squadrons exercised. Regimental Tactical Exercise for Junior Officers.	G.R.A.
—"—	9.1.17		Dull - cold. Snow fell heavily all morning. Lts Broomfield "C" & Davies "D" and Capt Hensman "D" to Hospital from Pioneer Battn. 6.1.17.	G.R.A.
—"—	10.1.17		Dull - cold - Heavy showers of sleet. Squadrons exercised. T. 2/Lieut A.I.B RITCHIE reported his arrival from X Reserve Regt.	G.R.A.
—"—	11.1.17		Dull - cold. Snow fell during morning. Brigade Tactical Exercise (indoors)	G.R.A.
—"—	12.1.17		Dull - cold. Showers of snow and sleet during day. Regimental Tactical Exercise. Squadrons exercised. Major Hon. R.N.D RYDER rejoined from Sick Leave	G.R.A.

Instructions regarding War Diaries and Intelligence Summaries are contained in F. S. Regs., Part II. and the Staff Manual respectively. Title Pages will be prepared in manuscript.

WAR DIARY ~~or INTELLIGENCE SUMMARY~~

(Erase heading not required.)

Army Form C. 2118

Place	Date	Hour	Summary of Events and Information	Remarks and references to Appendices
GAMACHES (Somme)	13.1.17		Dull - warmer. Squadrons exercised	G.R.A.
— " —	14.1.17		Dull - heavy snow fall during night - Cold. Squadrons exercised. 1 O.R from Base Major R BONSOR Major W.E ROYDS 3rd Corps Cavalry left to rejoin on completion of attachment. Lt Col C.S AUDRY Wiltshire Yeo. and Major A.N. AITKEN 13th L.H.R 1st A.N.Z.A.C joined	G.R.A.
— " —	15.1.17		Fine - frost during night - Squadrons exercised. Major A. MITCHELL 13th L.H.R left to rejoin on completion of attachment. Inspection of a loaded G.S limber wagon by G.O.C Brigade.	G.R.A.
— " —	16.1.17		Fine - very cold. - Hard frost during night. Commanding Officer inspected horses of A & D Sqdns at exercise. Following evacuated sick from Pioneer Bn.:- 14370 Pte J Griffiths, (Gastritis) 8147 Pte Carroll (Gonorrhoea) 9328 Pte Kerr (Scabies). 12 O.R to Pioneer Bn as reinforcements.	G.R.A.
— " —	17.1.17		Dull - heavy fall of snow during night and day. Regimental Tactical Exercise postponed. Following casualty reported from Pioneer Bn. - 1584 Pte T. SHADBOLT evacuated sick 14.1.17.	G.R.A.
— " —	18.1.17		Dull - thaw - rain in morning. Squadrons exercised.	G.R.A.

Instructions regarding War Diaries and Intelligence Summaries are contained in F. S. Regs., Part II. and the Staff Manual respectively. Title Pages will be prepared in manuscript.

WAR DIARY

~~INTELLIGENCE SUMMARY~~

(Erase heading not required.)

Army Form C. 2118

Place	Date	Hour	Summary of Events and Information	Remarks and references to Appendices
GAMACHES (Somme)	19.1.17		Dull - Frost during night. Squadrons exercised. Brigade Tactical Exercise. Following evacuated sick from Pioneer Bn:- 4738 Pte Burrows 1848 Pte O'Reilly 777 Pte Maxwell to Hospital - fractured rib. 3. OR from Base. 3. OR to Pioneer Bn as reinforcements. No 26371 Pte H. Morris to England for temporary commission in Infantry. Lt Col F W Mussenden rejoined from X Reserve Regt.	G.R.A.
— " —	20.1.17		Dull - hard frost - very cold. Squadrons exercised. 2/Lt A.C. ORCHIN and 6. OR to Divisional School. 2/Lt B H HOUSE and 2 NCO's from Divisional School. 7553 Pte O'Connell evacuated to Hospital.	G.R.A.
— " —	21.1.17		Dull - hard frost. Squadrons exercised. Divine Service C. of E. 10-0 am — Holy Communion 10.30 am 13394 Pte C W BIRKBECK to England to Cadet School for Temporary commission in RA.	G.R.A.
— " —	22.1.17		Bright - hard frost. Regimental Tactical Exercise. Squadrons exercised.	G.R.A.
— " —	23.1.17		Bright - very hard frost. Squadrons exercised. Lt Col C.S AUBRY - Wilts Yeo: and Major A N AITKEN 13th L.H.R, 1st A.N.Z.A.C. left to rejoin units on completion of attachment.	G.R.A.

1875 Wt. W593/826 1,000,000 4/15 J.B.C. & A. A.D.S.S./Forms/C. 2118.

Instructions regarding War Diaries and Intelligence Summaries are contained in F. S. Regs., Part II. and the Staff Manual respectively. Title Pages will be prepared in manuscript.

WAR DIARY

or

~~INTELLIGENCE SUMMARY~~

(Erase heading not required.)

Army Form C. 2118

Place	Date	Hour	Summary of Events and Information	Remarks and references to Appendices
GAMACHES (Somme)	24.1.17		Bright – hard frost. Squadrons exercised.	G.R.A.
—.—	25.1.17		Bright – hard frost. Squadrons exercised. Brigade Conference on Divisional Tactical Exercise. 2/Lt A.L. Williams rejoined from Pioneer Bn.	G.R.A.
—.—	26.1.17		Bright – hard frost. Squadrons exercised. Inspection of horses of A & B Sqdns by C.O. Following evacuated sick from Pioneer Bn.:– 6448 Pte SHAW 23.1.17. Following rejoined Pioneer Bn from Field Ambulance:– 4743 Pte BURROWS. 1 O.R to Hospital 24.1.17.	G.R.A.
—.—	27.1.17		Bright – hard frost. Squadrons exercised. Inspection of D Sqdn horses by C.O. T. Capt. D POPE wounded G.S.W. (thigh) 12.1.17. Following evacuated from Pioneer Bn to Ambulance Field Ambulance:– 14382 Pte Stubbins 5383 Pte Williams 6495 Pte Cooke. Following rejoined from Field Ambulance – 1848 Pte O'Reilly 7553 Pte O'Connell	G.R.A.
—.—	28.1.17		Bright – hard frost. Squadrons exercised. 2 O.R. to Pioneer Bn.	G.R.A.
—.—	29.1.17		Bright – hard frost. Squadrons exercised. No 6578 Sgt J. RILEY 8 Hussars to be 2/LIEUT. 8th Bn Yorkshire L.I. d/- 10.1.17.	G.R.A.

Instructions regarding War Diaries and Intelligence Summaries are contained in F. S. Regs., Part II. and the Staff Manual respectively. Title Pages will be prepared in manuscript.

WAR DIARY

~~INTELLIGENCE SUMMARY~~

(Erase heading not required.)

Army Form C. 2118

Place	Date	Hour	Summary of Events and Information	Remarks and references to Appendices
GAMACHES (Somme)	30.1.17		Hard frost. Bright morning, dull in afternoon. A little snow fell in course of the day. Squadrons exercised.	G.R.A.
"	31.1.17		Frost & snow during night. Bright but cold. Squadrons exercised.	G.R.A.

F.W. Mussenden
LIEUT. COLONEL,
COMMANDING VIII (K.R.I.) HUSSARS.

G.R.A. [illegible] CAPTAIN,
ADJUTANT VIII (K.R.I.) HUSSARS

1875 Wt. W593/826 1,000,000 4/15 J.B.C. & A. A.D.S.S./Forms/C. 2118.

Instructions regarding War Diaries and Intelligence Summaries are contained in F. S. Regs., Part II. and the Staff Manual respectively. Title pages will be prepared in manuscript.

WAR DIARY or ~~INTELLIGENCE SUMMARY.~~

(Erase heading not required.)

8th K.R.I. Hussars — Army Form C. 2118.

Confidential

Place	Date	Hour	Summary of Events and Information	Remarks and references to Appendices
GAMACHES (Somme)	1.2.17		Dull and cold. Snow fell during day. Squadrons exercised. Bombing display by 9th Hodson's Horse & 18th Lancers. Casualties reported from Pioneer Bn:- No 5495 Cpl E HANDLEY evacuated sick 28.1.17. No 6363 Pte WESTON evacuated sick 29.1.17	G.R.A.
— . —	2.2.17		Bright, hard frost. Squadrons exercised. Casualties reported from Pioneer Bn on 31.1.17:- 14345 Pte S. BEVAN Sick 16821 Pte OWENS Sick.	G.R.A.
— . —	3.2.17		Bright - hard frost. Inspection of horses at exercise by G.O.C. Brigade. Lieut L.W.D. WATHEN to be Acting Captain whilst Commanding 2nd Machine Gun Squadron d/- 26.11.16	G.R.A.
— . —	4.2.17		Bright - hard frost. Divine Service C of E 10.0 am. Holy Communion 10.30 am	G.R.A.
— . —	5.2.17		Dull - heavy fall of snow during night - warmer. Inspection of horses for casting by G.O.C. Following evacuated sick from Ambala Pioneer Bn:- 3741 Cpl W BROWN 14343 Pte V. GEORGE.	G.R.A.
— . —	6.2.17		Fine, cold, hard frost. Squadrons exercised. Roads very slippery. 14382 Pte F STUBBINS rejoined Pioneer Bn from Field Amb. 4.2.17. Undermentioned evacuated sick to AMBALA Field Ambulance 4.2.17:- 24710 Pte O'HALLORAN 5889 " HORREX.	G.R.A.

Instructions regarding War Diaries and Intelligence Summaries are contained in F. S. Regs., Part II. and the Staff Manual respectively. Title pages will be prepared in manuscript.

WAR DIARY
or
~~INTELLIGENCE SUMMARY.~~
(Erase heading not required.)

Army Form C. 2118.

Place	Date	Hour	Summary of Events and Information	Remarks and references to Appendices
GAMACHES (Somme)	7.2.17		Fine - very cold - hard frost. No 14370 Pte T. GRIFFITHS rejoined ARABIA Pioneer Bn from Hospital 4.2.17.	G.R.A.
—	8.2.17		Fine - cold - hard frost. Squadrons exercised. Brigade Tactical Exercise (indoor). Following casualty reported from Pioneer Battn :- No 2869 Pte C. Fitzgerald - sick - 6.2.17.	G.R.A.
—	9.2.17		Fine - cold - hard frost - Squadrons exercised	G.R.A.
—	10.2.17		Fine - cold - hard frost - Squadrons exercised - Following casualty reported from Pioneer Bn :- No 6134 Pte R Reynolds evacuated sick	G.R.A.
—	11.2.17		Fine - hard frost. Squadrons exercised.	G.R.A.
—	12.2.17		Dull - cold - slight thaw - Squadrons exercised. Following evacuated sick from Pioneer Bn :- 6470 Pte W Hennessy 25030 H Deakin 16591 G. Kay 9.2.17. No 14348 Pte S Bevan rejoined Pioneer Bn from Field Ambce 9.2.17. Capt L E WILLIAMS RAMC rejoined from leave - T/Lt J N CRUICKSHANK RAMC rejoined M How Field Ambce	G.R.A.
—	13.2.17		Dull - brighter later - cold wind. Slight thaw continued. Squadrons exercised.	G.R.A.
—	14.2.17		Bright, cold - some frost during night. Squadrons exercised. No. 6694 Pte Wheeler to Hospital - Pyrexia	G.R.A.

2353 Wt. W2514/1454 700,000 5/15 D. D. & L. A.D.S.S./Forms/C. 2118.

Army Form C. 2118.

Instructions regarding War Diaries and Intelligence Summaries are contained in F. S. Regs., Part II. and the Staff Manual respectively. Title pages will be prepared in manuscript.

WAR DIARY
or
~~INTELLIGENCE SUMMARY.~~
(Erase heading not required.)

Place	Date	Hour	Summary of Events and Information	Remarks and references to Appendices
GAMACHES (Somme)	15.2.17		Bright - cold - frost during night. Squadrons exercised. Brigade Tactical Exercise. Following evacuated sick from Pioneer Bn. 4743 Pte Burrows. 4256 Pte Turner 12.2.17. No 1626 Pte Power evacuated sick from Pioneer Bn 13.2.17.	G.R.A.
—	16.2.17		Dull - slight frost. Squadrons exercised. 19 Riding horses handed over to Canadian Horse Artillery Brigade. 3 Riding Horses handed over to No. 14. Machine Gun Squadron.	G.R.A.
—	17.2.17		Dull - thaw - much warmer. Squadrons exercised. No 22709 Pte Puncher evacuated Sick from Pioneer Bn 14.2.17.	G.R.A.
—	18.2.17		Fine - warm. Squadrons exercised. Divine Service C. of E. 10.0 am. Holy Communion 10.30 am. Lieut Col VO Thynne DSO Lieut D H Davy and 2/Lieut R S Forbes R. Wilts Yeo 15th Corps reported their arrival for attachment with 9 OR 10 RH 4 LD & 1 GS Wagon.	G.R.A.
—	19.2.17		Dull - warm. Squadrons inspected at exercise by C.O. Major Hon'ble R N D Ryder to Divisional School for attachment with 2 servants 3 horses. Lieut J C Brutton to Hospital - Rheumatism.	G.R.A.

2353 Wt. W2544/1454 700,000 5/15 D. D. & L. A.D.S.S./Forms/C. 2118.

Instructions regarding War Diaries and Intelligence Summaries are contained in F. S. Regs., Part II. and the Staff Manual respectively. Title pages will be prepared in manuscript.

WAR DIARY or INTELLIGENCE SUMMARY.

(Erase heading not required.)

Army Form C. 2118.

Place	Date	Hour	Summary of Events and Information	Remarks and references to Appendices
GAMACHES (Somme)	20.2.17		Dull - cold - rain. Inspection of horses of the Brigade at exercise by the Divisional Commander. The following rejoined AMBALA Pioneer Battn from Field Ambce:- 9328 Pte Kerr 25035 Pte Deakin. Following evacuated sick from Pioneer Battn - 5392 Pte Middleton	G.R.P.
—	21.2.17		Dull - Squadrons exercised. No 16182 Pte Burden to Hospital. Bronchitis	G.R.P.
—	22.2.17		Dull - foggy - cold. Squadrons exercised. Brigade Tactical exercise. Lieut W.M.D. HENRY and 2/Lt C.T. LINFORD reported their arrival from X Reserve Regt. 3 other ranks arrived from Base. 536 Pte Stearne evacuated to No 8 Field Ambce from Pioneer Bn.	G.R.P.
—	23.2.17		Dull - foggy - cold. Regimental Tactical exercise. 5779 Pte Lone evacuated sick from Pioneer Bn - 20.2.17.	G.R.P.
—	24.2.17		Fine - Squadrons exercised. No 4396 Pte Thucker rejoined Pioneer Bn from Hospital 20.2.17.	G.R.P.
—	25.2.17		Fine - Squadrons exercised. Lecture on Censorship. 1 O.R. evacuated sick from Pioneer Battn. Lieut G.A. ATKINSON-WILLES from Pioneer Bn to ~~Hospital~~ sick - to No 37 Rest Station	

2353 Wt. W2544/1454 700,000 5/15 D. D. & L. A.D.S.S./Forms/C. 2118.

Instructions regarding War Diaries and Intelligence Summaries are contained in F. S. Regs., Part II. and the Staff Manual respectively. Title pages will be prepared in manuscript.

WAR DIARY ~~or~~ INTELLIGENCE SUMMARY.

(*Erase heading not required.*)

Army Form C. 2118.

Place	Date	Hour	Summary of Events and Information	Remarks and references to Appendices
GAMACHES	26.2.17		Fine - Squadrons exercised & Regimental Tactical Exercise.	G.R.A.
(Somme).	27.2.17		Fine Squadrons exercised. Following ~~[illegible]~~ rejoined Pioneer Bn from AMBALA Field Amblce:- 5392 A Middleton. 4743 L Burrows. 24.2.17 2 Lieut T. B A EVANS-LOMBE and 1 OR reported arrival. 1 Charger and 1 OR from Base Remount Depot ABBEVILLE.	G.R.A.
—	28.2.17		Dull - cold. Squadrons exercised. Casualties reported from Pioneer Battn:- 4396 F Thacker 18707 A Bull to Ambala Field Ambulance 20.2.17 2 Lieut A I B RITCHIE to Pioneer Bn to replace Lieut G.A ATKINSON-WILLES	G.R.A.

K Currell
MAJOR,
COMMANDING VIII (K.R.I.) HUSSARS.

G.R.A. [signature]
CAPTAIN,
ADJUTANT VIII (K.R.I.) HUSSARS.

R

Serial No: 110.

Confidential

War Diary

of

VIII Kings Royal Irish Hussars

From 1st March to 31st March 1917

Vol 31

Instructions regarding War Diaries and Intelligence Summaries are contained in F. S. Regs., Part II. and the Staff Manual respectively. Title pages will be prepared in manuscript.

WAR DIARY or ~~INTELLIGENCE SUMMARY.~~

(Erase heading not required.)

8th (K.R.I.) Hussars

Army Form C. 2118.

Confidential.

Place	Date	Hour	Summary of Events and Information	Remarks and references to Appendices
GAMACHES	1.3.17		Dull, cold – Squadrons exercised. Brigade Tactical Exercise. Following rejoined Pioneer Bn from Field Ambce:– 6479 Pte W. Fennessy. 5889 Pte R Horrex 6616 Pte W. McCrath. 2/Lt J.D. Paton and 20 other ranks, with 43 horses rejoined from Fourth Army School	GRA.
GAMACHES	2.3.17		Fine – squadrons exercised.	GRA.
– " –	3.3.17		Dull – cold wind Slight frost Inspection of Horses at exercise by G.O.C. Brigade 1 other ranks to Corps HQ as Corps Flying Officer.	GRA.
—	4.3.17		Fine, slight frost during night. Sqdns exercised. Divine Service C of E 10 am. T/2/Lt R WHINYATES to be Actg Captain whilst Comdg W/32 Trench Mortar Battery from 29th May to 29th Dec: 1916. { Holy Communion 10.30 am	GRA.
—	5.3.17		Fine – some snow during night. Squadrons exercised. Lieut J.C. BRUTTON evacuated to England – sick 23.2.17. Regimental Staff Ride Captain W.E.P. CAIRNES assumed command of D Squadron	GRA

Instructions regarding War Diaries and Intelligence Summaries are contained in F. S. Regs., Part II. and the Staff Manual respectively. Title pages will be prepared in manuscript.

WAR DIARY
or
~~INTELLIGENCE SUMMARY.~~
(Erase heading not required.)

Army Form C. 2118.

Place	Date	Hour	Summary of Events and Information	Remarks and references to Appendices
GAMACHES	6.3.17		Fine. Squadrons exercised and carried out Musketry and Hotchkiss Gun practice. Major W E ROYDS & Major W H MANN – Corps Cavalry joined for attachment. Captain E.C. WELDON rejoined from 5th Cavalry Div School.	GRA
— —	7.3.17		Dull – cold wind. Brigade dismounted parade for presentation of medal ribbons. Squadrons exercised. 23 O.R. proceeded to join AMBALA Pioneer Sqn	GRA
— —	8.3.17		Dull – cold wind. Some frost & snow during night. Squadrons exercised. Brigade Tactical Exercise	GRA
— —	9.3.17		Dull – cold – frost during night. Squadrons exercised and carried out Musketry. Regimental Tactical Exercise for Junior Officers. Snow fell during day	GRA
— —	10.3.17		Dull – warmer. Squadrons exercised. Demonstration of Hotchkiss Guns & Rifles at 10.30 a.m. No 7533 Pte R Gibson evacuated sick – epilepsy. No 11432 L/Cpl Farrell & 11216 Pte Hayward evacuated sick from Pioneer Battn	GRA
— —	11.3.17		Dull – warm. Lecture "Artillery in the Attack" by Brig Gen WARDROP R.A. 10.30 a.m. Squadrons exercised.	GRA

2353 Wt. W2544/1454 700,000 5/15 D. D. & L. A.D.S.S./Forms/C. 2118.

Instructions regarding War Diaries and Intelligence Summaries are contained in F. S. Regs., Part II. and the Staff Manual respectively. Title pages will be prepared in manuscript.

WAR DIARY

~~or~~

~~INTELLIGENCE SUMMARY.~~

(Erase heading not required.)

Army Form C. 2118.

Place	Date	Hour	Summary of Events and Information	Remarks and references to Appendices
GAMACHES	12.3.17		Dull-drizzle-cold. Squadrons exercised. Regimental Staff Ride. 11432 L/c Farrell rejoined Pioneer Bn from C.C.S.	S.R.A.
— —	13.3.17		Fine. Squadrons exercised. Lecture for junior officers.	S.R.A.
— —	14.3.17		Dull-rain during night. Squadrons exercised. Inspection of explosives pack by G.O.C. Brigade. Reconnaissance for Junior Officers	S.R.A.
— —	15.3.17		Dull - fine at intervals. Squadrons exercised. Brigade Tactical Exercise	S.R.A.
— —	16.3.17		Dull - Squadrons exercised. Regimental Exercise for junior officers. Lieut C.A. ATKINSON-WILLES evacuated to England (sick) 3.3.17	S.R.A.
— —	17.3.17		Fine, bright sun. Squadrons exercised. Captain P.S. ALEXANDER 2/Lt R.A.W. KNIGHT, 2/Lt Hon W.M. STOURTON 2/Lt A.I.B. RITCHIE and 246 Other ranks returned from Pioneer Bn	S.R.A.
— —	18.3.17		Fine - bright sun. Pioneer Transport rejoined by road - Strength 1 Officer 2 RH 2 LD + 17 mules, with 1 Mess cart, 1 water cart, 1 G.S. wagon, 3 Limber wagons.	S.R.A.
— —	19.3.17		Dull. Orders received at 8.15 am to be ready to move Eastwards on 20th. Following evacuated sick:- 8274 Sgt CATT. Lumbago 1309 Pte ALLARDYCE 8249 Pte PEEVERS 2617 Pte CARR 7034 L/c McMENAMIN. 13 O.R. arrived from Base.	S.R.A.

2353 Wt. W2544/1454 700,000 5/15 D. D. & L. A.D.S.S./Forms/C. 2118.

Instructions regarding War Diaries and Intelligence Summaries are contained in F. S. Regs., Part II. and the Staff Manual respectively. Title pages will be prepared in manuscript.

WAR DIARY ~~or~~ INTELLIGENCE SUMMARY.

(Erase heading not required.)

Army Form C. 2118.

Place	Date	Hour	Summary of Events and Information	Remarks and references to Appendices
GAMACHES – HORNOY	20.3.17		Dull, very cold wind. Regiment paraded at 9.30 am. and marched via SENARPONT – LIOMER to HORNOY and went into billets – distance 18 miles	P.R.A.
HORNOY			14 horses of officers of dismounted detachment rejoined.	P.R.A.
HORNOY – WAILLY	21.3.17		Snow during night and morning. Regiment paraded at 9.0 am and marched via POIX to billets in WAILLY and LOEUILLY – distance 14 miles. Major (T. Lt Col) J VAN DER BYL rejoined from 5th Cav Div School	P.R.A.
WAILLY – CAYEUX	22.3.17		Slight frost and snow during night. Regiment paraded at 8 0 am and marched via ORESMAUX – JUMEL – AILLY – MORISEL – MOREUIL – DEMUIN to billets in IGNACOURT and CAYEUX-EN-SANTERRE – distance 25 miles – arrived 1 30 pm. Cpl E MAYHEW evacuated to No 26 C.C.S. – sick	P.R.A.
CAYEUX – Bois de Merehucourt	23.3.17		Slight frost and a good deal of snow during night. Paraded at 8 0 am and Regiment marched via CAIX – HARBONNIERES – PROYART – CAPPY to the Bois de MEREAUCOURT and went into bivouacs – distance 21 miles. Following evacuated:– 4378 Pte FOULDS (Sp Ankle) 5292 Pte A MIDDLETON (Boils) 11152 Pte PALMER (Gastritis) – to 1/3 S M Field Ambulance.	P.R.A.

2353 Wt. W2544/1454 700,000 5/15 D. D. & L. A.D.S.S./Forms/C. 2118.

Instructions regarding War Diaries and Intelligence Summaries are contained in F. S. Regs., Part II. and the Staff Manual respectively. Title pages will be prepared in manuscript.

WAR DIARY
or
~~INTELLIGENCE SUMMARY.~~
(Erase heading not required.)

Army Form C. 2118.

Place	Date	Hour	Summary of Events and Information	Remarks and references to Appendices
Bois de MEREAUCOURT – DEVISE	24.3.17		Hard frost - cold. Regiment paraded at 8.0 am. and marched via PERONNE to MON-EN-CHAUSSEE - 15 miles - and went into bivouac at DEVISE - 1½ miles - at 11.25 am. Squadrons watered and fed and off saddled.	G.R.A.
DEVISE	25.3.17	5.15 am	Hard frost and cold. 5.15 am Orders received to send one squadron to assist in the clearing up of situation at VILLERS FAUCON. "B" Squadron (Captain E.C. WELDON) detailed for this duty and returned and 4.30 pm - no casualties	G.R.A.
		5 o pm	Orders for working party of 50 men; and officers' patrols for 26th. N° 13168 Pte J PIGGOTT - Diarrhoea - to Mhow F.A.	
DEVISE	26.3.17	12 o mn	Dull - cold - rain. 12.0MN Orders received to send one squadron to support of Hodson's Horse at VAUX to be there by 6.0 a.m. A Sqdn (Major Hon: RND RYDER) left at 4.0 a.m. 4 Officers proceeded on	G.R.A.
		1.0 pm	patrol to reconnoitre villages. 1.0 pm Orders received that "A" Sqdn would be returned at 5 0 pm. being relieved by 2 Companies Cyclists. Working parties commenced work on a bridge on R. OMIGNON and village of DEVISE. A Sqdn returned at 11.0 p.m.	

2353 Wt. W2544/1454 700,000 5/15 D. D. & L. A.D.S.S./Forms/C. 2118.

Army Form C. 2118.

Instructions regarding War Diaries and Intelligence Summaries are contained in F. S. Regs., Part II. and the Staff Manual respectively. Title pages will be prepared in manuscript.

WAR DIARY

or

~~INTELLIGENCE SUMMARY.~~

(Erase heading not required.)

Place	Date	Hour	Summary of Events and Information	Remarks and references to Appendices
DEVISE	27/3/17		AMBALA Brigade line:- N to S. 18th Lancers MARQUAIX-HAMBLET-NOBESCOURT Fme-BERNES-FLECHIN. 9th Hodsons Horse POEUILLY-VILLÉVÊQUE-ETREILLERS Distance 10½ miles.	G.R.A.
		12 MN 26/27	12.0 MN 26/27. Orders received for Regiment to parade so as to be in the vicinity of NOBESCOURT Fme by 12.0 noon. Marched at 10.45 a.m. and reached Western outskirts of BOUCLY at 11.45 a.m. Watered and fed and moved to valley in K2(b) at 4.0 pm. Reconnoitred ground towards VILLERS FAUCON E28 & 23.	G.R.A.
VILLERS FAUCON		1.0 pm	Orders received at 1.0 pm that Regiment was to attack and take village of VILLERS FAUCON at 5.0 pm with assistance of a Howitzer Battery, X Battery RHA and 2 Armoured Cars & 1 Section No 4 M.G. Squadron (2Lieut W.P. Clowes 8th Hussars) Bombardment commenced at 4.20 pm and ceased at 5.10 pm.	
		5.0 pm	At 5.0 pm "D" Sqdn (Major J VANDERBYL) supported by "B" Squadron (Captain E.C. WELDON) proceeded to attack the village	G.R.A
		5.17 pm	~~Regiment~~ Report received that Regiment was holding S.W. and S outskirts both armoured cars out of action	
		5.40 pm	"C" Sqdn (Captain W.E.P. CAIRNES) sent to re-inforce.	
		6.0 pm	Message received - whole of village in our hands.	

2353 Wt. W2544/1454 700,000 5/15 D. D. & L. A.D.S.S./Forms/C. 2118.

Instructions regarding War Diaries and Intelligence Summaries are contained in F. S. Regs., Part II. and the Staff Manual respectively. Title pages will be prepared in manuscript.

WAR DIARY

~~or~~

~~INTELLIGENCE SUMMARY.~~

(*Erase heading not required.*)

Army Form C. 2118.

Place	Date	Hour	Summary of Events and Information	Remarks and references to Appendices
VILLERS FAUCON (cont^d)	27.3.17		1 Officer, 10 other ranks and 2 Machine Guns captured. Position consolidated and held during night. Squadrons relieved by Infantry and returned	
	28.3.17		to BOUCLY during morning 28th and thence to DEVISE. – reached at 3. 0 pm. "A" Squadron (Major Hon: R.N.D. RYDER remained in support in the BOIS DE TINCOURT till 8. 0 a.m. 28th when Squadron returned to BOUCLY and thence to DEVISE. Casualties as follows:–	GRA. GRA.
	27.3.17		Killed:– L/51. Pte. P. HICKEY	
			L/14352 Pte. J V MOONEY	
			Wounded:– Lieut R.F. HORNBY	
			5589 Sgt. R BIRTWISTLE — 6108 Corpl E PAULL	GRA.
			1283 Pte. E. HAVERTY. — 4954 Pte. J. BASSNETT	
			4198 " P. REDMOND (at duty). — 9446 " J. McKILLOP.	
			13576 " S. HAWKINS. — 24588 " A. DOYLE	
			3933 " P. BYFORD — 1579 Cpl SS. C FOULSHAM.	
			16171 " P. ORGAN. — 6678 Pte. A SHAW.	
			6147 " E. CHANDLER (at duty)	

2353 Wt. W2544/1454 700,000 5/15 D. D. & L. A.D.S.S./Forms/C. 2118.

Instructions regarding War Diaries and Intelligence Summaries are contained in F. S. Regs., Part II. and the Staff Manual respectively. Title pages will be prepared in manuscript.

WAR DIARY

~~INTELLIGENCE SUMMARY.~~

(*Erase heading not required.*)

Army Form C. 2118.

Place	Date	Hour	Summary of Events and Information	Remarks and references to Appendices
	27.3.17		Casualties contd:- Horses killed 5. Wounded 8 Wounded & missing 3.	G.R.A.
DEVISE	28.3.17		Wire from G.O.C 5th Cavalry Division to O.C. 8th Hussars:- Heartiest congratulations to you and all ranks for the dashing attack made by the Regiment on VILLERS FAUCON yesterday	G.R.A.
DEVISE | BOIS de MEREAUCOURT	29.3.17		Dull, cold, rain all day.- high wind. Orders received to march via DOINGT-PERONNE-BIACHES-HERBECOURT to bivouac in the BOIS de MEREAUCOURT. Marched at 12 0 noon and reached bivouac at 4 0 pm. Ground very bad, deep mud and no shelter for men or horses. Rain all night	G.R.A.
—— | WARFUSEE	30.3.17		Dull cold showers at frequent intervals. 7.30 am Orders received to march from BOIS de MEREAUCOURT to WARFUSEE-ABANCOURT at 10 30 am. Reached WARFUSEE at 2 0 pm. and went into billets - horses in open - men in huts. Captain E.B HOUSTON evacuated to Hospital - GASTRITIS.	G.R.A.
WARFUSEE	31.3.17.		Dull - cold - showers at intervals. Sqdns cleaned up. Captain E.B HOUSTON rejoined.	G.R.A.

F.W. Mussenden. LIEUT. COLONEL, COMMANDING VIII (K.R.I.) HUSSARS.

G.R.A. Atkinson CAPTAIN, ADJUTANT VIII (K.R.I.) HUSSARS.

2353 Wt. W2544/1454 700,000 5/15 D. D. & L. A.D.S.S./Forms/C. 2118.

11

Vol. 32 Serial No. 110.

Confidential:

War Diary

of

VIII King's Royal Irish Hussars

From 1st April to 30th April 1917

Vol. 32

Instructions regarding War Diaries and Intelligence Summaries are contained in F. S. Regs., Part II. and the Staff Manual respectively. Title pages will be prepared in manuscript.

WAR DIARY
or
~~INTELLIGENCE SUMMARY.~~
(Erase heading not required.)

8th (K.R.I.) Hussars

Army Form C. 2118.

Confidential

Place	Date	Hour	Summary of Events and Information	Remarks and references to Appendices
WARFUSEE-ABANCOURT	1.4.17		Fine early, dull later. Heavy showers of sleet & rain during day. Squadrons exercised. A, D Sqdns bathed. 10 Remounts from Base. Divine Service – voluntary – at 10.0 am & 6.30 pm.	G.R.A.
— " —	2.4.17		Dull cold. Frost during night – high wind. Squadrons exercised. Heavy fall of snow during afternoon. 2450 S.S. Greenway (Bronchitis) 834 Pte Stearne (Conjunctivitis) to Hospital.	G.R.A.
— " —	3.4.17		Dull, brighter later. Snow & frost during night. Squadrons exercised	
— " —	4.4.17		Dull, rain during night. Snow fell steadily during morning. Squadrons exercised. Inspection by C-in-C cancelled. 7521 Pte Baylon to Hospital. 3741 Cpl W Brown to be 2/Lieut 8th Bn Suffolk Regt 4-7-3-17	G.R.A.
— " —	5.4.17		Fine – warmer – Squadrons exercised. 14 ORs joined from Dismounted Reinforcements. 2/Lt T C WATSON & 2/Lt Hon W.M STOURTON rejoined from D.R. Captain P.S. ALEXANDER & 2/Lt. B.H HOUSE to D.R. 2/Lt D M LARKINS & H.E.A.E. BOLTON to Base, being surplus to Establishment	G.R.A.

2353 Wt. W2544/1454 700,000 5/15 D. D. & L. A.D.S.S./Forms/C. 2118.

Army Form C. 2118.

Instructions regarding War Diaries and Intelligence Summaries are contained in F. S. Regs., Part II. and the Staff Manual respectively. Title pages will be prepared in manuscript.

WAR DIARY
or
~~INTELLIGENCE SUMMARY.~~

(Erase heading not required.)

Place	Date	Hour	Summary of Events and Information	Remarks and references to Appendices
WARFUSEE-ABANCOURT	5.4.17		Following evacuated sick:- 14276 J. ROGERS - Rheumatism 5428 A BARKER Rheumatism 21048 S Clarke - Septic thumb. 6656 Sgt Pattison - discharge ear 6502 J Wright NYD	G.R.A.
— "	6.4.17		Fine - showers during afternoon Squadrons exercised. Orders received that Division would probably move to a bivouac area S of PERONNE on 8th.	G.R.A.
— "	7.4.17		Dull - rain & snow during night. Squadrons exercised	G.R.A.
— "	8.4.17		Dull - snow & rain. Squadrons exercised. Divine Service:- C of E 10.0 am. Holy Communion 10.30 am.	G.R.A.
— "	9.4.17		Bright at intervals - High wind - cold. Regiment at short notice (5 hours) to move from 12.0 mn 8/9 April. Squadrons exercised. 13 OR arrived from Base	G.R.A.
— "	10.4.17		Dull - showers of sleet & snow - high wind - cold. Squadrons exercised. Brigade inter-communication scheme with aeroplanes postponed.	G.R.A.
— "	11.4.17		Dull - showers of sleet & rain. Heavy fall of snow during afternoon and evening. 8.0 pm - Orders received to move to CAULAINCOURT at 10.55 am on 12th.	G.R.A.

Instructions regarding War Diaries and Intelligence Summaries are contained in F. S. Regs., Part II. and the Staff Manual respectively. Title pages will be prepared in manuscript.

WAR DIARY
or
~~INTELLIGENCE SUMMARY.~~
(Erase heading not required.)

Army Form C. 2118.

Place	Date	Hour	Summary of Events and Information	Remarks and references to Appendices
WARFUSEE-ABANCOURT	11 4 17		Major J. VAN DER BYL awarded D.S.O. 625 Pte P. CARVEY awarded Military Medal (Immediate Rewards).	G.R.R.
			Lieut C. A. ATKINSON-WILLES appointed ADJUTANT, d/- 5 4 1917	
		11 pm	Order to move cancelled.	
— —	12 4 17		Bright morning – rain and snow in afternoon and evening.	G.R.R.
			Brigade Route March at 2.0 pm	
			2375 Pte J HOPE to Hospital Haemorrhoids	
			Captain R B HOUSTON to Hospital Sprained ankle	
— —	13 4 17		Dull snow in morning. Squadrons exercised.	G.R.R.
			All ranks fitted with box respirators in gas chamber	
		7 pm	Orders to march to CAULAINCOURT WOOD via BRIE received.	
— —	14 4 17		Bright. Regiment marched at 9.30 am and reached CAULAINCOURT Wood at 4.0 pm and went into bivouac. Distance 24 miles	G.R.R.
CAULAINCOURT WOOD	15 4 17		Dull. Fine at intervals. Squadrons exercised.	G.R.R.
			Village and wood shelled intermittently throughout night by 5.9 Naval Gun at 12.0 mn 3.0 am & 6.0 am – no damage.	

Instructions regarding War Diaries and Intelligence Summaries are contained in F. S. Regs., Part II. and the Staff Manual respectively. Title pages will be prepared in manuscript.

WAR DIARY
or
~~INTELLIGENCE SUMMARY.~~
(Erase heading not required.)

Army Form C. 2118.

Place	Date	Hour	Summary of Events and Information	Remarks and references to Appendices
CAULAINCOURT WOOD	16.4.17		Dull - no rain. Squadrons exercised. Village and wood shelled by 5" Naval gun at 6.45 am. No damage.	G.R.A.
— —	17.4.17		Dull - rain all night. High wind. Squadrons exercised. French report 10,000 prisoners and all objectives gained.	G.R.A.
— —	18.4.17		Dull. Training for A & B Sqdns. Digging for C & D Sqdns	G.R.A.
— —	19.4.17		Dull & cold. Exercise for C & D. Digging for A & B — —	G.R.A.
— —	20.4.17		Dull. Squadron Training for A & B Sqdns. Digging for C & D — — 6236 L/c WALE to Hospital 12.4.17	G.R.A.
— —	21.4.17		Squadron Training for C & D Sqdns. Exercise & digging for A & B Sqdns Dull day - no rain. Lecture by Divisional Gas Officer.	G.R.A.
— —	22.4.17		Squadrons exercised. Divine Service C. of E. 10.0 am - Holy Communion 10.30 am No 5844 S.Q.M.S. Jackson to Machine Gun Depot on transfer. 6223 S.S. Byrne to Hospital	G.R.A.
— —	23.4.17		Dull Cold. A & B Sqdns Troop & Squadron Training. C & D Sqdns digging 2/Lt. W.P. CLOWES rejoined from 14th Machine Gun Squadron. 25045 Pte Stringer to BOULOGNE on transfer to R.E. 16893 Pte GOLDING to Hospital	G.R.A.

2353 Wt. W2544/1454 700,000 5/15 D. D. & L. A.D.S.S./Forms/C. 2118.

Instructions regarding War Diaries and Intelligence Summaries are contained in F. S. Regs., Part II. and the Staff Manual respectively. Title pages will be prepared in manuscript.

WAR DIARY
or
~~INTELLIGENCE SUMMARY.~~
(Erase heading not required.)

Army Form C. 2118.

Place	Date	Hour	Summary of Events and Information	Remarks and references to Appendices
CAULAINCOURT WOOD	24.4.17		Dull no rain. Cold. Squadron Training for A & C Squadrons. Digging & Exercise for B & D Sqdns. Brigade Tactical Exercise.	G.R.A.
—	25.4.17		Dull no rain. Squadron Training for B & D Sqdns. Digging for A & C	G.R.A.
—	26.4.17		Fine but cold. Squadron Training for A & C Sqdns. Digging and Exercise for B & D.	G.R.A.
—	27.4.17		Dull & cold. Squadron Training for B & D Squadrons. Exercise & digging for A & C Squadrons.	G.R.A.
—	28.4.17		Fine, but dull. Squadron Training for A & C Squadrons. Exercise & wiring for B & D Sqdns.	G.R.A.
—	29.4.17		Fine hot. Squadrons exercised. Parade Service C of E. 10.0 am. Holy Communion 10.30 a.m.	G.R.A.
—	30.4.17		Fine. Wood intermittently shelled during night. No casualties. B & D Sqdns. Squadron Training. A & C Sqdns – wiring & exercise.	G.R.A.

F.W. Mussenden – LIEUT. COLONEL, COMMANDING VIII (K.R.I.) HUSSARS.

G.R. A[illegible] CAPTAIN, A/ADJUTANT VIII (K.R.I.) HUSSARS.

2353 Wt. W2544/1454 700,000 5/15 D. D. & L. A.D.S.S./Forms/C. 2118.

ORDERLY ROOM
AWS2
31 MAY. 1917
8th K.R.I. HUSSARS

Serial No: 110.

Confidential

From 1st May to 30th June 1917.

War Diary

of

VIII King's Royal Irish Hussars

From 1st May 1917 to 31st May 1917

Vol. 33

WAR DIARY ~~or~~ ~~INTELLIGENCE SUMMARY.~~ Army Form C. 2118.

(Erase heading not required.)

VIII (K.R.I.) Hussars

Confidential

Instructions regarding War Diaries and Intelligence Summaries are contained in F. S. Regs., Part II. and the Staff Manual respectively. Title pages will be prepared in manuscript.

Place	Date	Hour	Summary of Events and Information	Remarks and references to Appendices
EAUCOURT WOOD.	1.5.17		Fine. "B" "C" & "D" Squadrons [illegible]. "A" Sqdn. [illegible]. Horses and lines inspected by Cavalry Corps Commander.	a.a.s
—	2.5.17		Fine. Regimental Exercise and Inspection by G.O.C. Brigade. [illegible] – "A" & "B" Echelons, Inspected by G.O.C. Division at 3.0 p.m. [illegible] G.H. ATKINSON-WILLES rejoined from England	a.a.s
—	3.5.17		Fine. [illegible] – [illegible]	a.a.s
—	4.5.17		Fine. Aeroplane dropped bombs on camp during early morning. [illegible]	a.a.s
—	5.5.17		Squadron [illegible] and [illegible]. "A" Sqdn. [illegible] (50 men) [illegible] [illegible] — Fine & hot. [illegible] in evening [illegible]	a.a.s
—	6.5.17		Rain during [illegible]. Fine day. Squadrons exercised.	a.a.s
—	7.5.17		[illegible] — Inspection of "A" Sqdn. [illegible] Commander [illegible] of [illegible]	a.a.s
—	8.5.17		[illegible] Regimental Parade cancelled	a.a.s

2353 Wt. W2544/1454 700,000 5/15 D. D. & L. A.D.S.S./Forms/C. 2118.

Instructions regarding War Diaries and Intelligence Summaries are contained in F. S. Regs., Part II. and the Staff Manual respectively. Title pages will be prepared in manuscript.

Army Form C. 2118.

WAR DIARY ~~or~~ ~~INTELLIGENCE SUMMARY.~~

(Erase heading not required.)

Place	Date	Hour	Summary of Events and Information	Remarks and references to Appendices
CAULAINCOURT WOOD	9.5.17		Squadron training. 30 men exchanged with Dismounted Reinforcements	aaw.
—	10.5.17		Fine and bright. Thunderstorm in the evening. Squadron training for all squadrons. Hotchkiss gun firing, Map reading and range finding in afternoon. Following officers rejoined from Dismounted Reinforcements — Capt P. S. ALEXANDER, 2 Lts HEALBOWEN, T.B.A. EVANS LOMBE, A.J.B. RITCHIE, C.T. LINFORD, M.R. RUSSELL, W.H. HARTLEY, B.H. HOUSE.	aaw.
—	11.5.17		Fine. Hot. Squadron training. No 4268 Sergt KELLY and No 626 L/Cpl GARVEY attended Army Commander's inspection of SECUNDERABAD Brigade and received their Military Medal ribbon. [illegible]	aaw.
—	[12].5.17		Fine — Squadron training for all Squadrons. Working party - 90 ORs - on "RED" line. Revd Father S. O'BRIEN joined from 4th Cavalry Division	aaw
—	13.5.17		Fine — Inspection of Dismounted Regiment by G.O.C. Brigade. R.C. [illegible] 6 p.m. Heavy thunderstorm during night	aaw
—	14.5.17		Dismounted Regiment paraded at 8 a.m. Strength 14 Officers 300 ORs — The Division having taken over a sector of the Line in relief of the Infantry — and marched to bivouacs at VERMAND where the Regiment halted for the night. Capt E.C. WOODS appointed Area Comdt ROISEL	aaw

2353 Wt. W2544/1454 700,000 5/15 D. D. & L. A.D.S.S./Forms/C. 2118.

Instructions regarding War Diaries and Intelligence Summaries are contained in F. S. Regs., Part II. and the Staff Manual respectively. Title pages will be prepared in manuscript.

WAR DIARY
or
INTELLIGENCE SUMMARY.
(Erase heading not required.)

Army Form C. 2118.

Place	Date	Hour	Summary of Events and Information	Remarks and references to Appendices
VERMAND BIHECOURT	[illegible]		[illegible] at 4-0 a.m. and [illegible] BIHECOURT and [illegible] [illegible] [illegible] as [illegible] [illegible] [illegible] [illegible] Returned 4-0 a.m. [illegible]	AAV
BIHECOURT	[illegible]		[illegible] quiet all day. Capt. P. S. ALEXANDER appointed [illegible] [illegible] [illegible] [illegible] [illegible] [illegible]	AAV

Instructions regarding War Diaries and Intelligence Summaries are contained in F. S. Regs., Part II. and the Staff Manual respectively. Title pages will be prepared in manuscript.

WAR DIARY
~~or~~
~~INTELLIGENCE SUMMARY.~~
(Erase heading not required.)

Army Form C. 2118.

Place	Date	Hour	Summary of Events and Information	Remarks and references to Appendices
BIHECOURT	17.6.17		Rain early - fine later. Working parties during night 17/18 as under:- 2 Officers 50 ORs - wiring between N corner of SOMMERVILLE Wood to E corner of PURPLE COPSE 9.30pm to 3.25 a.m 3 Officers 50 ORs - wiring round posts S of Eastern end of SOMMERVILLE Wood 9.40pm - 3.30 am 2 Officers 50 men widening and deepening Communication trench from SALT Trench 10 men entrenching at LONE TREE POST 10.0pm - 2.40 am 11960 L/c WOODS G S W right ankle - slight	ARS
BIHECOURT	18.6.17		Capt. C R L ADLERCRON joined Dismounted Regiment. RSM TITCHFORTH relieved R Q M S GREENSTREET. Fine - warmer Working parties during night 18/19 as under:- 20 men - loading party and road mending 2 Officers 50 ORs - wiring posts S. of SOMMERVILLE Wood 9.0pm - 3.0 am 2 Officers 50 ORs - wiring front of SOMMERVILLE Wood 8.30pm - 3.0 am No casualties.	ARS

Instructions regarding War Diaries and Intelligence Summaries are contained in F. S. Regs., Part II. and the Staff Manual respectively. Title pages will be prepared in manuscript.

WAR DIARY
~~or~~
~~INTELLIGENCE SUMMARY.~~
(Erase heading not required.)

Army Form C. 2118.

Place	Date	Hour	Summary of Events and Information	Remarks and references to Appendices
BIHUCOURT	19.5.17		[illegible] Working parties night of 19/20 as under: 2 officers 50 men work on strong points 10.0 pm – 3.15 am. 12 [illegible] – [illegible] on M.G. emplacements and wire at LONE TREE 10.15 pm 4.0 am. 40 [illegible] loading [illegible] trucks etc. 2 officers 50 men [illegible] 9.30 pm 4.10 am. [illegible]	a.a.w.
[illegible] (M 8 A to [illegible] BIHUCOURT) (Sheet 62C 1/40000)	20.5.17		[illegible] Regiment relieved [illegible], Canadian Cavalry Brigade in the front line [illegible] OMIGNON RIVER to [illegible] (M 8 a to M 2 c) during night 20/21st. C Squadron moved up to [illegible] at 9.0 pm and [illegible] from [illegible]. C Squadron [illegible] [illegible] 9.0 pm [illegible] 9.0 am [illegible] [illegible] [illegible] the enemy on our [illegible] [illegible] [illegible] [illegible]	Sheet 62C 1/40000 a.a.w.

WAR DIARY ~~or~~ INTELLIGENCE SUMMARY.

(*Erase heading not required.*)

Army Form C. 2118.

Instructions regarding War Diaries and Intelligence Summaries are contained in F. S. Regs., Part II. and the Staff Manual respectively. Title pages will be prepared in manuscript.

Place	Date	Hour	Summary of Events and Information	Remarks and references to Appendices
PONTRU SECTOR	2.5.17		Fine, clear. A quiet day on the whole. Enemy shelled the "Brown" line on the French side. Front line trenches improved, — Hotchkiss Gun emplacements wired, weather proof covers made. Revetting on road improved. Six positions and splinter proof covers commenced. In the "Brown" line trenches were improved – fire steps dug and improved. Hotchkiss Gun emplacements dug, wire repaired and improved. Two Officers patrols sent out to FISHERS CRATER which was reported held. No casualties. Six enemy HE shell fell in the valley in the rear of the [illegible] between 9.45 & 10.15 pm. 7 OR joined "Sick Area" from Base.	a.a.l.
—	3.5.17		Situation report 2.30 am – "Normal" Wet early, having rained all night. No casualties reported to 12.0 noon. A quiet day. Work on trenches continued, parapets strengthened – Hotchkiss gun emplacements completed. About 20 HE shells fell in front of wire of intermediate line S. of VADENCOURT. No casualties. 8574 Pte McLoughlin to Hospital (Sick).	a.a.l.

2353 Wt. W2544/1454 700,000 5/15 D. D. & L. A.D.S.S./Forms/C. 2118.

Instructions regarding War Diaries and Intelligence Summaries are contained in F. S. Regs., Part II. and the Staff Manual respectively. Title pages will be prepared in manuscript.

WAR DIARY
~~or~~
~~INTELLIGENCE SUMMARY.~~
(Erase heading not required.)

Army Form C. 2118.

Place	Date	Hour	Summary of Events and Information	Remarks and references to Appendices
POMPRY SECTOR	23.6.17		Fine and clear. A quiet day. Our front line shelled with a few H.E. about mid day. No damage. Following patrols went out:- Lt. WATSON + 15 men to continue work at ~~[illegible]~~ ROBINSON'S POST commenced by Lt ROBINSON'S party previous night. Working party unmolested and reported little movement of enemy. Lt. [illegible] + 8 men dug a small post at M.9.a.1.3 on S bank of river working from 10.0 pm to 3.0 a.m. A French patrol was met about M.9. Central. Nothing seen or heard of enemy. Lt. [illegible] + 8 men went out to M.2.d.0.2. Enemy patrol seen about 12.30 a.m. - estimated 12 to 18. Enemy retired hastily. A second enemy party seen at 2.30 a.m. N of Crater. Work on trenches continued throughout day and night. Casualties - 1839 Pte S. PERICO slightly wounded - at duty. Shell fire. 2040 Pte J. BENNETT + 6076 Pte E. CULLEN - Cum[?] injuries accidental.	aaw
———	24.6.17		Fine and bright. Genl. [illegible] visited BROWN line and expressed his pleasure at improvements made.	aaw

2353 Wt. W2544/1454 700,000 5/15 D. D. & L. A.D.S.S./Forms/C. 2118.

Instructions regarding War Diaries and Intelligence Summaries are contained in F. S. Regs., Part II. and the Staff Manual respectively. Title pages will be prepared in manuscript.

WAR DIARY
~~or~~
~~INTELLIGENCE SUMMARY.~~
(Erase heading not required.)

Army Form C. 2118.

Place	Date	Hour	Summary of Events and Information	Remarks and references to Appendices
PONTRU SECTOR 24th	24.6.17		Patrols went out as previous night. Enemy heard working in FISHERS CRATER & MG opened fire at 12.5 am. Patrol at M9 a 5.6 heard railway lines being removed and Motor transport on rear enemy lines. Work continued on trenches. Front line trench deepened & communication trenches dug. No casualties	A.a.w.
PONTRU SECTOR	25.6.17		Fine, clear. Wind dangerous 10.0 am veered round to S gts [illegible] noon. Received orders for relief by L.S.H. 1 OR to Hospital sick. Front line and Tumulus shelled by enemy with 5.9 during the afternoon. VADENCOURT heavily shelled for few minutes at 4.0 pm and 7.0 pm. [illegible] went out one being fired on. Two casualties – 16026 L/c RICHARDS C.S.W face & left leg. 4[illegible] S. ROGERS C.S.W right leg. RSM [illegible] slightly wounded – at duty. L.S. HORSE relieved the Regiment in the trenches during night 25/26. Commencing 9.30 pm relief complete 10.20 pm. Quiet – very little shelling	A.a.w.

2353 Wt. W2544/1454 700,000 5/15 D. D. & L. A.D.S.S./Forms/C. 2118.

Instructions regarding War Diaries and Intelligence Summaries are contained in F. S. Regs., Part II. and the Staff Manual respectively. Title pages will be prepared in manuscript.

WAR DIARY ~~or~~ ~~INTELLIGENCE SUMMARY.~~

(*Erase heading not required.*)

Army Form C. 2118.

Place	Date	Hour	Summary of Events and Information	Remarks and references to Appendices
			In Divisional Reserve	
Bihucourt	26.7		Very fine – hot. Squadrons occupied same bivouacs. Small working parties found. 1 OR to 36th Div for attachment to Infantry – new commission	a.a.w.
"	27.7		Fine hot. Parade Service RC 11.0 am. C of E 2.0 pm. A very quiet day. A certain amount of aerial activity. Canadians reported to have made a successful raid on [illegible] and [illegible] Wood taking 18 prisoners and killing several with slight casualties to themselves. Wiring and working parties were sent out [illegible] [illegible] [illegible] wood. No casualties.	a.a.w.
Bihucourt	28.7		Fine hot. Wiring and working parties sent out during night. [illegible] No casualties. 2/Lt N Coulson app[ointed] Town Major MONTECOURT & MERICOURT [illegible] Capt. B ALEXANDER detailed for duty with Cav Corps Div Reinforcements. 2 OR [illegible] RQMS GREENSTREET to M.G. Depot on promotion to Commissioned rank.	a.a.w.

Instructions regarding War Diaries and Intelligence Summaries are contained in F. S. Regs., Part II. and the Staff Manual respectively. Title pages will be prepared in manuscript.

WAR DIARY

~~or~~

~~INTELLIGENCE SUMMARY.~~

(Erase heading not required.)

Army Form C. 2118.

Place	Date	Hour	Summary of Events and Information	Remarks and references to Appendices
BIHECOURT	29.6.17		Fine & bright. Regiment returned to Bivouac at CAULAINCOURT wood, arriving 10.30pm. Lt C.S. Rowley & 2Lt Hon W.M. Stourton with 97 ORs remained as Dismounted Reinforcements at BIHECOURT. 1 OR to Hospital - sick	AAW.
CAULAINCOURT WOOD	30.6.17		Fine. Squadrons exercised.	AAW
—	31.6.17		Fine. Squadron training for all Squadrons.	AAW

F.W. Mussenden
LIEUT. COLONEL,
COMMANDING VIII (K.R.I.) HUSSARS.

A. Atkinson-Willes
LIEUT
ADJUTANT VIII (K.R.I.) HUSSARS.

2353 Wt. W2544/1454 700,000 5/15 D. D. & L. A.D.S.S./Forms/C. 2118.

R

Confidential

War Diary

of

VIII (King's Royal Irish) Hussars

From 1st June to 30th June 1917

Vol. 34

Instructions regarding War Diaries and Intelligence Summaries are contained in F. S. Regs., Part II. and the Staff Manual respectively. Title pages will be prepared in manuscript.

WAR DIARY ~~or~~ ~~INTELLIGENCE SUMMARY.~~

(Erase heading not required.)

8th (R. I.) Hussars

Army Form C. 2118.

Confidential.

Place	Date	Hour	Summary of Events and Information	Remarks and references to Appendices
CAULAINCOURT WOOD	1.6.17		Fine. Squadron Training. A & B practised night attack.	AAW
— —	2.6.17		Fine in morning – rain towards evening. 'C' Sqdn practised night attack	AAW.
— —	3.6.17		Fine. Divine Services – C. of E. 10.0 am RC. 5. 0 pm	AAW
			2 O.R.s to Hospital – sick.	
— —	4.6.17		Fine. Squadron training. 1. O.R. to Hospital sick.	AAW
— —	5.6.17		Fine. Dismounted Regiment paraded at 8 0 pm. Strength:- 17 Officers 300 other ranks, and took over a Sector of the line from LORD STRATHCONA'S HORSE	
VADENCOURT R.I. a. 1. 9. Sheet 62 C 1/40.000			Regimental Head Quarters – VADENCOURT Chateau.	
			'B' Squadron took over SALT TRENCH and reported all correct at 11.50 pm	AAW
			'A' Squadron took over CRESSY TRENCH and reported all correct at 11.45 pm	
			'D' Squadron took over TWIN CRATERS and report correct at 11.50 pm.	
			'C' Squadron took over the BROWN LINE and reported all correct at 12-30 am	
			Relief carried out quietly and without incident. In touch with French on our Right and with 18th (K.G.O.) LANCERS on our Left.	
			Enemy raided PONTRUET at about midnight using T.M. and Rifle Grenades.	

Instructions regarding War Diaries and Intelligence Summaries are contained in F. S. Regs., Part II. and the Staff Manual respectively. Title pages will be prepared in manuscript.

WAR DIARY
or
~~INTELLIGENCE SUMMARY.~~
(Erase heading not required.)

Army Form C. 2118.

Place	Date	Hour	Summary of Events and Information	Remarks and references to Appendices
VADENCOURT	6.6.17		Fine and hot. Very quiet along front. Enemy raided trench line on a kilometre front in vicinity of FAYET. Patrols sent out to FISHERS CRATER and beyond and towards LONE POST — nothing to report. Night passed quietly. No casualties.	ARW
"	7.6.17		Hot and close. Thunderstorm in afternoon. Very quiet all day. Patrols went out during night and found nothing to report. Work carried out during night in improvements to trenches, defences and wire. No casualties.	ARW
"	8.6.17		Hot and fine. Dull & close in afternoon. Patrols went out during night [illegible] being fired at from ELEVEN TREES. Work carried out on wire and improvements to trenches. No casualties.	ARW
"	9.6.17		Hot and close. A quiet day. CAPTAIN F.B. ALEXANDER arrived and relieved LT W.S. MANSFIELD. "C" Squadron relieved "A" in CRESSY TRENCH at 10 p.m. At 11.40 p.m. the enemy put a heavy barrage on SALT TRENCH and SOMERVILLE WOOD and raided the latter. Damage to wire and defences [illegible] by enemy fire. Casualties:- Captain F.C. WELDON wounded - shell splinters	ARW

2353 Wt. W2544/1454 700,000 5/15 D. D. & L. A.D.S.S./Forms/C. 2118.

Instructions regarding War Diaries and Intelligence Summaries are contained in F. S. Regs., Part II. and the Staff Manual respectively. Title pages will be prepared in manuscript.

WAR DIARY
or
~~INTELLIGENCE SUMMARY.~~
(Erase heading not required.)

Army Form C. 2118.

Place	Date	Hour	Summary of Events and Information	Remarks and references to Appendices
VADENCOURT	9.6.17 cont^d		4221 L/c E PAGE 6480 Pte T GAFFEY 3480 Pte BERESFORD 1686 Pte GRAY wounded all of B Squadron. 6 O.R's joined Back Area from Base	aaw
——	10.6.17		Hot but dull. Heavy thunderstorm at about 3.0 am lasting forty five minutes. Some telephones put out of action by storm. Work continued on wiring and improvements to trenches. No casualties. Lt ROWLEY joined from Back area.	aaw
——	11.6.17		Dull & hot. A quiet day. Wiring and working parties sent out during night. No casualties	aaw
——	12.6.17		Hot but dull. Slight rain in afternoon. TUMULUS and SALT TRENCH shelled by enemy 4.2 Howitzer during afternoon. DEAN COPSE and CAUBRIERES WOOD shelled by enemy all afternoon. 'D' Squadron relieved 'B' in SALT TRENCH at midnight. Wiring and working parties went out. SECUNDERABAD Brigade raided ASCENSION WOOD. ZERO hour 2 a.m. 'X' & 'N' Batteries put down a barrage.	aaw
——	13.6.17		Fine. Cool breeze. 2Lt. BOLTON relieved 2Lt. MATTHEWS who proceeded on urgent leave. Major & VAN-DER-BYL, DSO, attended a parade of CANADIAN Brigade and received medal ribbon from Corps Commander. Considerable hostile shelling during night over whole of Brigade Sector	aaw

2353 Wt. W2544/1454 700,000 5/15 D. D. & L. A.D.S.S./Forms/C. 2118.

Instructions regarding War Diaries and Intelligence Summaries are contained in F. S. Regs., Part II. and the Staff Manual respectively. Title pages will be prepared in manuscript.

WAR DIARY
or
INTELLIGENCE SUMMARY.
(Erase heading not required.)

Army Form C. 2118.

Place	Date	Hour	Summary of Events and Information	Remarks and references to Appendices
YTRES COURT	13.6.17 Cont		Regimental Transport at VERMAND bombed by enemy aircraft. No casualties.	AAW
— " —	14.6.17		Very hot. Work on wire and trenches carried out during night. Considerable shelling during night. Captain P. S. ALEXANDER took out a patrol of 7 men of C Sqdn to clear up situation East of FISHER'S CRATER. An enemy sentry was [illegible] and taken prisoner – wounded. He died early next day.	AAW
— " —	15.6.17		Very hot. A quiet day and night. No casualties. A Sqdn relieved B in MUSTARD QUARRY, relief completed at midnight. Wiring and working parties were out. No casualties. 3 OR's to Hosp. Sick	AAW
— " —	16.6.17		Very hot. Quiet. Working and wiring parties were out. No casualties.	AAW
— " —	17.6.17		Very hot. Quiet. Some shelling in early morning. Quiet night. Usual working parties found. No casualties.	AAW
— " —	18.6.17		Hot. Thunderstorm in afternoon. 9th Horse raided St HELENE TRENCH, killed 5 Germans & took 3 prisoners. 2Lt W. H. HARTLEY & 2 troops 'A' formed Right Flank Guard to raiding party & all H.Qrs were in BROWN LINE. Little retaliation to our bombardment. Casualties:- 1274 Pte N. MORAN – wounded. 15 OR's joined Base Camp from [illegible]	AAW

2353 Wt. W2544/1454 700,000 5/15 D. D. & L. A.D.S.S./Forms/C. 2118.

Instructions regarding War Diaries and Intelligence Summaries are contained in F. S. Regs., Part II. and the Staff Manual respectively. Title pages will be prepared in manuscript.

WAR DIARY

or

~~INTELLIGENCE SUMMARY.~~

(Erase heading not required.)

Army Form C. 2118.

Place	Date	Hour	Summary of Events and Information	Remarks and references to Appendices
VADENCOURT	19.6.17		Dull - Very wet night. Capt P S ALEXANDER and LT D.W DALY with 30 ORs patrolled to ST HELENE TRENCH to cut the wire. Were fired on by rifle and machine gun fire and had to retire, having cut only 5 yards. No casualties. Instructor of Catering visited Back Area bivouac & subsequently reported messing arrangements good.	AAW
- -	20.6.17		Dull. Raining heavily in evening. Capt P.S. ALEXANDER and 2LT M R RUSSELL with 30 men patrolled to ST HELENE trench and cut 12 yards wire and cleared tracks through. They were bombed and came under Machine Gun fire. Patrol returned 2.0 am. No casualties. Work carried out on trenches and wiring. Divisional Commander inspected horses of the Regiment and expressed his satisfaction at the condition. Lt W.A.D HENRY to [illegible] Cavalry Entrenching Battalion for duty.	AAW AAW
- -	21.6.17		Cooler, with rain in afternoon. ~~[illegible]~~ LT D.W DALY & M R RUSSELL & 30 men patrolled to ST HELENE trench where they were bombed by the enemy. Casualties - LT D W DALY slightly wounded. 8208 Sgt BRYSON wounded, Pte [illegible] Pte BURKE - severely wounded. 13264 Pte Goddard - wounded.	AAW

2353 Wt. W2544/1454 700,000 5/15 D. D. & L. A.D.S.S./Forms/C. 2118.

Instructions regarding War Diaries and Intelligence Summaries are contained in F. S. Regs., Part II. and the Staff Manual respectively. Title pages will be prepared in manuscript.

WAR DIARY
~~or~~
~~INTELLIGENCE SUMMARY.~~
(Erase heading not required.)

Army Form C. 2118.

Place	Date	Hour	Summary of Events and Information	Remarks and references to Appendices
VADENCOURT	21.6.17 Contd		Wiring and trench work carried out. Capt. C.R.L. ADLERCRON [illegible] from [illegible] Entrenching Battalion.	RAW
—	22.6.17		[illegible] 18th Lancers raided ST HELENE trench – they penetrated as far as ST HELENE village. Usual work during night in wiring and trench digging. No casualties.	RAW
—	23.6.17		Cold. Some rain in afternoon. Very quiet day. VERMAND [illegible] during day. Usual work during night. No casualties. [illegible] during night by [illegible] Lancers. [illegible] complete 12.45 a.m. Squadrons marched back to bivouacs at [illegible]COURT independently. [illegible] and [illegible] [illegible] 90 O.R.s [illegible] VERSAILLES 20 [illegible]	RAW
[illegible]	[illegible]		Squadron [illegible]	RAW
	[illegible]		[illegible]	RAW
	[illegible]		[illegible] Capt. HEATHCOTE [illegible] of B Squadron. Capt. C.R.L. ADLERCRON assumed command of B Sqdn. Capt. [illegible] VAN DER BYL DSO to [illegible] Corps [illegible]	RAW

2353 Wt. W2544/1454 700,000 5/15 D. D. & L. A.D.S.S./Forms/C. 2118.

Instructions regarding War Diaries and Intelligence Summaries are contained in F. S. Regs., Part II. and the Staff Manual respectively. Title Pages will be prepared in manuscript.

WAR DIARY
or
~~INTELLIGENCE~~ SUMMARY
(Erase heading not required.)

Army Form C. 2118

Place	Date	Hour	Summary of Events and Information	Remarks and references to Appendices
CAULAINCOURT WOOD	27.6.17		Fine. Squadron training. SQMS. Bulcock rejoined from Base. Heavy storm during afternoon.	aaw
— " —	28/6/17		Heavy rain early. Commanding Officer's parade cancelled.	aaw
— " —	29/6/17		Fine. Commanding Officer inspected A & B Squadrons at Drill.	aaw
— " —	30/6/17		Commanding Officer inspection "C" & "D" Squadrons at Drill. Cancelled owing to Rain	aaw

F.W. Mussenden –
LIEUT. COLONEL,
COMMANDING VIII (K.R.I.) HUSSARS.

A Atkinson-Willes Lieut.
ADJUTANT VIII (K.R.I.) HUSSARS.

1875 Wt. W593/826 1,000,000 4/15 J.B.C. & A. A.D.S.S./Forms/C. 2118.

Serial No: 110.

Confidential

War Diary

of

VIII Kings Royal Irish Hussars

From 1st July to 31st July 1917

Vol. 35.

Instructions regarding War Diaries and Intelligence Summaries are contained in F. S. Regs., Part II. and the Staff Manual respectively. Title Pages will be prepared in manuscript.

WAR DIARY
or
~~INTELLIGENCE SUMMARY~~
(Erase heading not required.)

8th (K.R.I.) Hussars

Confidential.

Army Form C. 2118

Place	Date	Hour	Summary of Events and Information	Remarks and references to Appendices
CAULAINCOURT WOOD	1.7.17		Fine but dull. Divine Service C of E. 10.30 am R.C. 9.0 am. 1. O.R. from Hospital.	aaw
— " —	2.7.17		Fine. The Commanding Officer inspected C & D Squadrons at Drill. A & B Squadrons – Squadron Training. 8 O.R's joined from British Cavalry Entrenching Battalion.	aaw
— " —	3.7.17		Squadron Training. – Inspection of Regimental Transport by Divisional Commander	aaw
— " —	4.7.17		Very wet early, cleared about 8.0 am. Squadron Training for all Squadrons.	aaw
— " —	5.7.17		Fine. Squadron Training.	aaw
— " —	6.7.17		Fine. Squadron Training. Camp shelled at 6.30 a.m and again at 8.15 pm. No damage.	aaw
— " —	7.7.17		Fine. Squadron Training. Received orders to move from CAULAINCOURT WOOD at 1.0 pm. Squadrons moved independently to the valley N of TERTRY 3 remounts received and posted to D Squadron.	aaw
BIVOUAC N of TERTRY	8.7.17		Very heavy thunderstorm and rain. Fine evening.	aaw
— " —	9.7.17		Dismounted Reinforcements rejoined Regiment from VENDELLES LIEUT W.A.D HENRY rejoined from British Cavalry Entrenching Battalion.	aaw

1875 Wt. W593/826 1,000,000 4/15 J.B.C. & A. A.D.S.S./Forms/C. 2118.

Instructions regarding War Diaries and Intelligence Summaries are contained in F. S. Regs., Part II and the Staff Manual respectively. Title Pages will be prepared in manuscript.

WAR DIARY
or
INTELLIGENCE SUMMARY
(Erase heading not required.)

Army Form C. 2118

Place	Date	Hour	Summary of Events and Information	Remarks and references to Appendices
BIVOUAC N. of TERTRY	10.7.17		Fine, Squadron Training.	AAW
— " —	11.7.17		Fine, Inspection of the Regiment by the Commanding Officer, in Field Service Marching Order.	AAW
— " —	12.7.17		Fine, Squadron Training.	AAW
— " — / BUIRE	13.7.17		Hot. Regiment paraded at 1.15 p.m. in Field Service Marching Order and moved to Brigade Starting Point 1000x E of ESTREES-EN-CHAUSSEE. Marched via BOIS de BIAS – CARTIGNY to BUIRE and bivouacked for the night. CAPT. E.C. WOODS, 2LTS. BOLTON, LINFORD and HARTLEY and RITCHIE with 94 ORs. remained behind as Dismounted Reinforcements to follow by rail. Billeting party proceeded to SUZANNE.	AAW
BUIRE / SUZANNE	14.7.17		Reveille 4 a.m. Fine, hot. Marched at 6.0 am via COURCELLES – DOINGT – PERONNE – CLERY – MARICOURT to SUZANNE. – Arrived 10.30 am and bivouaced. Billeting party left at 5.0 pm for MORLANCOURT.	AAW
SUZANNE / VILLE sous CORBIE	15.7.17		Fine. Regiment paraded 7.15 am, watered and proceeded to Starting Point – the Church SUZANNE. 8.0 am. Marched via BRAY – MORLANCOURT to VILLE sous CORBIE. Arrived 10.15 am and went into billets – horses in open.	AAW
VILLE sous CORBIE / SARTON	16.7.17		Fine. Regiment paraded at 5.30 a.m. and proceeded to the Starting Point – the cross roads 400x S of U in BUIRE – Marched via BAIZIEUX – LEALVILLERS – LOUVENCOURT to SARTON – about 13 miles. Arrived 10.15 am. Billeting party left at 2.30 pm for ST. MICHEL.	AAW

1875 Wt. W593/826 1,000,000 4/15 J.B.C. & A. A.D.S.S./Forms/C. 2118.

Instructions regarding War Diaries and Intelligence Summaries are contained in F. S. Regs., Part II. and the Staff Manual respectively. Title Pages will be prepared in manuscript.

WAR DIARY
or
INTELLIGENCE SUMMARY
(Erase heading not required.)

Army Form C. 2118

Place	Date	Hour	Summary of Events and Information	Remarks and references to Appendices
SARTON – ST. MICHEL	17.7.17		Fine. Regiment paraded 5.20 am and moved to Starting point near HALLOY. Brigade marched at 6.0 am. via LUCHEUX – IVERGNY to WANIN where Regiment watered and fed. Continued march at 11.0 am via HOUVIN – BUNEVILLE – to ROELLECOURT (Brigade H.Qrs) arrived 12 noon. Regiment went into bivouac at ST MICHEL – very dirty and crowded.	aaw
ST. MICHEL	18.7.17		Wet. Squadrons exercised. "D" Squn moved to ROCOURT ST LAURENT.	aaw
ST. MICHEL	19.7.17		Dull. Squadrons exercised.	aaw
ST. MICHEL	20.7.17		Dull. Squadrons exercised.	aaw
ST. MICHEL	21.7.17		Fine. Squadrons paraded. C.O. inspected horses for casting.	aaw
ST. MICHEL	22.7.17		Fine. Divine Service C. of E. 10.0 am. R.C. 10.0 am.	aaw
ST. MICHEL	23.7.17		Fine. Hot. Squadrons paraded. Tactical exercise for young officers under Senior Major.	aaw
ST. MICHEL	24.7.17		Fine. Hot. Regimental Tactical Exercise. Lecture by Gas Officer at Bde H.Q. at 2.0 pm for all Officers.	aaw
ST. MICHEL	25.7.17		Hot. Some showers. Brigade Inter-communication scheme with aeroplanes. Regiment paraded 7.0 am. returned 4.0 pm. Useful information given by planes.	aaw

1875 Wt. W593/826 1,000,000 4/15 J.B.C. & A. A.D.S.S./Forms/C. 2118.

Instructions regarding War Diaries and Intelligence Summaries are contained in F. S. Regs., Part II. and the Staff Manual respectively. Title Pages will be prepared in manuscript.

WAR DIARY

~~or~~

~~INTELLIGENCE SUMMARY~~

(Erase heading not required.)

Army Form C. 2118

Place	Date	Hour	Summary of Events and Information	Remarks and references to Appendices
St. Michel	26.7.17	—	Fine. Squadrons exercised. Official photographer took "C" Squadron for cinematograph.	a.a.w
St. Michel	27.7.17	—	Fine. Hot. Squadrons exercised. Hotchkiss gun firing. Lieut D W DALY rejoined from Hospital.	a.a.w
St. Michel	28.7.17	—	Fine. Hot. Musketry and exercise.	a.a.w
St. Michel	29.7.17		Very heavy thunderstorm all morning. Major J. VAN DER Byl, DSO rejoined from 14th Corps.	a.a.w
St. Michel	30.7.17		Wet. Squadrons exercised. Staff Ride for junior officers, under Senior Major. C.O. Comdg the Brigade.	a.a.w
St. Michel	31.7.17	—	Fine. Regimental Tactical Exercise.	a.a.w

F.W. Mussenden – LIEUT. COLONEL, COMMANDING VIII (K.R.I.) HUSSARS.

A. Atkinson Willes Lieut ADJUTANT VIII (K.R.I.) HUSSARS.

1875 Wt. W593/826 1,000,000 4/15 J.B.C. & A. A.D.S.S./Forms/C. 2118.

Serial No: 110. R

Confidential.

War Diary

of

VIII (King's & Royal Irish) Hussars

From 1st August to 31st August 1917.

Vol 36.

Instructions regarding War Diaries and Intelligence Summaries are contained in F. S. Regs., Part II. and the Staff Manual respectively. Title pages will be prepared in manuscript.

WAR DIARY or ~~INTELLIGENCE SUMMARY.~~

(Erase heading not required.)

8th (K.R.I.) Hussars

Army Form C. 2118.

Confidential.

Place	Date	Hour	Summary of Events and Information	Remarks and references to Appendices
ST. MICHEL SUR TERNOISE (PAS DE CALAIS)	1.8.17		Wet. Squadrons exercised	aaw
	2.8.17		Wet. Squadrons exercised.	aaw
	3.8.17		Wet. Brigade exercise with aircraft cancelled. Squadrons exercised.	aaw
	4.8.17		Wet. Squadrons exercised.	aaw
	5.8.17		Dull. Divine Service C of E. 10.0 am. R.C. 9.0 am.	aaw
	6.8.17		Staff Ride for junior officers. 4 Officers proceeded to AIRE to attend a demonstration in bridging.	aaw
	7.8.17		Fine. Regimental Exercise near BRYAS.	aaw
	8.8.17		Fine morning. Heavy thunderstorm in evening. Musketry for A Sqdn. Squadron parade – B C & D.	aaw
	9.8.17		Fine. Colonel F.W. MUSSENDEN left to take over command of British Cavalry Reinforcements at ROUEN. Squadron Parade. A & B: Lewis Gun firing.	aaw

A7092 Wt. W128 9/M1293 750,000. 1/17. D. D & L Ltd. Forms/C2118/14.

Instructions regarding War Diaries and Intelligence Summaries are contained in F. S. Regs., Part II. and the Staff Manual respectively. Title pages will be prepared in manuscript.

WAR DIARY
or
~~INTELLIGENCE SUMMARY.~~
(Erase heading not required.)

Army Form C. 2118.

Place	Date	Hour	Summary of Events and Information	Remarks and references to Appendices
ST. MICHEL SUR TERNOISE	10.8.17		Fine. Brigade Exercise. Regiment paraded 7 0 am and returned 1 30 pm. Officers class in rapid wiring.	aaw
	11.8.17		Exercise. Regimental Horse Show in afternoon, eliminating for Brigade Show. Wet afternoon.	aaw
	12.8.17		Fine. Parade Service R.C. 10 0 am. Brigade Horse Show.	aaw
	13.8.17		Showery. Squadron Parades.	aaw
	14.8.17		Fine. Squadron Parades.	aaw
	15.8.17		Fine. Showers at intervals. Divisional Horse Show held at BRYAS. Regiment took 1st in Pack Horse and 2nd in NCOs & men's jumping.	aaw
	16.8.17		Fine. Squadrons paraded. CO inspected "A" & "D" Sqdn at jumping.	aaw
	17.8.17		Fine. Squadron parades. C.O inspected "B" & "C" Sqdns at jumping. C.O tested Hotchkiss Gun Drill of all Squadrons.	aaw
	18.8.17		Fine. Squadrons paraded.	aaw
	19.8.17		Fine. Divine Service C of E 9 0 am. R C 9. 0 am.	aaw
	20.8.17		Fine. Squadrons paraded.	aaw
				aaw

Army Form C. 2118.

Instructions regarding War Diaries and Intelligence Summaries are contained in F. S. Regs., Part II. and the Staff Manual respectively. Title pages will be prepared in manuscript.

WAR DIARY
~~or~~
~~INTELLIGENCE SUMMARY.~~
(Erase heading not required.)

Place	Date	Hour	Summary of Events and Information	Remarks and references to Appendices
ST. MICHEL SUR TERNOISE	21.8.17		Fine. The Divisional Commander inspected the Brigade in Field Service Marching Order near OCOCHE at 10.0 am	aaw
	22.8.17		Fine. Squadron Parades.	aaw
	23.8.17		Fine Squadron Parades.	aaw
	24.8.17		Regimental Tactical Exercise in the vicinity of BUNEVILLE. General Rankin held a Gymkhana which was attended by a French General. "C" Squadron performed a Musical Ride.	aaw
	25.8.17		Fine. Squadron Parades.	aaw
	26.8.17		Fine Squadrons exercised	aaw
	27.8.17		Squadrons paraded. Staff Ride for junior officers under Senior Major.	aaw
	28.8.17		Squadrons paraded.	aaw
	29.8.17		Wet. Squadrons paraded. D.D.R. Cavalry Corps inspected all mares with a view to earmarking for breeding purposes.	aaw
	30.8.17		Fine. Squadron parades.	aaw
	31.8.17		Showery. Brigade Tactical Exercise postponed. Squadrons exercised.	aaw

[signature] MAJOR, COMMANDING VIII (K.R.I.) HUSSARS.

A. A. Willis Lieut
ADJUTANT VIII (K.R.I.) HUSSARS.

A7092 Wt. W128 9/M1293 750,000. 1/17. D. D & L. Ltd. Forms/C2118/14.

K

Serial No. 110.

Confidential

War Diary

of

VIII (King's Royal Irish) Hussars

From 1st September to 30th September 1917

Vol 37

Instructions regarding War Diaries and Intelligence Summaries are contained in F. S. Regs., Part II. and the Staff Manual respectively. Title pages will be prepared in manuscript.

WAR DIARY or ~~INTELLIGENCE SUMMARY.~~

(Erase heading not required.)

8th K R I Hussars

Confidential

Army Form C. 2118.

Place	Date	Hour	Summary of Events and Information	Remarks and references to Appendices
St MICHEL SUR TERNOISE P. de C.	1.9.17		Corps Horse Show. Regt took 2nd in Pack ponies. A wet afternoon.	aaw
	2.9.17		A wet morning. Church parade cancelled.	aaw
—"—	3.9.17		Fine. A.D.V.S. inspected the horses of the Regiment.	aaw
—"—	4.9.17		Fine. Squadron Parades. Musketry for 'A' Squadron.	aaw
—"—	5.9.17		Fine. Hot. Regimental Tactical Exercise in the vicinity of OSTREVILLE, attended by Divisional Commander and Brigadier.	aaw
—"—	6.9.17		Fine morning. Parades under Squadron arrangements. Heavy storm in the afternoon.	aaw
—"—	7.9.17		Fine but dull. Squadron Training. Brigade Tactical Scheme for Signallers and Despatch Riders.	aaw
—"—	8.9.17		Fine. C.O. inspected Subaltern Officers' Chargers and Subaltern Officers at Riding School. Parades under Squadron arrangements.	aaw
—"—	9.9.17		Fine. Divine Services, C. of E. and R.C. 10.0 am.	aaw
—"—	10.9.17		Fine. Parades under Squadron arrangements. Musketry for 'D' Squadron on the MENCHY BRETON Range.	aaw

A7092 Wt. W128.9/M1293 750,000. 1/17. D. D & L. Ltd. Forms/C2118/14.

Army Form C. 2118.

Instructions regarding War Diaries and Intelligence Summaries are contained in F. S. Regs., Part II. and the Staff Manual respectively. Title pages will be prepared in manuscript.

WAR DIARY
~~or~~
~~INTELLIGENCE SUMMARY.~~

(Erase heading not required.)

Place	Date	Hour	Summary of Events and Information	Remarks and references to Appendices
ST. MICHEL SUR TERNOISE P. de C.	11.9.17		Fine. Squadron Training. Musketry for "C" Sqdn on the MONCHY BRETON Range	AAW
	12.9.17		Fine. Regimental Tactical Exercise – practising inter-communication	AAW
— " —	13.9.17		Fine. Squadron Parades. 42 Other ranks proceeded to the Base – 20 as re-inforcements, the remainder for transfer to Infantry	AAW
— " —	14.9.17		Fine. The Regiment paraded 8.45 am to take part in a Brigade Route March. Starting point – OSTREVILLE 9.30 a.m. Gas Helmets were worn for 3/4 hour.	AAW
— " —	15.9.17		Fine. Equitation for Subaltern Officers. Squadrons exercised.	AAW
— " —	16.9.17		Fine. Divine Service – R.C. 9.0 am.	AAW
— " —	17.9.17		Fine. Squadron Parades. Musketry for "B" Squadron on MONCHY BRETON Range	AAW
— " —	18.9.17		Fine. Regimental Tactical Exercise – practising attack on a convoy.	AAW
— " —	19.9.17		Fine. Squadron Parades. Musketry for "A" Squadron on MONCHY BRETON Range. C.O. inspected B & C Squadrons at Foot-drill in afternoon. 2/LT. W.P. CLOWES instructed in German Machine Gun	AAW
— " —	20.9.17		Wet morning – Fine later. Squadron Parades. AMBALA Brigade Gymkhana in afternoon. "C" Sqdn did a Musical Ride. Captain L.C. WOODS, 2 servants, & 4 horses, left to take charge of Brigade party building huts, etc.	AAW

Army Form C. 2118.

Instructions regarding War Diaries and Intelligence Summaries are contained in F. S. Regs., Part II. and the Staff Manual respectively. Title pages will be prepared in manuscript.

WAR DIARY ~~or INTELLIGENCE SUMMARY.~~

(Erase heading not required.)

Place	Date	Hour	Summary of Events and Information	Remarks and references to Appendices
St MICHEL SUR TERNOISE P de C	21.9.17	—	Fine. Squadron Parades.	AAW
	22.9.17	—	Fine. The G.O.C. Brigade inspected the Regiment at Foot-drill.	AAW
— " —	23.9.17	—	Fine. Divine Service R.C. 10.0 am. Captain J E BLAKISTON HOUSTON arrived from BASE	AAW
— " —	24.9.17	—	Fine. Squadron Parades. Musketry for "D" Sqdn in morning on ROCOURT ST LAURENT Range; "C" Sqdn in afternoon.	AAW
— " —	25.9.17	—	Fine. Regimental Tactical Exercise - practising intercommunication. Captain J E B HOUSTON posted to "D" Sqdn. Captain C.R.L. ADLERCRON posted to "C" Sqdn	AAW
— " —	26.9.17	—	Fine. Squadron parades. Musketry for "A" Sqdn on ROCOURT Range. C.O. inspected "B" Sqdn at Drill.	AAW
— " —	27.9.17	—	Fine. Squadron parades. Musketry for "B" Squadron on ROCOURT Range.	AAW
— " —	28.9.17	—	Fine. Brigade Route March. Gas Helmets were worn.	AAW
— " —	29.9.17	—	Fine. Squadrons exercised. 9 Other ranks to Base - surplus to establishment.	AAW
— " —	30.9.17	—	Fine. Divine Service R.C. 10.0 am.	AAW

J. H. Mort. LIEUT. COLONEL, ~~COMMANDING VIII (K.R.I.) HUSSARS.~~

A. Atkinson Willes. Lieut. ADJUTANT VIII (K.R.I.) HUSSARS.

A7092 Wt. W125.9/M1293 750,000. 1/17. D. D & L. Ltd. Forms/C2118/14.

(110) R

Confidential

War Diary

of

VIII (King's Royal Irish) Hussars

From 1st October to 31st October 1917

Vol. 38.

Instructions regarding War Diaries and Intelligence Summaries are contained in F. S. Regs., Part II. and the Staff Manual respectively. Title pages will be prepared in manuscript.

WAR DIARY or INTELLIGENCE SUMMARY. VIII (K.R.I.) Hussars

(Erase heading not required.)

Army Form C. 2118.

Confidential

Place	Date	Hour	Summary of Events and Information	Remarks and references to Appendices
St MICHEL SUR TERNOISE	1.10.17		Fine. Squadrons paraded.	a.a.w.
— " —	2.10.17		Fine. Regimental Tactical Exercise in the vicinity of LA THIEULOYE.	a.a.w.
— " —	3.10.17		Dull. Squadron Training. Musketry for "D" Squadron.	a.a.w.
— " —	4.10.17		Dull. Colder. Squadrons paraded. C.O. inspected C Squadron at dismounted work. Musketry for H.Qrs. Very wet evening.	a.a.w.
— " —	5.10.17		Fine. Brigade Staff Ride cancelled. Conference of Commanding Officers at Brigade H.Q.	a.a.w.
— " —	6.10.17		Wet. 24 Cast horses proceeded to Railhead. Squadrons exercised.	a.a.w.
	7.10.17		Regiment paraded 6.30 am and proceeded to Brigade Starting Point at PRYAS. Cold and bright early, but rained all afternoon. Brigade marched 7.20 am via PERNES, LILLERS, ST VENANT to the STEENBECQUE area. Watered and fed at LA BASSEE Canal. Reached STEENBECQUE about 3.20 pm. Horses in open – men found cover in barns etc. Expect to move to WORMHOUDT 10.0 am tomorrow.	a.a.w.
— " —	8.10.17		After a very wet night weather changed. Regiment received orders to stand fast, and remained in billets all day. Very wet evening.	a.a.w.

A7092 Wt. W12S.9/M1293 750,000. 1/17. D. D & L. Ltd. Forms/C2118/14.

Instructions regarding War Diaries and Intelligence Summaries are contained in F. S. Regs., Part II. and the Staff Manual respectively. Title pages will be prepared in manuscript.

WAR DIARY
or
~~INTELLIGENCE SUMMARY.~~
(Erase heading not required.)

Army Form C. 2118.

Place	Date	Hour	Summary of Events and Information	Remarks and references to Appendices
STEENBECQUE	9.10.17		Fine morning. Squadrons exercised round billets – Heavy rain in evening. 100 horses got under cover – remainder in open.	AAW
– " –	10.10.17		Very wet. Regiment remained in billets expecting to move.	AAW
– –	11.10.17		Regiment paraded 8.0 am and moved to Brigade Starting Point – cross roads AIRE-HAZEBROUCK – ST VENANT-HAZEBROUCK. Marched via HAZEBROUCK-STEENVOORDE to WATOU area – arrived just after mid-day. H.Q, C & D Squns at TRAPPISTES Farm; A & B Squns at Hike Camp. All horses in open – men under cover.	AAW
WATOU Area				
– –	12.10.17		Wet. Squadrons exercised. 8 Remounts received.	AAW
– –	13.10.17		Very wet. Squadrons exercised. Received at 1.0 am orders to move	AAW
– –	14.10.17		Fine. Regiment paraded 8.30 am and moved to Brigade Starting Pt. ½ mile E of STEENVOORDE. Brigade marched at 9.30 am via STEENVOORDE – STAPLE – EBLINGHEM – to RENESCURE area. Regiment went into old billets at CAMPAGNE – 2.15 pm.	AAW
CAMPAGNE				
CAMPAGNE	15.10.17		Brigade continued the march. Regiment paraded 8.30 am and proceeded to Brigade Starting Point – ARQUES Church. Brigade marched at 9.0 am to THIEMBRONNE area via [redacted] WIZERNES. – Regiment billeted in FAUQUEMBERGUES, very crowded – the Portuguese occupying most of the area.	AAW
FAUQUEMBERGUES				

Army Form C. 2118.

Instructions regarding War Diaries and Intelligence Summaries are contained in F. S. Regs., Part II. and the Staff Manual respectively. Title pages will be prepared in manuscript.

WAR DIARY
or
~~INTELLIGENCE SUMMARY.~~
(Erase heading not required.)

Place	Date	Hour	Summary of Events and Information	Remarks and references to Appendices
FAUQUEMBERGUES / MARESQUEL	16.10.17		Fine. The Brigade continued the march – 8th Hussars leading. Moved off at 9.0 am via FRUGES – RUISSEAUVILLE – PLANQUES – to MARESQUEL area. H.Q. & "D" Squadron billeted in ECQUEMICOURT – very crowded. A.B. & C Sqdns in MARESQUEL with Bde H.Qrs. All billets very crowded. Horses in open.	[illegible]
—	17.10.17		Fine. Squadrons exercised and cleaned up.	[illegible]
—	18.10.17		Squadrons exercised. Capt EDWARDS & Capt. PARKINS to 5th Divisional Artillery on transfer. Lieut. PAKT to Cadet School for Commission.	[illegible]
—	19.10.17		Fine. Sqdns exercised. "D" Sqdn moved from ECQUEMICOURT to BEAURAINVILLE. "B" Sqdn moved from MARESQUEL to BEAURAIN Chateau.	[illegible]
BEAURAINVILLE	20.10.17		Fine. H.Q. moved from ECQUEMICOURT to BEAURAINVILLE – rather crowded. Squadrons exercised. Clearing up generally.	[illegible]
—	21.10.17		Fine. Parade Service C. of E. for "D" Sqdn & H.Q. 10.30 am. Parade Service R.C. BEAURAINVILLE 8.0 am.	[illegible]
—	22.10.17		Fine. Squadron training. Colonel MUSSENDEN arrived from ROUEN.	[illegible]
—	23.10.17		Wet. C.O's inspection of "A" Squadron cancelled.	[illegible]
—	24.10.17		Fine. Brigade Tactical Exercise – defence of a convoy in the vicinity of CAMPAGNE LES HESDIN.	[illegible]
—	25.10.17		Very stormy. Squadrons exercised. Colonel MUSSENDEN returned to ROUEN. Following officers arrived from Base:– 2Lts C.W. ROFF, S.M. MONTGOMERY, W.E. DENT, R.E.F. CHIRNSIDE, T.K.V. GRAHAM.	[illegible]

Army Form C. 2118.

Instructions regarding War Diaries and Intelligence Summaries are contained in F. S. Regs., Part II. and the Staff Manual respectively. Title pages will be prepared in manuscript.

WAR DIARY
or
~~INTELLIGENCE SUMMARY.~~
(Erase heading not required.)

Place	Date	Hour	Summary of Events and Information	Remarks and references to Appendices
BEAURAINVILLE	26.10.17		Very wet. Regimental Scheme cancelled.	aaw
— " —	27.10.17		Fine. C.O. inspected A Sqdn billets. Squadrons exercised.	aaw
— " —	28.10.17		Fine. Parade Service. C. of E. at MARESQUEL 10.30 am R.C's BEAURAINVILLE 9.0 am 8 Officers' Chargers arrived.	aaw
— " —	29.10.17		Wet. C.O. inspected A Sqdn in Drill Order. G.O.C. took Staff Ride for young officers. Troop foot ball competition commenced.	aaw
— " —	30.10.17		Very cold and wet. C.O. inspected "B" Sqdn.	aaw
— " —	31.10.17		Fine. Brigade Tactical Exercise.	aaw

J. M. Mort
LIEUT. COLONEL,
COMMANDING VIII (K.R.I.) HUSSARS.

A. Atkinson-Willes Lieut
ADJUTANT VIII (K.R.I.) HUSSARS.

A7092 Wt. W128 9/M1293 750,000. 1/17. D. D & L. Ltd. Forms/C2118/14.

R

(110)

Confidential

War Diary

of

VIII King's Royal Irish Hussars

From 1st February to 28th February 1918

Vol. 42

Instructions regarding War Diaries and Intelligence Summaries are contained in F. S. Regs., Part II. and the Staff Manual respectively. Title pages will be prepared in manuscript.

WAR DIARY or ~~INTELLIGENCE SUMMARY.~~ VIII K.R.I. Hussars

(Erase heading not required.)

Army Form C. 2118.

Confidential

Place	Date	Hour	Summary of Events and Information	Remarks and references to Appendices
SECTOR A I	1/2/18		Foggy - cold wind. 2/Lt C W REES took out a patrol of 12 O.R's at 6 o p.m and occupied a position between FISHER'S CRATER and the St HELENE TRENCH wire to act as Right flank guard to two strong patrols of 18th Lancers and 9th H.H. No enemy encountered and no fire drawn. Work continued on posts and new belts of wire	aaw
BEAUCOURT - AILLY LE HAUT CLOCHER			Mounted portion of Regiment paraded 10.30 am and marched via St OUEN - GORENFLOS - ERGNES - to AILLY-LE HAUT CLOCHER (HQ, A & D) - "C" Squadron in FAMECHON - "B" in BUSSUS BUSSUE	
SECTOR A I	2/2/18		Clear, but still cold. Enemy registered on TUMULUS at about 8.30 a.m with about 12 H.E. Lt J.E.H. BRADISH-ELLAMES and 2Lt W.H. HARTLEY took out a patrol of 32 O.R's at 11.30 p.m. Party proceeded through gaps in wire of St HELENE TRENCH and reconnoitred the trench and village finding both unoccupied; thence to wire of PEN TRENCH which appeared very strong. A good deal of movement and noise heard here. Bright moonlight and absence of cover made detailed reconnaissance impossible. Party returned 4.15 a.m. Work continued on posts. New belt of wire completed.	aaw
— " —	3/2/18		Fine. Quiet day. Regiment was relieved in the line on night 3rd/4th by the 7th Dragoon Guards and marched to LE VERGUIER. Relief completed 10. o p.m. Lieut C.S. ROWLEY & J.D. PATON with 2 M.G.O.s & 5 batmen rejoined Back Area details from Divisional School.	aaw

A7092 Wt. W128/9/M1293 750,000. 1/17. D. D & L. Ltd. Forms/C2118/14.

Instructions regarding War Diaries and Intelligence Summaries are contained in F. S. Regs., Part II. and the Staff Manual respectively. Title pages will be prepared in manuscript.

WAR DIARY
or
INTELLIGENCE SUMMARY.
(Erase heading not required.)

Army Form C. 2118.

Place	Date	Hour	Summary of Events and Information	Remarks and references to Appendices
~~Sector~~ LE VERGUIER	4/2/18		The LE VERGUIER position consists of 4 forts. The Regiment was disposed as follows:- "A" Sqdn - Fort DYCE, "B" Sqdn Fort LEES, "C" Sqdn Fort GREATHEAD "D" Sqdn Fort BELL. Condition of trenches fair to bad. Squadrons worked 5 hours daily on improvements.	aaw
— —	5/2/18		Work on defences continued. The Major General Comdg and Fifth Army Commander inspected the defences. At 11.0pm our neighbours having sent "S O S" signal, several of our batteries opened, but it proved a false alarm.	aaw
— —	6/2/18		Work continued on forts. Quiet day - weather clear	aaw
— —	7/2/18		Lts CLIFFORD and CLEMENTS relieved by Lieuts HENRY and DENT. Enemy shelled Fort LEES area with 60 H.E's about 3.0pm. Lieut W.A.O. HENRY severely wounded. Corpl Cox (H.Q) slightly wounded - at duty. Work continued on forts.	aaw
— —	8/2/18		Work continued on forts. Enemy fired 4 shells on Fort DYCE. No casualties. Lieut T.D. PATON [illegible] left Back Area for Forward Area.	aaw
— —	9/2/18		Enemy shelled valley S.E of LE VERGUIER from 10.0 am to 12.30 pm searching for a battery. Work on forts continued. 2/Lt M.R. RUSSELL joined from Back Area	aaw

A7092 Wt W128/9/M1293 750,000 1/17 D. D. & L. Ltd. Forms/C2118/14.

Instructions regarding War Diaries and Intelligence Summaries are contained in F. S. Regs., Part II. and the Staff Manual respectively. Title pages will be prepared in manuscript.

WAR DIARY
or
~~INTELLIGENCE SUMMARY.~~
(Erase heading not required.)

Army Form C. 2118.

Place	Date	Hour	Summary of Events and Information	Remarks and references to Appendices
AILLY LE HT CLOCHER	26/2/18		Fine. Exercise; 18 Lancers & 9 H.H. left to entrain for the East. Forward party continued work on roads.	aaw
— " —	27/2/18		Fine. Exercise. Forward party continued work on roads.	aaw
— " —	28/2/18		Fine. Exercise. Forward party continued work on roads.	aaw

J H Mort. LIEUT. COLONEL,
~~COMMANDING~~ VIII (K.R.I.) HUSSARS.

A. A. Willis Lieut
ADJUTANT VIII (K.R.I.) HUSSARS.

B.

(110).

Confidential

War Diary

of

8th King's Royal Irish Hussars

From 1st November to 30th November 1917

Vol. 39.

Instructions regarding War Diaries and Intelligence Summaries are contained in F. S. Regs., Part II. and the Staff Manual respectively. Title pages will be prepared in manuscript.

WAR DIARY
or
~~INTELLIGENCE SUMMARY.~~
(Erase heading not required.)

VIII (K.R.I.) Hussars

Confidential

Army Form C. 2118.

Place	Date	Hour	Summary of Events and Information	Remarks and references to Appendices
BEAURAINVILLE	1/11/17		Wet. C.O's inspection of C Sqdn cancelled	AW
—	2/11/17		Wet. Regimental Staff Ride cancelled.	AAW
—	3/11/17		Dull. Divisional Route March. Regiment paraded 9.20 am.	AAW
—	4/11/17		Fine. Parade Service for R.C's. Captain W.E.P. CHARNES proceeded to U.K. on duty	AAW
—	5/11/17		Fine. Squadron training.	AAW
—	6/11/17		Fine. Squadron Training	AAW
—	7/11/17		Wet. Brigade Tactical Exercise – under [illegible] St DENOEUX. Received orders to move on 9th	AAW
—	8/11/17		Dull. Sqdns exercised	AAW
—	9/11/17		Wet. Regiment paraded 8.0 am and marched to LONGUEVILLETTE (HQ. A & D) and HARDINVAL (B & C). Arrived 3 0 pm. All horses under cover except D	
LONGUEVILLETTE				AAW
—	10/11/17		Dull, but fine. Regiment paraded at 9.15 am and marched to BAVELINCOURT and arrived 1.30 pm. All horses under cover. HQ. A & B in [illegible]COURT, & BAVELINCOURT, C Sqdn in ESSART, D in BEHENCOURT	
BAVELINCOURT				AAW

Army Form C. 2118.

Instructions regarding War Diaries and Intelligence Summaries are contained in F. S. Regs., Part II. and the Staff Manual respectively. Title pages will be prepared in manuscript.

WAR DIARY
or
~~INTELLIGENCE SUMMARY.~~
(Erase heading not required.)

Place	Date	Hour	Summary of Events and Information	Remarks and references to Appendices
BAVINCOURT – SIZANNE	11/1/17		Fine. Regiment paraded at 3.15pm and marched to Camp No 17 – near SIZANNE. Arrived about 8.15pm. 75% of Horses under cover.	AAW
– – CANTIGNY	12/1/17	–	Fine – Foggy morning. Regiment paraded at 3.45pm and marched to Brigade Starting Point near L'ECLUSIER from where the Brigade marched to CANTIGNY – arriving 8.0pm. All horses under cover.	AW
CANTIGNY	13/1/17	–	Fine. Foggy. No exercise allowed in daylight.	AW
	14/1/17	–	Foggy & cold. Squadrons exercised in the vicinity of billets. Cleaning up & [illegible] billets. 11 ORs joined from Base. 2/Lt C. W. Ross to Hospital – sick.	AW
– –	15/1/17	–	Foggy. Squadrons exercised. [illegible] Williams to Cadet School – new commission.	AW
– –	16/1/17	–	Foggy. Squadrons exercised.	AW
– –	17/1/17	–	Foggy. Squadrons exercised. Lt Home proceeded to Hotchkiss Gun Course [illegible] of C. Os at Div. HQ.	AW
– –	18/1/17	–	Dull. [illegible]	AW
– –	19/1/17	–	Fine. Cold. Orders received to move to forward concentration area on the night 19/20. Squadrons exercised early.	AW

A7092 Wt. W128.9/M1293 750,000. 1/17. D. D. & L. Ltd. Forms/C2118/14.

Instructions regarding War Diaries and Intelligence Summaries are contained in F. S. Regs., Part II. and the Staff Manual respectively. Title pages will be prepared in manuscript.

WAR DIARY
or
~~INTELLIGENCE SUMMARY.~~
(Erase heading not required.)

Army Form C. 2118.

Place	Date	Hour	Summary of Events and Information	Remarks and references to Appendices
N.W. of FINS S. of MARCOING	20/11/17		Regiment paraded at 1.0 am. and joined the Brigade which marched via BOUCLY – FINCOURT Wood – EQUANCOURT to forward concentration area at BOIS d'DESSART N.W. of FINS – arriving there at day break. Off saddled for two hours and fed. Saddled up at 9.0 am and stood to. At 2.0 pm Brigade moved forward via BEAUCAMP – VILLERS PLOUICH to an area 1½ miles S of MARCOING. Bivouached for the night – horses remained saddled up. Cold – wet night.	AHW
S. of MARCOING RIBECOURT	21/11/17	12.0 noon	Fine rain all day. Horses remained saddled up – no water since yesterday morning – Orders received to move at a moment's notice. Moved forward to support 1st Cav. Div. and marched via MARCOING to RIBECOURT where the Regiment bivouached. Orders received to off-saddle until mid-night – Further orders received to remain off-saddled, but ready to move at 7.0 am. Still no water for horses. Rained all night but slightly warmer.	AHW
RIBECOURT EQUANCOURT	22/11/17		Fine, dull. Regiment paraded at 7.15 am and moved to EQUANCOURT via HAVRINCOURT and METZ and halted W. of FINS at 12.0 noon for 2 hours. Off saddled and watered – first time since 7.0 am 20th. 2.0 pm – Moved to EQUANCOURT. – Horses in open – some men got shelter. Received orders at mid night to move at 6.30 am.	AHW
EQUANCOURT BRAY	23/11/17		Regiment paraded at 7.15 am and marched to BRAY via ETRICOURT – MOISLAINS – BOUCHAVESNES – CLERY – MARICOURT – about 20 miles. Reached BRAY about 12.30 pm. Wet. Some cover for men and horses.	AHW

A7092 Wt. W128.9/M1293 750,000. 1/17. D. D & L. Ltd. Forms/C2118/14.

Instructions regarding War Diaries and Intelligence Summaries are contained in F. S. Regs., Part II. and the Staff Manual respectively. Title pages will be prepared in manuscript.

WAR DIARY
or
~~INTELLIGENCE SUMMARY.~~
(Erase heading not required.)

Army Form C. 2118.

Place	Date	Hour	Summary of Events and Information	Remarks and references to Appendices
BRAY	24/11/17	—	Fine. Received orders to stand to at ½ hour's notice after 8 a.m.	Aw.
—	25/11/17	—	Fine. Colder. Bn standing to ready to move at ½ hours notice.	Aw.
—	26/11/17	—	Rain. [illegible] cancelled. Men bathed and cleaned up. Orders received to move to TERTRY area	Aw.
CAUVIGNY FARM	27/11/17	—	Regiment paraded 9.15 a.m. and proceeded to [illegible] NW of CAPPY [illegible] via CAPPY - ESTREES - VILLERS CARBONNEL - BRIE - MONS-en-CHAUSSEE to Camp near TERTRY. Arrived 2.30 pm. Huts unfinished, leaky and very dirty.	Aw.
—	28/11/17	—	Fine. [illegible] and cleaned up and improved camp.	Aw.
—	29/11/17	—	Fine. [illegible] Capt. HOLLOWAY & 2/Lt [illegible] & [illegible] returned from ROUEN. [illegible] [illegible] for the trenches.	Aw.
VILLERS FAUCON	30/11/17	—	Fine. Received [illegible] 9.30 am to move at once in a Northerly direction [illegible] [illegible] and dump made. [illegible] [illegible] [illegible] 10 a.m. [illegible] to VILLERS FAUCON where we halted for ½ hour. Moved on at 1.30 pm [illegible] [illegible] [illegible] GOUZEAUCOURT [illegible] through N.W. edge of EPEHY [illegible] [illegible] [illegible] heavy M.G. fire from [illegible] [illegible] [illegible] [illegible]	Ref. Map [illegible] [illegible]

A7092 Wt. W128 9/M1293 750,000. 1/17. D. D & L. Ltd. Forms/C2118/14.

Instructions regarding War Diaries and Intelligence Summaries are contained in F. S. Regs., Part II. and the Staff Manual respectively. Title pages will be prepared in manuscript.

WAR DIARY
or
INTELLIGENCE SUMMARY.
(Erase heading not required.)

Army Form C. 2118.

Place	Date	Hour	Summary of Events and Information	Remarks and references to Appendices
	30/11/17		Contd. 2Lt T C Whitson [illegible] from A Sqdn was [illegible] C.O. ordered Major Ryder to take his Squadron (A) on Gauche Wood. On crossing the sky line they came under heavy shell and M.G. fire from Chapel Crossing and Gauche Wood. The Squadron occupied the sunken road 1000x West of the Wood, & attacks pushed out on Gauche Wood again came under heavy M.G. fire, Major Ryder was killed and 16 O.R's killed and wounded. By 2 opm Lt Simmons who had assumed command held the sunken road W of Gauche Wood with 13 men with 9th Hodson Horse on his right, and repelled a strong counter attack of the enemy debouching from Gauche Wood. The C.O. having withdrawn "C" Sqdn from the right, led the Regiment across the Peronne-Heudicourt railway and moved via the N.W. corner of Genin Well Copse (where several casualties were caused by shrapnel and H.E.) in a N.E. direction on Gauche Wood. Again came under heavy shell fire on crossing the ridge and being held up by fire, it became necessary to turn S.W. and [illegible] the [illegible] Gouzeaucourt Road about 600x N of Revelon Farm. Regiment moved to S.W. corner of Genin Well Copse and dismounted about 3 opm and moved up in support of A Squadron. "C" Squadron ordered to reconnoitre towards Gauche Wood but came under heavy fire from the railway and Chapel crossing and withdrew to the sunken road after repeated attempts.	W.6. Sheet 62C

A7092 Wt. W128 9/M1293 750,000. 1/17. D. D & L. Ltd. Forms/C2118/14.

Instructions regarding War Diaries and Intelligence Summaries are contained in F. S. Regs., Part II. and the Staff Manual respectively. Title Pages will be prepared in manuscript.

WAR DIARY
or
~~INTELLIGENCE SUMMARY~~
(Erase heading not required.)

Army Form C. 2118

Place	Date	Hour	Summary of Events and Information	Remarks and references to Appendices
W.6 Sheet 62c	30/11/17		15 Lancers relieved the Regiment about 7 a.m. Withdrew for the night to the valley W. of GENIN WELL COPSE.	
			Casualties during day — Killed — Major Hon. R N D Ryder	
			5699 Sergeant R Wass	
			1514 L/C T Surdsolt	
			1415 " C Flynn	
			24512 " H Wright	
			Wounded — Lt. T C Wilson	
			13511 Sgt. Shepherd J. 2343 Cpl. Hosmer R 7803 Cpl. Bennett	
			2422 S.S. L Mulcock 12368 Pte. A Marsh 1622 J Scarlett	
			13512 J Shreeve 4011 A Gregg 5324 W Chimpken	
			4360 A Hudson 7017 H. Walker 7012 Cpl. Cousens J	
			818 L/C J McCann 7574 N Woods 14225 F Martina	
			2163 L Sheeran 1330 S Perigo 1804 T. Blake	
			1140 J Rynne 4225 H Curtis 301220 A Twydale	
			276664 W Musgrave 26714 R Jordan 25033 T Deakin	
			6257 Cpl. Pinchin (since died of wounds) 13776 J Carroll	
			6567 Cpl. R Walters 6624 Sgt. T Jones Interpreter Pourois	
			Missing — 6234 L/C E Case 6563 C Read 26776 A Wilson	
			Animal Casualties — Killed 20 horses 1 Mule Missing 32 horses 3 mules	
			Wounded 21 horses	

[illegible signature]
LIEUT. COLONEL,
COMMANDING VIII (K.R.I.) HUSSARS.

A. Atkinson [illegible] Lieut.
ADJUTANT VIII (K.R.I.) HUSSARS.

1875 Wt. W593/826 1,000,000 4/15 J.B.C. & A. A.D.S.S./Forms/C. 2118.

110.

8th K.R.I. Hussars

CONFIDENTIAL.

WAR DIARY.

VOL. 40.

December 1917

Aust Cav Bde

War Diary Vol. 40.

Dec 1917

Instructions regarding War Diaries and Intelligence Summaries are contained in F. S. Regs., Part II. and the Staff Manual respectively. Title pages will be prepared in manuscript.

WAR DIARY
or
~~INTELLIGENCE~~ SUMMARY.
(Erase heading not required.)

8th (K.R.I.) Hussars

Confidential.

Army Form C. 2118.

(1414) 8.H.

Place	Date	Hour	Summary of Events and Information	Remarks and references to Appendices
REVELON FARM	1/12/17		Fine. Cold. Received orders at 9.0am to move to the S.W. of REVELON Farm; remained there all day. Very cold. 9th H. and 18 Lancers still in the line after a successful attack on GAUCHE Wood.	
HEUDICOURT			In the evening, the Regiment rejoined the Brigade near HEUDICOURT Station and bivouacked for the night.	
— " —	2/12/17		Very cold night. The Regiment moved up dismounted to support the SEC'BAD BDE and remained in the valley S.W. of REVELON FARM all day. Returned to the horses about 8.0pm.	
— " —	3/12/17		Fine, Cold. Received Orders to move back to VILLERS FAUCON. Marched at 11.30am and bivouacked in same valley as on 30th Nov:	
VILLERS FAUCON REVELON FM	4/12/17		Moved from VILLERS FAUCON dismounted at 2.0pm and took over the Support Line from REVELON FARM – GOUZEAUCOURT road to CHAPEL HILL from Royal West Surreys. Very cold – hard frost. A quiet night.	
— " —	5/12/17		Fine and bright. Enemy fairly [illegible] aerial activity all day. The [illegible] relieved the Regiment in the line. A & B Squadrons relieved about 9.0pm "C" & "D" Sqdns relieved 12.30am 6/12/17. Marched across country back to horses. [illegible] E. Collins wounded slightly at duty. B [illegible] [illegible]	

A7092 Wt. W125 9/M1293 750,000. 1/17. D. D. & L. Ltd. Forms/C2118/14.

Army Form C. 2118.

Instructions regarding War Diaries and Intelligence Summaries are contained in F. S. Regs., Part II. and the Staff Manual respectively. Title pages will be prepared in manuscript.

WAR DIARY
~~or~~
~~INTELLIGENCE SUMMARY.~~
(Erase heading not required.)

Place	Date	Hour	Summary of Events and Information	Remarks and references to Appendices
VILLERS FAUCON	6/12/17		Cold bright day. Returned from trenches about 2.30 am. Men very tired having had very little sleep since 30th Nov.	
— " —	7/12/17		Dull. Not so cold. C O inspected horses in the lines at Stable hour.	
— " — CARTIGNY	8/12/17		The Brigade marched from VILLERS FAUCON at 12.30 pm via ROISEL and BOUCLY to CARTIGNY and occupied the same stables and huts as before	
— " —	9/12/17		Wet. Squadrons rested and cleaned up.	
— " —	10/12/17		Bright. Cold. Regiment stood to, saddled up, from 8.0 am till 9.30 am. Squadrons exercised after 9.30 am and bathed during the day.	
— " —	11/12/17		Cold wind - dull. The Regiment stood to from 6.30 am till 8.0 am, ready to move to the Corps Sector if wanted.	
— " —	12/12/17		Fine, bright. Stood to from 6.30 am till 8.0 am. Squadrons exercised after 10.0 am in the vicinity of stables.	
— " —	13/12/17		Dull. Received orders at midnight to be saddled up ready to move at 7.0 am. Off saddled at 9.0 am but stood to all day at an hour's notice.	
— " —	14/12/17		Dull - wet. Still standing to at one hour's notice.	
— " —	15/12/17		Fine - frosty. Still standing to at one hour's notice.	
— " —	16/12/17		Fine, cold. Stand to cancelled at 8.0 am. A digging party of 150 men with 50 horseholders proceeded to HERVILLY where they dismounted and proceeded to the Intermediate line to dig.	

A7092 Wt. W128 9/M1293 750,000. 1/17. D. D & L. Ltd Forms/C2118/14.

Instructions regarding War Diaries and Intelligence Summaries are contained in F. S. Regs., Part II. and the Staff Manual respectively. Title pages will be prepared in manuscript.

WAR DIARY

~~or~~

~~INTELLIGENCE SUMMARY.~~

(Erase heading not required.)

Army Form C. 2118.

Place	Date	Hour	Summary of Events and Information	Remarks and references to Appendices
CARTIGNY	17/12/17		Heavy snowfall. Digging party went up under Major McCURELL – returned about 10.0pm. No 6602 Pte Powell to Hospital – fractured leg.	
— " —	18/12/17		Bright – hard frost. Snow on roads frozen hard making it very difficult for traffic. No digging party.	
— " —	19/12/17		Fine. Very hard frost. 150 men went digging under Lt. S ROWLEY and marched back on foot arriving 10.0pm.	
— " —	20/12/17		Very cold – hard frost. 67 Remounts arrived. No digging party.	
— " —	21/12/17		Very cold. Hard frost. C.O. inspected last joined remounts – a fairly good lot. A party of 25 men went to TERTRY to build huts.	
— " —	22/12/17		Hard frost & night and not so cold.	
— " —	23/12/17		Cold – Bright. Service for R.C's 8.30 am. Brigade Head Quarters moved to TERTRY.	
— " —	24/12/17		Very cold – snow. A digging party of 200 O.Rs. paraded at 1.30pm. Lorries did not arrive until 3.30pm. On arrival at TEMPLEUX LE GUERARD no R.E. guide could be found. Party returned about 9.0pm – no work done.	
— " —	25/12/17		Cold – snow. The C.O. went round men's dinners mid-day. Divine Service for Roman Catholics at 10.0am.	
— " —	26/12/17		Fine – Cold. Squadrons exercised. Lieut Kent and 3 O.Rs. were sent on Hotchkiss Gun Course.	

Instructions regarding War Diaries and Intelligence Summaries are contained in F. S. Regs., Part II. and the Staff Manual respectively. Title pages will be prepared in manuscript.

WAR DIARY
or
INTELLIGENCE SUMMARY.
(Erase heading not required.)

Army Form C. 2118.

Place	Date	Hour	Summary of Events and Information	Remarks and references to Appendices
CARTIGNY	27/12/17		Cold - Bright. Exercise	
—"—	28/12/17		Very cold - wind - snow. Conference for Commanding Officers at Brigade H.Qrs. 10.0 a.m. Orders to move on the 29th received. Lieut Ladenburg to Hospital	
TERTRY.	29/12/17.		Fine Cold. The Regiment moved from CARTIGNY to TERTRY squadrons moving independently. Roads were very bad & slippery. Some improvement done to huts etc. but still there is a lot to be done.	
—"—	30/12/17.		Fine. Still thaw. Parade service for Roman Catholics 10.0 a.m. Lieut CHIRNSIDE & 2Lieuts EVANS-LOMBE, M.R. RUSSELL } to Hospital	
—"—	31st		Fine - warmer. Men employed in erecting huts & cookhouses. Lieut. ARMSTRONG left the Regiment to join 3rd Brigade Tank Corps.	

J. Vander Byl
MAJOR,
COMMANDING VIII (K.R.I.) HUSSARS.

A7092 Wt. W128.9/M1293 750,000. 1/17. D. D & L. Ltd. Forms/C2118/14.

Instructions regarding War Diaries and Intelligence Summaries are contained in F. S. Regs., Part II. and the Staff Manual respectively. Title pages will be prepared in manuscript.

WAR DIARY
or
INTELLIGENCE SUMMARY.
(Erase heading not required.)

January 1918.

[illegible] Confidential

Army Form C. 2118.

110

Place	Date	Hour	Summary of Events and Information	Remarks and references to Appendices
[illegible]	1/1/18		Hard frost – bright – Work in camp continued. Walls round huts and horse lines commenced – Cook houses taken in hand.	[illegible]
	2/1/18		Squadrons exercised and continued work in camp	[illegible]
	3/1/18		Squadrons exercised and continued building.	[illegible]
	4/1/18		Very cold [illegible]. Work in camp continued. Capt. E. B. [illegible] and Capt. P. [illegible] attended a Gas Course	[illegible]
	5/1/18		Hard frost. Squadrons exercised and continued work in camp.	[illegible]
	6/1/18		[illegible] 11.0 a.m. R.C.s at TREFCON 10.0 a.m. [illegible] [illegible] Evans-[illegible] for course at Divisional School	[illegible]
	7/1/18		[illegible] Rain all night. Lieuts Rowley & STANILAND attended a Gas Course	[illegible]
	8/1/18		[illegible] all day	[illegible]
	9/1/18		[illegible] Snowed all afternoon	[illegible]
	10/1/18		Thawing. C.O. inspected huts and horse lines	[illegible]
	11/1/18		[illegible] continued.	[illegible]
	12/1/18		[illegible] continued	[illegible]

A7092 Wt. W125/9/M1293 750,000. 1/17. D. D. & L. Ltd. Forms/C2118/14.

Army Form C. 2118.

Instructions regarding War Diaries and Intelligence Summaries are contained in F. S. Regs., Part II. and the Staff Manual respectively. Title pages will be prepared in manuscript.

WAR DIARY
or
~~INTELLIGENCE SUMMARY.~~

(Erase heading not required.)

Place	Date	Hour	Summary of Events and Information	Remarks and references to Appendices
TERTRY	13/1/18		Fine. Parade Service R.C. 10.0. am.	AHW
— " —	14/1/18		Fine. Ready to at one hours notice required. Walls round huts nearly complete. Captain J.C. BRUTTON arrived from England to attend Divisional School.	AHW
— " —	15/1/18		Wet. Regiment bathe at Brigade Baths.	AHW
— " —	16/1/18		Blowing a gale. – Rain. Lieut A.I.B. RITCHIE left for 3rd Brigade Tank Corps. Capt J.C. BRUTTON to Divisional School	AHW
— " —	17/1/18		Lieuts H.E.A.E. BOLTON, A.C. ORCHIN and D.M. LARKINS proceeded to U.K. to join Royal Flying Corps.	AHW
— " —	18/1/18		Wet. Working party of 220 paraded under Captain ~~E.B. Houston~~ P.S. ALEXANDER at 7.30 am and proceeded to work near LE VERGUIER. 100 Officers and men under Captain E.B. HOUSTON, paraded at 1.30pm for ceremonial presentation of Medals. Parade cancelled at last moment.	AHW
— " —	19/1/18		Fine. Working party of 220 paraded at 7.30 am under Capt Alexander. 100 Officers & men under Capt E.B. HOUSTON paraded for ceremonial presentation of medals. Sergt. W. SEXTON received D.C.M. Ptes. Owens & Hamilton received Military Medals.	AHW
— " —	20/1/18		Working party as on 19th. Lt. N. COULSON went to Fifth Army Musketry Camp for a course.	AHW

A7092 Wt. W128 9/M1293 750,000. 1/17. D. D & L. Ltd. Forms/C2118/14.

Instructions regarding War Diaries and Intelligence Summaries are contained in F. S. Regs., Part II. and the Staff Manual respectively. Title pages will be prepared in manuscript.

WAR DIARY
or
~~INTELLIGENCE SUMMARY.~~
(Erase heading not required.)

Army Form C. 2118.

Place	Date	Hour	Summary of Events and Information	Remarks and references to Appendices
TERRY.	21/1/18		Wed. Working party 120 strong, went up at 3.0pm and returned 8.30pm	AHW
——	22/1/18		Tue. Usual working party went up.	AHW
——	23/1/18		Wed. Lieut. F.S. Romney proceeded to Fifth Army Infantry School for course. Lecture on Intelligence at Divisional Canteen. [illegible]	AHW
——	24/1/18		Thur. Lieut. W.A.D. [illegible] rejoined from Divisional Signal Course	AHW
——	25/1/18		Fri. Advance party went into the line.	AHW
Se[illegible]	26/1/18		Sat. Dismounted [illegible] 3.10 pm and [illegible] trenches [illegible] Relief complete 9.30pm. "D" Sqdn [illegible] [illegible] "A" Sqdn [illegible] Post and [illegible] [illegible] Quarry. "C" Sqdn [illegible] 3 [illegible] [illegible] [illegible] Quarry [illegible] Post [illegible] [illegible] [illegible] [illegible] 6 pm and 50 men [illegible] [illegible] [illegible] Enemy quiet.	AHW
——	27/1/18		Sun. Enemy quiet. [illegible] at all posts, and wire [illegible] [illegible] [illegible] 9 pm [illegible]	AHW
——	29/1/18		[illegible] and [illegible] [illegible] aircraft activity [illegible] [illegible] [illegible] [illegible] [illegible] A.A. guns. [illegible] post [illegible] wiring continued. No casualties.	AHW

A7092 Wt. W125 9/M1293 750,000. 1/17. D. D. & L. Ltd. Forms/C2118/14.

Instructions regarding War Diaries and Intelligence Summaries are contained in F. S. Regs., Part II. and the Staff Manual respectively. Title pages will be prepared in manuscript.

WAR DIARY
or
~~INTELLIGENCE SUMMARY.~~
(Erase heading not required.)

Army Form C. 2118.

Place	Date	Hour	Summary of Events and Information	Remarks and references to Appendices
SECTOR A1	29/1/18		2/Lt W H HARTLEY and 10 men A Sqdn went out at 2.0 am and reconnoitred FISHER'S CRATER and low ground to S.E. No sign of enemy. Low ground very boggy. Returned 4.30 am. No casualties. A bright clear day. Aerial activity. Enemy otherwise quiet. Work on wiring and posts continued. 2/Lieut B H HOUSE relieving Lieut W.S. MANSFIELD.	
TERTRY			Back area camp at TERTRY bombed by E A at 10.0 pm. Casualties :- 13361 Pte R LEWIS, 29660 Pte R HOLLIDAY, 7021 Pte A BOYLAN, 614 Pte L CHANDLER and 45483 Cpl M WHITE - all of "B" Squadron wounded.	A.W.
SECTOR A1	30/1/18		Lieut C. T. CLIFFORD took out a patrol of 10 men "D" Sqdn at 2.0 am. Reconnoitred PRUE COPSE and wire of St HELENE Trench. Low ground by [illegible] ; wire of latter in bad repair. No sign of enemy except that a hostile M.G. fired in their direction when at PRUE COPSE. Work on trenches and wire. Weather fine and clear. Bright moonlight and frost at night. "B" Sqdn relieved "C" in R half sub-sector. "D" Squadron relieved "A" in L half sub-sector. Lt Hon W M STOURTON took out a patrol at 5.30 pm and acted as Right flank guard to 15 Lancers strong patrol. Returned at 7.30 pm without having met any enemy.	
TERTRY			No 29660 Pte R HOLLIDAY died of wounds. Back area details paraded at 9.30 am with led horses and proceeded to Brigade Starting Point E. end of MONS-EN-CHAUSSEE. Marched via BRIE - FOUCAUCOURT to MARCELCAVE. Lieut W S MANSFIELD left for duty with AGRICULTURAL DIRECTORATE. Lt E A STANILAND and Lt D W DALY to CAV. CORPS EQUITATION SCHOOL.	A.W.

A7092. Wt. W128 9/M1293 750,000. 1/17. D. D & L. Ltd. Forms/C2118/14.

Instructions regarding War Diaries and Intelligence Summaries are contained in F. S. Regs., Part II. and the Staff Manual respectively. Title pages will be prepared in manuscript.

WAR DIARY

or

~~INTELLIGENCE SUMMARY.~~

(Erase heading not required.)

Army Form C. 2118.

Place	Date	Hour	Summary of Events and Information	Remarks and references to Appendices
SECTOR A.1	31/1/18		Very foggy. Work on trenches and wire carried on in day time. 2Lt. B. H. House [illegible] took out a patrol of 12 ORs from "C" Sqdn and acted as R[illegible] gun guard to strong patrols of 9th Lt. and 18th Lancers whose object was to sweep the country between Victoria Cross Roads, Mix Wood and Fishers Crater. Patrol returned 7.0 pm having encountered no enemy and drawing no fire. Night was dark until moonrise owing to fog. Enemy quiet. [illegible] ORs to hospital sick.	[illegible]
MARCELCAVE			Mounted portion of Regiment paraded at 8.15 am and marched via Villers Bretonneux – Amiens – Montieres – Vignacourt to Bernaville (HQ A & D) and St Ouen (B & D). Fine – very cold. 4 ORs from Base.	

[illegible signature]
MAJOR,
COMMANDING VIII (K.R.I.) HUSSARS.

[illegible signature] Lieut.
ADJUTANT VIII (K.R.I.) HUSSARS.

A7092 Wt. W128 9/M1293 750,000. 1/17. D. D & L. Ltd. Forms/C2118/14.

1917-1918

5TH CAVALRY DIVISION

AMBALA CAVALRY BDE

9TH HODSON'S HORSE

JAN 1917-MAR 1918

TO EGYPT: 5.MTD BDE
AUS MTD DIV

SERIAL NO. 109

Confidential

War Diary

of

9th HODSON'S HORSE.

FROM 1st January 1917 191 TO 31st January 1917 191

Army Form C. 2118.

Instructions regarding War Diaries and Intelligence Summaries are contained in F. S. Regs., Part II, and the Staff Manual respectively. Title pages will be prepared in manuscript.

WAR DIARY
9th Hodsons Horse
~~INTELLIGENCE SUMMARY.~~

(Erase heading not required.)

Vol VII

Hour, Date, Place.	Summary of Events and Information.	Remarks and references to Appendices.
Jan 1st – 31st MONTIÈRES	In billets. Staff rides, bombing, hotchkiss gun, etc training carried out.	HG
Jan 2d – 31st	The regt supplied a company of 269 all ranks for the Ambala Pioneer Battn ~~unit~~ which for a few days was attached to XIVth corps and afterwards to 6th corps.	HG.
	A number of officers and NCO's attended various courses of instruction during the month at the Divnl: School AULT.	HG.

9th Hodsons Horse

WAR DIARY

or

INTELLIGENCE SUMMARY.

(Erase heading not required.)

Vol VIII

Army Form C. 2118.

Instructions regarding War Diaries and Intelligence Summaries are contained in F. S. Regs., Part II, and the Staff Manual respectively. Title pages will be prepared in manuscript.

Hour, Date, Place.	Summary of Events and Information.	Remarks and references to Appendices.
MONTIÈRES Feb 1st – 28th	In billets. Staff rides and individual training in Hotchkiss, bombing and musketry carried out	LG
	a dismounted company of 251 all ranks was maintained during the month with the Ambala Pioneer Battn attached to 6th Corps	LG
Feb 23rd	Captain E. LORIMER 37th Lancers and Lieut R.A. CARR WHITE 31st Lancers joined the regiment	LG
Feb 25th	2Lieut W. D. WOELLWARTH rejoined the regt.	LG
" 25th	Lieut (actg Capt) G. B. REEVES was accidentally killed	LG.

L. Graham Capt
Adjutant
for O.C. 9 Hodsons Horse.

Instructions regarding War Diaries and Intelligence Summaries are contained in F. S. Regs., Part II, and the Staff Manual respectively. Title pages will be prepared in manuscript.

WAR DIARY
or
INTELLIGENCE SUMMARY.
(*Erase heading not required.*)

9th Horse
Vol IX

Army Form C. 2118.

Hour, Date, Place.	Summary of Events and Information.	Remarks and references to Appendices.
March 1st to 20th. MONTIERES	In billets. Sqdn training, regt exercises and musketry carried out. A working party of about 260 men was maintained with the Ambala Pioneer Battn att: 6th corps. This party returned to the regt on 18th March.	
March 20th	Regt marched to billets at SELINCOURT	
March 21st	Regt marched to Billets at FLEURY	
March 22nd	regt marched to billets at DEMUIN	
March 23rd	regt marched to bivouac at BOIS de MEREAUCOURT	
March 24th	regt took up an outpost line from ETREILLERS - BEAUVOIS - CAULAINCOURT - POUILLY with hdqrs at MONCHY L'agache. During the night A sqdn occupied VILLEVEQUE.	
March 25th	HdQrs moved to TERTRY, the same outpost line being held by the regt until March 28th, many reconnaisances of the enemy's positions in BOIS D'HOLNON, ATTILLY, MARTEVILLE, VERMAND being carried out and constant touch maintained with the enemy.	
March 28th	Regt concentrated and went into billets at MONCHY L'agache	
March 29th	Regt marched to bivouac at BOIS de MEREAUCOURT	
March 30th	Regt marched to billets at WARFUSEE-ABANCOURT.	

[signature]
Lt Colonel Commdg
9 Hodsons Horse.

Army Form C. 2118.

Vol 10

Instructions regarding War Diaries and Intelligence Summaries are contained in F. S. Regs., Part II, and the Staff Manual respectively. Title pages will be prepared in manuscript.

WAR DIARY
9th Hodsons Horse
or
~~INTELLIGENCE SUMMARY.~~

(Erase heading not required.)

Hour, Date, Place.	Summary of Events and Information.	Remarks and references to Appendices.
1st – 14th April WARFUSEE	In billets	[illegible]
14th April	Marched to bivouac in wood between TERTRY and CAULAINCOURT	[illegible]
14th – 30th April	In bivouac. Troop, sqdn and regimental training carried out. Dismounted reinforcements in bivouac near BRIE.	[illegible]

Fu Graham Capt & Adjt
for O.C. 9th Horse.

Instructions regarding War Diaries and Intelligence Summaries are contained in F. S. Regs., Part II, and the Staff Manual respectively. Title pages will be prepared in manuscript.

WAR DIARY

9th Hodsons or Horse. VOL XI

~~INTELLIGENCE SUMMARY.~~

(Erase heading not required.)

Army Form C. 2118.

Hour. Date. Place.	Summary of Events and Information.	Remarks and references to Appendices.
1st to 15th May	In bivouac between TERTRY and CAULAINCOURT.	
15th to 28th May	A trench regt of about 300 all ranks was formed and attached to Secunderabad Bde, & was in support to 7th D. Gs from 15th to 21st May, when it relieved the latter regt in the front line South East of LE VERGIER. Held front line till night of 28/29 May and then returned to bivouac.	
23rd May	Jemadar SIRDAR KHAN was wounded	
28th to 31st May	In bivouac between TERTRY and CAULAINCOURT	
3rd May	2Lieut R. H. R. CUMMING joined the regt.	
	Leo Graham Capt adjt for O.C. 9 Hodsons Horse.	

Instructions regarding War Diaries and Intelligence Summaries are contained in F. S. Regs., Part II. and the Staff Manual respectively. Title pages will be prepared in manuscript.

WAR DIARY
or
~~INTELLIGENCE SUMMARY.~~
(Erase heading not required.)

Army Form C. 2118.

Place	Date	Hour	Summary of Events and Information	Remarks and references to Appendices
	JUNE			
	1st–5th		In bivouac between TERTRY and CAULAINCOURT	
	5th		On the 5th, a French regiment of 300 all ranks marched to VADENCOURT and went into Brigade reserve.	
	12th		B and C Sqdns relieved 2 Sqdns of the 18 Lancers in HODSONS POST and the BROWN LINE respectively, A and D Sqdns remaining in reserve at VADENCOURT	
	15/16		On the night 15/16th B and C Sqdns relieved the two Sqdns of the 18th Lancers in DRAGOON POST – A2.1 post and LONE TREE – SOMMERVILLE wood respectively.	
	17/18th		On the night 17/18th the two troops of C Sqdn holding SOMMERVILLE WOOD were withdrawn to the BROWN LINE	
	12th to 18th		A and D Sqdns, while in reserve carried out continuous practice of a proposed raid on ST HELENE trench and neighbourhood	
	18/19th		On the night of 18/19th the raid was successfully carried out on ST HELENE trench, ST HELENE village and neighbourhood by D Sqdn under Capt M. VIGORS and A Sqdn under Capt C. F. L. STEVENS respectively. 3 prisoners were taken, several Germans killed in the open or in dugouts, and many dugouts bombed and burnt. The casualties to raiding party were 1 British officer (Lieut G WILSON) and 6 men slightly wounded.	

Instructions regarding War Diaries and Intelligence Summaries are contained in F. S. Regs., Part II. and the Staff Manual respectively. Title pages will be prepared in manuscript.

WAR DIARY

or

~~INTELLIGENCE SUMMARY.~~

(Erase heading not required.)

Army Form C. 2118.

Place	Date	Hour	Summary of Events and Information	Remarks and references to Appendices
	JUNE			
	19/20th		On the night of 19/20th A and D sqdns relieved 2 sqdns of 18th Lancers in HODSONS POST and BROWN LINE respectively.	
	20/21		On the night of 20/21st A and D sqdns relieved B and C sqdns in DRAGOON POST – A2.1 post and LONE TREE post respectively; B sqdn coming back to HODSONS POST and C sqdn to BROWN LINE (during the period the regt was in the trenches, patrols went out nightly from the two forward squadrons and a large amount of work was done improving the defences of that part of the line held by the regt)	
	23/24th		On the night of 23/24th the regt was relieved by the 34th POONA HORSE and marched back to bivouac.	
	24th/1030		In bivouac between TERTRY and CAULAINCOURT	

[signature]
Captain
Adjutant
for O.C. 9th Hodsons Horse

2353 Wt. W2544/1454 700,000 5/15 D. D. & L. A.D.S.S. Forms/C. 2118.

Army Form C. 2118.

WAR DIARY . 9th Hodson's Horse
or
INTELLIGENCE SUMMARY.
(*Erase heading not required.*)

Instructions regarding War Diaries and Intelligence Summaries are contained in F. S. Regs., Part II, and the Staff Manual respectively. Title pages will be prepared in manuscript.

Hour, Date, Place.	Summary of Events and Information.	Remarks and references to Appendices.
Field 4-7-17	Major C. H. Rowcroft proceeded to Marseilles to assist in re-organisation of Indian Labour Corps.	[illegible]
" 8-7-17	Dismounted reinforcements rejoined the regiment	[illegible]
" 13-7-17	Regiment marched from Hirsonc	[illegible]
" 26-7-17	1 IO & 20 ORI returned to Base for return to India	[illegible]
" 26-7-17	1 IO & 3 ORI Proceeded for duty to ROUEN	[illegible]

[illegible] for Lt. Col.
Comdg. 9th Hodson's Horse

Army Form C. 2118.

WAR DIARY
or
INTELLIGENCE SUMMARY.
(Erase heading not required.)

Instructions regarding War Diaries and Intelligence Summaries are contained in F. S. Regs., Part II, and the Staff Manual respectively. Title pages will be prepared in manuscript.

Hour, Date, Place.	Summary of Events and Information.	Remarks and references to Appendices.
1917 August 1st to Aug 31st OSTREVILLE and MARQUAY	In billets. Brigade and Squadron training and musketry carried out.	L.G.
August 9th	Capt J. A. C. MAY-SOMERVILLE 11th Lancers joined the Regiment	K.
	L. Graham Capt adjt for Lt Colonel Comndg 9th Hodson's Horse.	

Serial No. 109.

Army Form C. 2118.

WAR DIARY.

9th Hodsons Horse

or

INTELLIGENCE SUMMARY.

(*Erase heading not required.*)

1917

Instructions regarding War Diaries and Intelligence Summaries are contained in F. S. Regs., Part II, and the Staff Manual respectively. Title pages will be prepared in manuscript.

Hour, Date, Place.	Summary of Events and Information.	Remarks and references to Appendices.
Sept 1st to Sept 30th OSTREVILLE	In billets. Regimental & squadron training and musketry carried out	R
Sept 15th	2 Lieut. G. W. NINNIS joined the Regiment.	R
Sept: 17th	2 Lieuts. M. E BENDLE and J. E. WALKER joined the Regiment.	R

Leo Graham Capt & Adjutant
for O.C.
9th Hodsons Horse.

Instructions regarding War Diaries and Intelligence Summaries are contained in F. S. Regs., Part II, and the Staff Manual respectively. Title pages will be prepared in manuscript.

WAR DIARY or ~~INTELLIGENCE SUMMARY.~~

(*Erase heading not **required**.*)

9th Hodson's Horse

October

Army Form C. 2118.

109

Hour, Date, Place.	Summary of Events and Information.	Remarks and references to Appendices.
October 1st – 7th OSTREVILLE	In billets, Squadron & Regimental Training & musketry carried out	[illegible]
October 7th	marched to billets at TENNAY. In billets until 11th	[illegible]
October 11th	marched to bivouac near WATAU. In bivouac until 14th	[illegible]
October 14th	marched to billets at WARDRECQUES	[illegible]
October 15th	marched to billets at THIEMBRONNE	[illegible]
October 16	marched to billets at CAYRON ST MARTIN	[illegible]
October 16th – 31st	In billets at CAYRON ST MARTIN. Squadron training and staff rides carried out.	[illegible] [illegible]
October 7th TENNAY	2/Lieut D.T. LONG joined the Regiment	[illegible]
October 24th CAYRON ST MARTIN	2/Lieut I.G.F. PIERCE joined the Regiment	[illegible]

J. C. Graham Capt Adjt
for O.C. 9th Horse.

Instructions regarding War Diaries and Intelligence Summaries are contained in F. S. Regs., Part II. and the Staff Manual respectively. Title pages will be prepared in manuscript.

WAR DIARY
or
~~INTELLIGENCE~~ SUMMARY.
(Erase heading not required.)

9th Hodson's Horse

~~November 1917~~

Army Form C. 2118.

109.

December 1917

Place	Date	Hour	Summary of Events and Information	Remarks and references to Appendices
CAVRON ST MARTIN	1-11-17 to 8-11-17		In billets. Sqdn and Regimental Training carried out.	
"	2-11-17		2nd Lieut E. H. GASTRELL joined the Regt.	
OUTRE BOIS	9-11-17		Regt marched to ~~___~~ OUTRE BOIS and went into billets	
FRANVILLERS	10-11-17		Regt marched to FRANVILLERS and went into billets	
BRAY	11-11-17		Regt marched to BRAY and went into billets	
BRUSLE	12-11-17		Regt marched to camp just west of BRUSLE	
"	20-11-17	1.30am	Regt marched from BRUSLE to BOIS DESSART in readiness to move forward if operations by III Army were successful. About 12.30 pm Regt moved forward to valley 1½ miles east of VILLERS PLOUICH where Bde was ordered to halt. Regt bivouaced for the night.	
	21-11-17	2 pm	Regt moved up to MARCOING on orders being received by Bde to support the 1st Cav Divn. These orders were subsequently cancelled and Regt marched to bivouac just west of RIBECOURT where it halted for the night.	
EQUANCOURT	22-11-17		Regt marched to camp at EQUANCOURT	
ETINEHEN	23-11-17		Regt marched to billets at ETINEHEM.	
"	2[illegible]-11-17		2nd Lieut J. R. N. MURPHY joined the Regt	
TERTRY	27-11-17		Regt marched to camp East of TERTRY	

2353 Wt. W2544/1454 700,000 5/15 D. D. & L. A.D.S.S. Forms/C. 2118.

Instructions regarding War Diaries and Intelligence Summaries are contained in F. S. Regs., Part II. and the Staff Manual respectively. Title pages will be prepared in manuscript.

Army Form C. 2118.

WAR DIARY
or
~~INTELLIGENCE~~ SUMMARY.

(*Erase heading not required.*)

Place	Date	Hour	Summary of Events and Information	Remarks and references to Appendices
TERTRY	27-11-17 to 30-11-17		In camp at TERTRY	
"	30-11-17		Orders received about 8.30 am to march north at once. Bde concentrated at X roads east of ESTREES EN CHAUSSEE and marched to a point 3/4 mile N.W. of PEIZIERE (EPEHY) where it received orders to cooperate on the right of the Guards Divn counter attack on GOUZEAUCOURT and fill the gap between that village and GAUCHE WOOD which was to be attacked by 8th Hussars. The Regt proceeded mounted, with C sqdn under Major A.I. FRASER DSO as advanced sqdn and D sqn in close support, via REVELON FARM, through a belt of wire 1 mile to the north of that place, and advanced on the Sunken road 1 mile south of GOUZEAUCOURT. C sqn, just before arriving at the sunken road was met with heavy machine gun and rifle fire and was forced to dismount and continue the advance on foot. Major FRASER, while leading his sqdn, was killed in the sunken road by an enemy sniper or M.G. D sqdn, which had advanced through a heavy shell and machine gun fire, and had arrived mounted at a point 300 yds west of the sunken road was ordered at 3-35 pm to dismount and prolong the line to the right of C sqdn, along a bank running parallel to and 100 yds west of the Sunken road and at the same time a report having been received that 300 of the enemy were debouching from GAUCHE wood, A and B sqns were ordered to join the remainder of the Regt. While leading A sqdn up Major F. St J. ATKINSON was mortally wounded by a shell. B sqn then prolonged the line to the right of D sqn, with A sqn in support. At nightfall the sunken road was occupied by C, D and B sqns with A sqn in support and the led horses sent back to HEUDICOURT. During the advance Ressaidar HARBANT SINGH and Jemadar MIR AHAM KHAN were wounded and 2nd Lieut T.R.K. MURPHY slightly wounded, remaining at duty.	

[signature] Lt Colonel Commdg.

2353 Wt. W2544/1454 700,000 5/15 D. D. & L. A.D.S.S. Forms/C 2118.

A P P E N D I X "B".

On the morning of the 20th. November the Brigade was composed as follows :-

8th.Hussars, 9th.H.Horse, 18th.Lancers, M.G.Sqdn,
"A" Battery R.C.H.A. and Light Ammunition Column,
5th. Field Squadron (less 2 troops), Mhow F.A. Pack Sect.

<u>20th.November</u>
6.20 am. Arrived at BOIS DE DESSART, concentration Area at ZERO hour. Dawn was breaking, and the guns started. All horses in the Brigade were watered and fed.
At 11 am. the Brigade was warned that it might move forward at any moment which it eventually did at 12.40 pm. in rear of Sec'bad Cav.Bde.
The advance was slow and the Brigade reached R.9.a. via VILLERS PLOUICH at 2.10 pm.
Shortly afterwards it was ordered to follow Sec'bad Bde. through MARCOING to 1st. Objective NIERGNIES, 18th.Lcrs. formed Advanced Guard to Brigade and started, followed by 9th.H.Horse , 8th.Hussars, Field Troop R.E., "A" Battery R.C.H.A., Mhow F.A. Pack Section, but Sec'bad Bde. Advanced Guard failed to cross the BEAUREVOIR-MASNIERES line , and the Brigade bivouacked practically where it was.

<u>21st.November.</u>
11 am. 9th.H.Horse was allowed to start watering one troop at a time at VILLERS PLOUICH. At 3 pm. the Brigade was put at the disposal of G.O.C. 1st. Cav.Divn. whose right (2nd. Cav.Bde) was being heavily (counter-) attacked in NOYELLES. Brigade arrived via MARCOING to a position of readiness about L.21.d. at 3.45 pm.
Its services were not required and it moved into bivouac S.W. of RIBECOURT about K.30 c. at 6.30 pm.
9th.H.Horse were ready to go up to the line till ....

.......12 midnight 21st/22nd, when they would be relieved in this duty by 8th.Hussars .

21st.November. 11.30 pm. Orders were received that Brigade was rejoin the 5th. Cavalry Division at 10 am. on 22nd.

22nd.November 7.30 am. Brigade ordered to rejoin 5th. Cavalry Division at FINS and EQUANCOURT, arriving at 10.30 am.

All horses were watered with the exception of some of the 9th.H.Horse which watered at VILLERS PLOUICH on morning of 21st., and the horses of "A" Battery R.C.H.A., which watered at MARCOING, returning thither from RIBECOURT at 8 pm. 21st. The horses of the Brigade had not been watered for 48 hours , but it had rained continuously from midday 20th.and there had been a good deal of moisture on the grass.

At 2 pm. Brigade moved to an area West of EQUANCOURT and most of the men got under cover in huts for the night.

----oOo----

Army Form C. 2118.

109

WAR DIARY or ~~INTELLIGENCE SUMMARY~~.

(Erase heading not required.)

9th Hodson's Horse

Instructions regarding War Diaries and Intelligence Summaries are contained in F. S. Regs., Part II. and the Staff Manual respectively. Title pages will be prepared in manuscript.

December 1917

Place	Date	Hour	Summary of Events and Information	Remarks and references to Appendices
Sunken road 1 mile S of GOUZEAUCOURT	30-11-17	11 p.m.	Regt less A sqn occupying sunken road 1 mile S. of GOUZEAUCOURT with 8th Hussars on right and 1 squadron 20th Hussars on left, with A squadron in support behind bank 100 yds in rear.	
do	30-11-17	11-30 pm	8th Hussars on right were relieved by 18th Lancers	
do	1-12-17	5 AM	A squadron moved up into sunken road.	
do	1-12-17	7-30 AM	18th Lancers attacked GAUCHE WOOD in conjunction with Guards Divn and Tanks. Line of Regt was prolonged to the right taking over that portion of the sunken road previously occupied by 18th Lancers. This line was held during the day.	
do	do	4-15 pm	A Squadron moved forward and took up a position on the right of the Guards Divn and ½ mile S. of GAUCHE wood.	
do	do	6-6.30 p.m.	Sunken road heavily shelled. Jemadar (woordie major) Sardar Khan wounded. Capt: H. Dodding Essex Yeo. att: slightly wounded remaining at duty.	
do	2-12-17		In early morning the Regt was relieved by 4th D.G's and 20th Deccan Horse, and marched back to bivouac 1 mile S. of HEUDECOURT. Total casualties from 30-11-17: 2 British Officers killed, 2 wounded slightly at duty, 3 Indian officers wounded, 8 ORs killed and 38 ORs wounded. 6 ORs wounded slightly at duty.	
	3-12-17		Marched to bivouac at VILLERS FAUCON.	
	4-12-17		Regt marched dismounted up to VAUCHELETTE FARM and took ~~up~~ over the Brown Line N.W. of the farm. D Sqn remaining in support in a sunken road 400 yds to the South. On the march up Ressaidar Hardit Singh was mortally wounded by a machine gun bullet 1 mile S.W. of VAUCHELETTE FARM.	

2353 Wt. W2544/1454 700,000 5/15 D. D. & L. A.D.S.S. Forms/C. 2118.

Army Form C. 2118.

Instructions regarding War Diaries and Intelligence Summaries are contained in F. S. Regs., Part II. and the Staff Manual respectively. Title pages will be prepared in manuscript.

WAR DIARY
or
INTELLIGENCE SUMMARY.
(Erase heading not required.)

Place	Date	Hour	Summary of Events and Information	Remarks and references to Appendices
VAUCHELETTE Farm	5-12-17	8.30pm	Regt was relieved by a company of Durham L.I. and marched back to bivouac at VILLERS FAUCON. Total casualties 1 Indian officer mortally wounded. 1 ORs wounded	
VILLERS FAUCON	8-12-17		Marched to camp at BRUSLE.	
BRUSLE	21-12-17		Marched to camp between TERTRY and CAULAINCOURT.	
TERTRY area	21-12-17 to 31-12-17		In camp between TERTRY and CAULAINCOURT.	

J.E. Graham Capt. Adjt
for O.C. 9 Hodson's Horse

Army Form C. 2118.

(109.)

WAR DIARY

or 9 Hodsons Horse.

~~INTELLIGENCE SUMMARY.~~

(Erase heading not required.)

Instructions regarding War Diaries and Intelligence Summaries are contained in F. S. Regs., Part II, and the Staff Manual respectively. Title pages will be prepared in manuscript.

January 1918.

Hour, Date, Place.	Summary of Events and Information.	Remarks and references to Appendices.
TERTRY 1-31 Jany 1918	In camp between TERTRY & CAULINCOURT.	MD
	Digging parties supplied in cavalry corps area.	
26/31 Jany	Dismounted regiment 270 strong. in trenches on right of Corps front East of VADENCOURT. 9HH in reserve in Brown line between PONTRU & LE VERGUIER	MD
HARBONNIERES 30 Jan	Remainder of regiment marched to HARBONNIERES.	MD
FLESSELLES 31 "	" " " FLESSELLES.	MD
TERTRY 19 "	Capt EVF SEYMOUR joined the regiment.	MD

M Dundas
Capt
for OC 9HH.

Instructions regarding War Diaries and Intelligence Summaries are contained in F. S. Regs., Part II. and the Staff Manual respectively. Title pages will be prepared in manuscript.

WAR DIARY
or
INTELLIGENCE SUMMARY.
(Erase heading not required.)

Army Form C. 2118.

Place	Date	Hour	Summary of Events and Information	Remarks and references to Appendices
MOUFLERS	1.2.18		Horses of the Regt. marched to the MOUFLERS area and were billeted H. Qrs. at MOUFLERS, A & B Sqdns L'ETOILE, C Sqdn. BRUCAMPS, D Sqdn. VILLERS SOUS AILLY.	
VADENCOURT area	1.2.18 to 15.2.18		Dismounted Regt. of 270 ranks under Major H. L. Dyce M.C. held the line EAST of VADENCOURT. Patrolling was regularly carried out. A flank guard of 25 men cooperated in a raid carried out by the 15th Lancers on the night of 12/13th.	
do	15.2.18		Trench Regt. were relieved by 15th Hussars and marching to near VERMAND proceeded by rail to ROISEL.	
ROISEL SALEUX	16.2.18		Trench Regt proceeded by rail to SALEUX from where they were conveyed by lorries to billets as above.	
MOUFLERS	26.2.18		The Regt. marched to PROUZEL area and were billeted, H. Qrs. at PROUZEL, A & B Sqns at PLACHY-BUYON, C Sqn. at NAMPTY and D Sqdn. at NEUVILLE sous LOEUILLY. Regt. entrained at SALEUX for MARSEILLES. Dismounted men remained at PLACHY-BUYON under Lt. W. D. Woolhouth and entrained on 1-3-18 for TARANTO	
			F.W. Messervy Capt & Adjt for O.C. 9th H. Horse.	

2353 Wt. W2544/1454 700,000 5/15 D. D. & L. A.D.S.S. Forms/C. 2118.

Army Form C. 2118.

Instructions regarding War Diaries and Intelligence Summaries are contained in F. S. Regs., Part II. and the Staff Manual respectively. Title pages will be prepared in manuscript.

WAR DIARY

~~INTELLIGENCE SUMMARY~~

(Erase heading not required.)

Place	Date	Hour	Summary of Events and Information	Remarks and references to Appendices
MARSEILLES	1.3.18 2.3.18		The Regt. arrived at MARSEILLES and went into camp.	
"	5.3.18		The Regt. embarked on H.T. HYDASPES, which carried all animals of the Regt. less C Sqn. & Transport, H.T. CITY OF BENARES, which carried C Sqn. & Transport animals, and H.T. ELLENGA which carried the dismounted men.	
MARSEILLES	6.3.18		Regt. sailed from MARSEILLES.	
ALEXANDRIA	15.3.18		Regt. reached ALEXANDRIA after an uneventful voyage, losing one horse only.	
"	16.3.18.		Regt. disembarked and entrained to TEL EL KEBIR.	
TEL EL KEBIR	17.3.18 to 31.3.18		In camp at TEL EL KEBIR. Individual and Sqn. training carried out.	

F. O. Messervy Capt & adjt
for O.C. 9th H. Horse

1917-1918

5TH CAVALRY DIVISION

AMBALA CAVALRY BDE

18TH K.G.O. LANCERS

JAN 1917 - MAR 1918

~~FROM FRANCE~~

TO EGYPT - AUGT. MTD DIV

. SMTD. BDE

SERIAL NO 180

Confidential

War Diary

of

18th LANCERS.

FROM 1st January 1917 1917 TO 31st January 1917 191

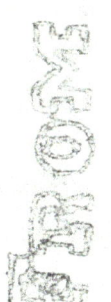

Vol VII

Army Form C. 2118.

Instructions regarding War Diaries and Intelligence Summaries are contained in F. S. Regs., Part II. and the Staff Manual respectively. Title pages will be prepared in manuscript.

WAR DIARY
or
~~INTELLIGENCE SUMMARY.~~
(Erase heading not required.)

18 Lancers

January 1917

Place	Date	Hour	Summary of Events and Information	Remarks and references to Appendices
BAZINVAL	1.1.17		Regt in billets on BRESLE R.	Maps DIEPPE ABBEVILLE LENS AMIENS 1/100,000
LONGROY-GAMACHES	2.1.17		5 BOs, 260 OR proceeded, as part of Ambala Pioneer Battn, by rail to 14 Corps. They were encamped between TRONES and BERNAFAY Woods and were employed in making a light railway on the MORVAL-LESBOEUFS Ridge. 3 Men D Sqn ~~[illegible]~~ wounded by shell fire on 6.1.17.	
ST ADELAIDE				
GOUSSEAUVILLE	6.1.17			
LE LIEU DIEU	8.1.17		Pioneer Battalion moved to AGNEZ-LES-DUISANS, near ARRAS. Employed under 9th Divn, VI Corps of 3rd Army in making a railway.	
			In London Gazette of Jan 1st 1917, Lt Col Ricketts, Capt (Temp LtCol) Hills both attached to Infy. + Capt (Temp) Major Risley (attd RFA) were awarded the DSO, these officers together with Capt (Temp LtCol) C.H. Marsh were also mentioned in Despatches of 2.1.17.	
	13.1.17		Ris. Major Ahmedyar Khan + Ris Sundar Singh were awarded Order of British India, 2nd Class and 1941 Dfr Bhagwan Singh, 1575 K. Dfr Khuda Bux Khan (now Jemadar), 1595 Sowar Lal Singh, 2686 L. Mohd Sharif Khan attd Ambala M. Gun Sqn, 2466 L. Hidayat Khan attd Ambala M.G. Sqn, 4155 Havildar TAZAKHAN RHA attd 18 Lancers, were awarded Indian Distinguished Service Medal. Ressaidar Tawakkil Khan was ordered to attend an investiture + was decorated by H.M the King with the order of British India 2nd Class for his excellent service in Persia at the outbreak of war, in connection with the Turko-Persian Boundary Commission, under Major A.H. Brooke 18 Lancers	

2353 Wt. W2544/1454 700,000 5/15 D. D. & L. A.D.S.S. Forms/C. 2118.

Instructions regarding War Diaries and Intelligence Summaries are contained in F. S. Regs., Part II. and the Staff Manual respectively. Title pages will be prepared in manuscript.

WAR DIARY
or
~~INTELLIGENCE~~ SUMMARY.
(Erase heading not required.)

18 Lancers
January 1917

Army Form C. 2118.

Place	Date	Hour	Summary of Events and Information	Remarks and references to Appendices
~~[illegible]~~	12.1.17		Lt C. G. Royston left to join R.F.C as an observer, in the wing being raised for work with the Cavalry Corps.	
~~[illegible]~~	23.1.17		Capt R. Dening rejoined from 6 weeks attachment to 5th Cav Div staff. Capt [illegible] about the middle of this month went to Ambala Bde, officiating as Staff Captain.	
	26.1.17		Lt W. B. Bletsoe IAR rejoined regt from Ambala M.G. Sqn.	
Summary BALINVAL LINGARY St ADELAIDE GOUTJEAVILLE LE LIBOURG			During the last 10 days of this month intense cold prevailed between 15 & 20 degrees of frost, & occasional snow. During January, owing to the absence of the Pioneer Batts, only sufficient men remained to keep the horses exercised. Tactical & Theoretical Training of officers & N.C.Os, map-reading, lectures etc were carried out periodically. 1 Bde Tactical Exercise & a Regt Tactical exercise (without troops) & lecture was carried out weekly. BOs, IOs & N.COs attended the Divl school at AULT for courses, including ~~[illegible]~~ Bombing & general instruction.	
	31.1.17		Ris Major Ahmedyar Khan, Jem Dhurman Khan & AL Dfr Baz Khan S/A proceeded to England to take part in the opening of Parliament procession, & form part of the Imperial Escort.	

A5834 Wt. W4973/M687 750,000 8/16 D. D. & L. Ltd. Forms/C.2118/13.

Instructions regarding War Diaries and Intelligence Summaries are contained in F. S. Regs., Part II. and the Staff Manual respectively. Title pages will be prepared in manuscript.

WAR DIARY

or

~~INTELLIGENCE SUMMARY~~. 18th K.G.O. Lancers

(Erase heading not required.)

January 1917.

Army Form C. 2118.

Place	Date	Hour	Summary of Events and Information	During January 1917 Men	During January 1917 Followers	13/11/14 to 31/1/17 Men	13/11/14 to 31/1/17 Followers		Remarks and references to Appendices
			Indian Fighting men & Regl: Public Followers	Men	Followers	Men	Followers		
			Casualties – To Hospital sick	14	-	313 x	10 x	x Includes men evacuated temporarily to I.C.F.A. as well as those to "out-of Divl. Area".	
			— do — wounded.	3		29	-		
			Killed in action.	-		6	-		
			Died of disease.	1 °		8	-	° Pneumonia	
			Transferred to other Units & Followers						
			Surplus to India			19	5	⊗ During Jany, 25 men came up to Regt, but 54 men who rejoined from M.G. Sqdn +signal troop, on these units being made all British, were sent down to Marseilles, plus 2 followers – this gives the two minus numbers opposite Reinforcements from base etc. No horses were returned from these units.	
			New formations – Used for new formations.	-54 ⊗	-2 ⊗	106	2		
			Strength of Dismounted Reinforcements on 31.1.1917.	-	-	125	5		
			Reinforcements – from Base & other Units	-29 ⊗	-2 ⊗	405	16		
			Returned from Hospital	4	-	130	2		
			Horses & Mules.	Horses	Mules	Horses	Mules	x 8 wounded in action	
			Casualties – Evacuated Lame & Sick	4	-	368 x	31		
			Used for new formations.	-	-	201	62		
			Transferred Surplus.	-	-	46	40		
			Reinforcements from Base & other Units	4	-	547	115		

31/1/17

V. [illegible] Lt Col.
Comdg 18th Lancers

T2134. Wt. W708–776. 500000. 4/15. Sir J. C. & S.

Instructions regarding War Diaries and Intelligence Summaries are contained in F. S. Regs., Part II. and the Staff Manual respectively. Title pages will be prepared in manuscript.

Vol VIII

WAR DIARY
or
~~INTELLIGENCE SUMMARY.~~
(Erase heading not required.)

8th Lancers

February 1917.

Army Form C. 2118.

Place	Date	Hour	Summary of Events and Information	Remarks and references to Appendices
BAZINVAL LONGROY-GAMACHES ST ADELAIDE FOUSSEAYVILLE LE LIEU-DIEU	1-2-17		Regiment in billets on BRESLE river. Pioneer Battalion still away at AGNEZ-LES-DUISANS near ARRAS. Employed under 9th Div. VI Corps of IIIrd Army in making a railway. Owing to this continued absence of the Pioneer Battalion, training, during the whole month, has been restricted to the tactical & theoretical training of Bos, I.O, N.C.O.s. The training of "specialists" in Hotchkiss gunning and Bombing was proceeded with. One Brigade & one Regimental Tactical Exercise was carried out weekly. Officers & N.C.O.s attended the Divisional School at AULT for courses in Hotchkiss gunning, Bombing & General Instruction. The following appeared in Daily Orders D.A.G. Part III No. 103 of 8-12-16 "Lt. Col. (Temp. Bde. General) F. A. Maxwell, V.C. C.S.I D.S.O. awarded a bar to his Distinguished Service Order for subsequent acts of conspicuous gallantry". In the first week of this month, Capt. F. Gwatkin, who was acting Staff Captain at Bde Hdqrs, proceeded to 5th Cav. Div. Hdqrs as officiating G.S.O III. Capt R. Denning proceeded to Brigade Hdqrs as officiating Staff Captain.	Maps — DIEPPE ABBEVILLE LENS AMIENS 1/100,000.
	10-2-17		The Regiment beat the "Medical Services" in the preliminary rounds of the Divisional football tournament (for Indian Cav.)	
	24-2-17		The Regiment beat the 34th P. Horse in the semifinals of Divisional football tournament	

Instructions regarding War Diaries and Intelligence Summaries are contained in F. S. Regs., Part II. and the Staff Manual respectively. Title pages will be prepared in manuscript.

WAR DIARY
or
~~INTELLIGENCE SUMMARY.~~
(Erase heading not required.)

18 Lancers.
February 1917.

Army Form C. 2118. (2)

Place	Date	Hour	Summary of Events and Information	Remarks and references to Appendices
	22-2-17		Lieut. W.B. Blatsoe proceeded to England on duty, to report to the Indian Office, in connection with his obtaining a permanent commission in the Indian 28/2/17 Army —	
	24-2-17		Major S.C. Corbyn rejoined the regiment on the completion of three weeks tour of duty in LONDON, in charge of parties of Indian Officers visiting England —	
			After the opening of Parliament (on 5th Feb) by H.M. the King, R.M. Malik Ahmad Yar Khan was presented by the King with the Order of British India II class for "specially good work as a ½ Squadron Commander"	
	26-2-17.		Capt. W.R.P. Henry (12th Cav:) attd. 18 Lancers proceeded to PARIS en route to MARSEILLES for tour of duty for two months at the Base.	
			During the first 18 days of the month intense cold prevailed, between 15 & 20 degrees of frost.	

Instructions regarding War Diaries and Intelligence Summaries are contained in F. S. Regs., Part II. and the Staff Manual respectively. Title pages will be prepared in manuscript.

WAR DIARY
or
~~INTELLIGENCE SUMMARY.~~
(*Erase heading not required.*)

18th K.G.O. Lancers
February 1917.

Army Form C. 2118.

Place	Date	Hour	Summary of Events and Information					Remarks and references to Appendices
			Indian Fighting men & Regl: Public Followers.	During February 17		13/11/14 to 28/2/17		
				Men	Followers	Men	Followers	
			Casualties – To Hospital sick	23	-	336 x	10 x	x Includes men evacuated temporarily to I.C.F.A. as well as those to "out of Divisional Area".
			— do — wounded.	-	-	29	-	
			Killed in action	-	-	6	-	
			Died of disease	-	-	8	-	
			Transferred to other Units & Followers	-	-			
			surplus to India			19	5	
			New formations – Used for new formation	-	-	106	2	
			Strength of Dismounted Reinforcements on 28.2.1917	.	.	109	5	
			Reinforcements – From Base or other Units	2	-	407	16	*· 8 wounded in action
			Returned from Hospital	11	-	141	2	
			Horses & Mules	Horses	Mules	Horses	Mules	
			Casualties – Evacuated lame & sick	3	-	371 x	31	
			Used for new formations			201	62	
			Transferred surplus	2	-	48	40	
			Reinforcements from Base & other units	3	-	550	115	

[signature] Major
Comdg 18th Lancers

28/2/17

A5834 Wt. W4973 M687 750,000 8/16 D. D. & L. Ltd. Forms/C.2118/13.

Instructions regarding War Diaries and Intelligence Summaries are contained in F. S. Regs., Part II. and the Staff Manual respectively. Title pages will be prepared in manuscript.

WAR DIARY
or
~~INTELLIGENCE SUMMARY.~~
(Erase heading not required.)

Vol IX

ADJUTANT'S OFFICE No. 26 R Date 1/4/17 18th K. G. O. LANCERS

Army Form C. 2118.

18 Lancers March 1917.

Place	Date	Hour	Summary of Events and Information	Remarks and references to Appendices
BAZINVAL LONGRIY ST ADELAIDE GOUSSEAUVILLE LIEU-DIEU	1.3.17 to 17.3.17		Regt in billets on BRESLE River. { Lt Webster proceeded to Rouen as a training officer 7.3.17 / Capt Henry — do — Marseilles — do — 2.3.17 } Work as during Feb. 1917.	Maps 1/100,000 Dieppe Abbeville Lens Amiens
	17.3.17		Pioneer Battn rejoined. Divn on 48 hours notice to move.	
	18.3.17		Regt received orders to move on 20th.	
	19.3.17			
VILLERS CAMPSART DROSMESNIL	20.3.17	9.am	Regt marched via SENARPONT to Billet at VILLERS-CAMPSART (A, B, HQ) and DROSMESNIL (C & D). – arrived 1 pm. – Remainder of Bde in vicinity. Capt Lorimer 37th Horse joined regt – Dismounted Sqdn moved to GAMACHES under Lt Benfield.	
FREMONTIERS VELENNES UZENNEVILLE	21.3.17	8.30 am	Regt marched via POIX to billet at UZENNEVILLE (A), FREMONTIERS (B, HQ) VELENNES (C & D). – arrived 12 noon – remainder of Bde in vicinity. Lt Fitzpatrick to 1.C.F. Ambulance sick on 20.3.17 & Lt Williams (from Pioneer Battn on 10.3.17. Lt Bletsoe struck off strength (to England for permanent commission) from 22.2.17. Lt Watson IAR rejoined from Rouen 19.3.17. Lt Forbes appointed Regt Transport officer from 20.3.17. & appointed Qr Mr from 13 Jan 17 vice Lt Royston to R.F. Corps	
	22.3.17	7.30 am	Regt marched via CONTY – AILLY-SUR-NOYE – CASTEL to billet at HANGARD (A Sqn) and DEMUIN (B, C, D, HQ) – Fall of snow during day & frost at night.	
	23.3.17	8am	Regt marched via MARCELCAVE – HARBONNIERES – PROYART – FROISSY – CAPPY – FRISE to BOIS-DE-MEREAUCOURT (S of FEUILLERES) where regt ~~was~~ bivouacked with rest of Bde. B echelon at HERBECOURT – Horses repo with Regt. Weather very cold for the time of year – slight frost at nights	Map 1/100,000
	24.3.17	8am	Regt marched via BIACHES, crossing SOMME at PERONNE, then again at DOIGNT, through CARTIGNY to HANCOURT. Regt HQ & B Sqn in reserve at HANCOURT	ST QUENTIN

A5834 Wt. W4973 M687 750,000 8/16 D. D. & L. Ltd. Forms/C.2118/13.

Instructions regarding War Diaries and Intelligence Summaries are contained in F. S. Regs., Part II. and the Staff Manual respectively. Title pages will be prepared in manuscript.

WAR DIARY
or
~~INTELLIGENCE SUMMARY.~~ 1st Lancers March 1917

(Erase heading not required.)

Army Form C. 2118.

(2)

Place	Date	Hour	Summary of Events and Information	Remarks and references to Appendices
HANCOURT BERNES FLECHIN MARQUAIX HAMELET	24/3/17		HANCOURT – Arrived about noon. C Sqn at FLECHIN and BERNES – in touch with 9th Horse at POEUILLY. D Sqn thence to HAMELET, A Sqn MARQUAIX – 1 section No 14 M.G. Sqn at BERNES. Patrols sent out gained touch with enemy. 3 Hostile M Guns at K1 C15. 1 M.G. in trench running from VENDELLES towards BERNES – ROISEL occupied by enemy – 1 Troop A Sqn watching it, remainder A Sqn withdrawn to TINCOURT – TINCOURT WOOD held by 3 hostile M.Gs. at K7 & 15, K1 C05, K1 C15. MARQUAIX shelled – Touch not yet gained with Canadian Cav Bde. Casualties during day ORI 1 (missing) (A Sqn). Horses killed 1, missing 2 (all C Sqn) – ORI missing owing to Roisel being thought to be in our hands & A Sqn moving up to it about 7 pm, & finding our infy post had left it & Germans reoccupied it.	Map 1/40,000 Sheet 62C
	25/3/17		SOYECOURT reported held by enemy, enemy observed in VENDELLES, a Cavalry patrol seen N of VENDELLES – line of wire (hostile) running from direction JEANCOURT past VENDELLES and SOYECOURT towards VERMAND – Trench strongly held by enemy in front of B DE LA CROIX, with dismounted men & 2 M Gs. Rifle fire opened on patrol from FM South of STA. FM seemed strongly held. Enemy in ROISEL – MARQUAIX shelled – Hostile Cavy patrols on hill K 9 central, and W of VENDELLES – About 25 shells (small) on FLECHIN during day – 1 Troop A Sqn sent to TINCOURT WOOD which had been taken by Canadian Cav Bde – 1 Coy Warwick Regt moved up there & troop rejoined A Sqn. 4 German aeroplanes over HANCOURT flying towards PERONNE during afternoon – 2 Platoons 3rd Corps Cyclist Battn attached to Regt – 1 to A Sqn TINCOURT, 2nd at Regt HQ HANCOURT – Infantry detachments at BERNES, FLECHIN, NOBESCOURT FM, HAMELET and MARQUAIX withdrawn during night 24/25. 2 Troops B Sqn occupied FLECHIN during night & relieved by 2 troops C Sqn on morning 25th	

Instructions regarding War Diaries and Intelligence Summaries are contained in F. S. Regs., Part II. and the Staff Manual respectively. Title pages will be prepared in manuscript.

WAR DIARY
or
INTELLIGENCE SUMMARY.
(Erase heading not required.)

18th Lancers March 1917

Army Form C. 2118.

(3)

Place	Date	Hour	Summary of Events and Information	Remarks and references to Appendices
	25/3/17 contd		1 Battn Oxfords 1/4th at TINCOURT, 1 Battn GLOSTERS at BOUVRINCOURT in reserve. Casualties – OR1 wounded 1 (A sqn). Reports sent in to Bde on villages BERNES, FLECHIN, MARQUAIX – M.G. section (14 M.G. sqn) moved from BERNES to MARQUAIX	
	26/3/17		C & D sqns as before – with patrols out. A & B sqns at MARQUAIX and HAMELET respectively at 10am, when 1 (or 2) Coys 1/4 Oxfords attacked ROISEL. B sqn were unable to cooperate effectively as ground S of ROISEL was too marshy & intersected – A sqn cooperated on N flank – clearing hill K9 & K3 of enemy M.G.s, & about 10 mounted & 15 dismounted men and occupying it with a post about K9 a 88 until relieved by 2 platoons of 1/4 Oxfords at 7.30 pm. Sqdn was held up by M.G. & rifle fire when trying to proceed towards K10. – Very wet windy & cold day, considerably hindering observation & movement. – VILLERS FAUCON held by enemy infantry. FLECHIN heavily shelled for 40 mins by 4 to 6 light field guns killing & wounding 8 horses C sqn. Horses consequently withdrawn to HANCOURT. BERNES shelled intermittently and a few shells on HANCOURT – MONTIGNY FM rarely held by enemy during day – but held at night. Copses to W of it always held. ROISEL was entered by infantry at 1pm, attack having commenced at 10.30 am – after a light bombardment, & cleared of enemy by 3 pm – Armoured Car Battery cooperating. A sqn at TINCOURT night 26/27 – ROISEL being held by Oxfords. D sqn from pt 114 to ROISEL relieved by 2 Coys LINCOLN Regt – 1 Coy 2/7 Sherwood Foresters & 2 Platoons 2/5 Sherwood Foresters arrived HANCOURT, 1 platoon each BERNES and FLECHIN of 2/5 Sherwood Foresters. A good	

A5834 Wt. W4973 M687 750,000 8/16 D. D. & L. Ltd. Forms/C.2118/13.

(4)

Army Form C. 2118.

Instructions regarding War Diaries and Intelligence Summaries are contained in F. S. Regs., Part II. and the Staff Manual respectively. Title pages will be prepared in manuscript.

WAR DIARY
or
~~INTELLIGENCE SUMMARY.~~ 18 Lancers
March 1917
(Erase heading not required.)

Place	Date	Hour	Summary of Events and Information	Remarks and references to Appendices
HANCOURT etc.			Many infantry coming up evening 26th. Casualties - I.O. 1 (Jem Jagat Singh) wounded, ORI killed 1 (D), ORI wounded 6 (2A, 2B, 2C), ORI missing 1 (C), animals killed 3, wounded 9, missing 1.	
	27/3		BERNES and FLECHIN shelled throughout morning - 1 Battn Leicester Regt arrived HANCOURT midday - 1 Sec 4 MG Sqn - returned from MARQUAIX to Regt HQ at HANCOURT - report called for on SOYECOURT line by Bde - Excellent work done by No 1995 L Dfr MOBARA KHAN L/C, No 1830 Dafr SHER MOHD KHAN, 17 Cav attd + 2558 Sr MOHD NIWAZ KHAN R/C - Report submitted to Bde. - 8 Hrs took VILLERS FAUCON during day - A Sqn being ready to support - but not called upon. Casualties - Nil.	
	28/3	5 am	B Sqn moved to VILLERS FAUCON to act as Corps Troops to detachment holding it relieving 2 sqdns 8 Hrs. Patrolled towards STE EMILIE Pt 137 (E 17) and TEMPLEUX LE GUERARD - patrols unable to cross ST EMILIE - ROISEL railway line owing to fire. Sqdn assisted 1 Coy of BUCKS Regt to construct defences in VILLERS FAUCON - Horses withdrawn to K9 owing to continuous shell fire on VILLERS-FAUCON. Sqdn withdrawn at 7 15 pm under orders Ambala Bde & rejoined at HANCOURT at 12.20 AM on 29th. During the day A, C & D sqns concentrated at HANCOURT, the line having been taken over by infantry.	
	29/3	12 noon.	Regt marched W with Ambala Bde via PERONNE, HALLE, BIACHES to previous bivouac at BOIS DE MEREAUCOURT - wet windy & cold day with hail	

A5834 Wt. W4973 M687 750,000 8/16 D. D. & L. Ltd. Forms/C.2118/13.

(5) ~~4~~

Army Form C. 2118.

Instructions regarding War Diaries and Intelligence Summaries are contained in F. S. Regs., Part II. and the Staff Manual respectively. Title pages will be prepared in manuscript.

WAR DIARY
or
INTELLIGENCE SUMMARY.
(*Erase heading not required.*)

18 Hussars
March 1917

Place	Date	Hour	Summary of Events and Information	Remarks and references to Appendices
	30/3	10.30 AM.	Regt marched with Bde to WARFUSEE-ABANCOURT via CAPPY and CHUIGNOLLES. Billeted in W end of village – whole Bde being in this & LAMOTTE villages	Map 1/100,000 AMIENS.
	31/3		Day spent in cleaning up etc.	
Summary			The task of the Bde in the operations described was to hold the line BEAUVOIS – POEUILLY – FLECHIN – BERNES – MARQUAIX, French Cav being to S and Canadian Cav Bde to N – 9 H.H. held from S end of Bde line to POEUILLY inclusive & the Regt thence to MARQUAIX & at one time Bde TINCOURT & later VILLERS-FAUCON. The intention was to hold this line to enable the infantry to come up & dig in on it – at same time to seize any localities not strongly held by the enemy – The enemy rearguards consisted of infantry with M.G's & some Cavalry – Villages generally seem to have been held by 50 to 100 men. Their rifle fire was on the whole bad. The country is very open and almost ideal for Cavalry. but the weather was very unfavourable. Cold, windy & stormy – The villages were all systematically burnt & blown up & trees cut down in the most thorough way & often included quite valueless trees.	
			Lieut Flood proceeded to Rouen as a training officer on 20/3/17	
			Capt F. Gwatkin appointed G S O 3 5 Cav Divn on 31.3.17	

(6)

Army Form C. 2118.

Instructions regarding War Diaries and Intelligence Summaries are contained in F. S. Regs., Part II. and the Staff Manual respectively. Title pages will be prepared in manuscript.

WAR DIARY
or
~~INTELLIGENCE SUMMARY.~~ 18th K.G.O. Lancers
March 1917

(Erase heading not required.)

Place	Date	Hour	Summary of Events and Information	Remarks and references to Appendices

Indian Fighting men & Regl: Public Followers	During March 17 Men	During March 17 Followers	13/11/14 to 31/3/17 Men	13/11/14 to 31/3/17 Followers
Casualties – To Hospital Sick	8	-	344x	10x
— do — wounded	8	-	37	-
Killed in action	1	-	7	-
Died of disease	-	-	8	-
Missing in action	1	-	1	-
Prisoner in action	1	-	1	-
Transferred to other Units & Followers Surplus to India	1	-	20	5
New formations – Used for new formation			106	2
Strength of Dismounted Reinforcements on 31. 3. 17			98	5
Reinforcements. From Base or other Units	– 5	-	402	16
Reinforcements. Returned from Hospital	14	-	155	2
Horses & Mules	Horses	Mules	Horses	Mules
Casualties – Evacuated lame & sick	16 ~~74~~	-	38[illegible]x	31
Casualties – Used for new formation	-	-	201	62
Casualties – Transfd Surplus	-	-	48	40
Reinforcements from Base & other Units	5	-	555	115

x Includes men evacuated temporarily to I.C.F.A. as well as those to "out of Divisional are."

x. Includes:-
8 wounded in action
4 Killed — do —
3 Missing — do —

1. DAG Rosn Vai Ambala Bde &
2. C.G.S. Simla India
3. Retained

A5834 Wt. W4973/M687 750,000 8/16 D. D. & L. Ltd. Forms/C.2118/13.

31/3/17

V. Musprat Lt Col
Comdg 18th K.G.O Lancers

Instructions regarding War Diaries and Intelligence Summaries are contained in F. S. Regs., Part II. and the Staff Manual respectively. Title pages will be prepared in manuscript.

18 Lancers

WAR DIARY
or
~~INTELLIGENCE SUMMARY.~~
(Erase heading not required.)

APRIL 1917

ADJUTANT'S OFFICE No. 27 R Date 1/5/17. 18th K.G.O. LANCERS

Vol 10

Army Form C. 2118.

Place	Date	Hour	Summary of Events and Information	Remarks and references to Appendices
MARLY WARFUSEE-ABANCOURT	1.4.17		Regt in billets - Day employed in cleaning up arms, equipt & saddlery - B echelon rejoined regt on 31.3.17 having been divisionalized since 23.3.17	AMIENS SH17 1/100000 St. QUENTIN 18 1/100000
	2.4.17 to 8.4.17		Days spent in cleaning up - Exercising horses - Hotchkiss gun firing on a range close to WARFUSEE and practising coming into action w. Box with new equipment - (latter equipment is a much more serviceable one than the former) - Drill & fitting Box respirators and adapting them to Cavalry - it having been found that carried on the back, they soon the haversacks wore out owing to the jolting. Dismounted Men rejoined regt on 5th & moved to camp at MARLY, just N.E of CHUIGNOLLES on 6th. Lt Col Muspratt evacuated to C.C. Stn at CAYEUX on 5th with Ulcer on toe. Major Corbyn assumed command of regt. Weather very cold, snowy, wet & windy - 1½ Sqns billetted in village - remainder in large wooden huts, and horses in temporary stables at N.W. edge of village. Men's health good.	
	9.4.17 14.4.17	10.AM	Regiment marched via FOUCAUCOURT - ESTREES - BRIE - MONS-EN-CHAUSSEE - ESTREES-EN-CHAUSSEE to area between TERTRY & CAULAINCOURT, & bivouacked in woods by ST MARTIN DES PRES. 4.15 pm B echelon came along with regiment. Weather very cold & wet. Horses suffered badly from the effects of the cold, and only ½ of horse rugs of the regiment were available, remainder were lost to 9 H.H.!	
	15-4-17 to 19-4-17		Rain & snow curtailed training to any great extent. Every effort was made to erect shelters for the men & horses. All villages & farms in this area have been destroyed by the enemy; with the result that there is no cover for horses.	
	20-4-17 to		With improvement in the weather Squadron training commenced - & the Bde made arrangements for a range for Hotchkiss Guns. The regiment daily provided working parties (from 30 & 70 men) for the purpose of filling in	

A5834 Wt. W4973 M687 750,000 8/16 D. D. & L. Ltd. Forms/C.2118/13.

15th Lancers.

WAR DIARY
or
~~INTELLIGENCE SUMMARY.~~
(Erase heading not required.)

April 1917

Army Form C. 2118.

(2)

Instructions regarding War Diaries and Intelligence Summaries are contained in F. S. Regs., Part II. and the Staff Manual respectively. Title pages will be prepared in manuscript.

Place	Date	Hour	Summary of Events and Information	Remarks and references to Appendices
CAULAINCOURT TERTRY area. Reg.	20-4-17 to 30-4-17		Craters, made by the enemy before retiring at practically every X roads. Also working parties were taken for clearing up & repairing the roads through the villages – all the houses having been blown up & many of the walls falling straight across the road. On 29-4-17 the Ambala Bde supplied working parties (about 60 per regt) to undertake the wiring & construction of M.Gun emplacements on the IV Corps "Red Line" from CAULAINCOURT to POEUILLY (both places inclusive.)	ST QUENTIN 3:18 1/100000
Summary			The Bde (with the Divn) after resting at HARTUCKE a fortnight, moved up to the forward area by TERTRY in conjunction with the attack the French were about to make on the HINDENBURG LINE defences N. & S.E. of ST QUENTIN. This attack failed on 17th & 18th, & consequently the regiment (& Bde) continued working. The "Red Line" is practically the line of outposts held by the regiment in the last week of March.	
			The body of [illegible] Fulab Shah, who was killed by M.Gun fire while patrolling in front of the enemy's wire in neighbourhood ~~of [illegible]~~ [illegible] of HARVILLY, was found covered thickly with earth. The Germans had removed all valuables such as his watch & ring.	
			L.D. [illegible] Khan [illegible] was awarded I.O.M. II Class on 9-4-17 for showing "great initiative & great determination [illegible] in command of a patrol". This was in connection with a report called for by Bde a	

A5834 Wt. W4973 M687 750,000 8/16 D. D. & L. Ltd. Forms/C.2118/13.

Instructions regarding War Diaries and Intelligence Summaries are contained in F. S. Regs., Part II. and the Staff Manual respectively. Title pages will be prepared in manuscript.

18 Lancers

WAR DIARY
or
~~INTELLIGENCE SUMMARY.~~

(*Erase heading not required.*)

April 1917.

Army Form C. 2118.

(3)

Place	Date	Hour	Summary of Events and Information	Remarks and references to Appendices
TERTRY CAULAINCOURT			27-3-17 on SOYÉCOURT line.	ST QUENTIN Sh 18 1/100000.
	11-4-17		Major V.A.S. Keighley proceeded to MARSEILLES.	
	13-4-17		Capt J. Gratkin rejoined regiment from G.S.O. III 5th Cav Divn.	
	16-4-17		Col Muspratt was evacuated to England, & consequently struck off the strength of the regiment from that date.	
	25-4-17		2/Lt T.A.C. Fitzpatrick rejoined the Dismounted men from Base ROUEN.	
			The Dismounted men under Lt BENFIELD moved up to BRIE on 16-4-17 from FOUCAUCOURT. They have been employed on mending roads in the vicinity of their camp.	

Instructions regarding War Diaries and Intelligence Summaries are contained in F. S. Regs., Part II. and the Staff Manual respectively. Title pages will be prepared in manuscript.

Army Form C. 2118.

WAR DIARY
or
~~INTELLIGENCE SUMMARY.~~
(Erase heading not required.)

18th K.G.O. Lancers.
April 1917

Place	Date	Hour	Summary of Events and Information	Remarks and references to Appendices
			(see table below)	

Indian Fighting men & Regl Public Followers	During April 17 Men	During April 17 Followers	13/11/14 to 30/4/17 Men	13/11/14 to 30/4/17 Followers
Casualties – To Hospital Sick	19	1	363x	11x
— do — wounded	-	-	37	-
Killed in action	-	-	7	-
Died of disease	1	-	9	-
Missing in action	-	-	1	-
Prisoner in action	-	-	1	-
Transferred to other Units & Followers Surplus to India	1	-	21	5
New formations – Used for new formation.	-	-	106	2
Strength of Dismounted Reinforcements on 30.4.17	-	-	100	5
Reinforcements – From Base & other Units	26	1	428	17
Reinforcements – Returned from Hospital	12	1	167	3
Horses and Mules.	**Horses**	**Mules**	**Horses**	**Mules**
Casualties – Evacuated lame & sick	21	2	408⁂	33
Casualties – Used for new formation	-	-	201	62
Casualties – Transferred Surplus	-	-	48	40
Reinforcements from Base & other Units	23	1	578	116

x Includes men evacuated temporarily to I.C.F.A. as well as those to "out-of Divisional Area." –

⁂ Includes: –
8 wounded in action
4 killed — do —
3 missing — do —

[illegible] Major
Comdg 18th Lancers

30/4/17

A5834 Wt. W4473/M687 750,000 8/16 D. D. & L. Ltd. Forms/C.2118/13.

Instructions regarding War Diaries and Intelligence Summaries are contained in F. S. Regs., Part II. and the Staff Manual respectively. Title Pages will be prepared in manuscript.

18 Lancers.

WAR DIARY
or
~~INTELLIGENCE SUMMARY~~
(Erase heading not required.)

May 1917

VOL XI

Army Form C. 2118.

ADJUTANT'S OFFICE. No. 28 B. Date 1/6/17. 18th K. G. O. LANCERS.

(1)

Place	Date	Hour	Summary of Events and Information	Remarks and references to Appendices
TERTRY - CAULAINCOURT area.	1-5-17 to 12-5-17		These days were spent in Squadron training & a certain amount of Regimental Drill; Hotchkiss gun firing on a range close to camp; map reading, & fire control. The country in this area affords facilities for Squadron training, far better than any met with up to the present date; the country & villages are left in the state in which the Germans held them; lines of wire & trenches, defending most of the tactical points. Moreover there have been no crops to hinder the movements of troops, as has always been the case before. Every third day the regiment has supplied the Bde working party on the IVth Corps red line.	St QUENTIN Sh. 18. 1/100000.
	8.5.17		Dismounted Reinforcements moved up in motor lorries from the camp at BRIE to a camp on W. edge of BOIS DE HOLNON, for work on IV Corps "Brown" line	(AMIENS SH.17).
	9.5.17		Lt PRINSEP. 3rd Skinners Horse. and 2/Lt BULLOCK, U.L.IA., joined the regiment from the base ROUEN.	
	13.5.17		Dismounted Reinforcements rejoined the regiment.	
	15.5.17		5th Cav Div took over part of the line. The Ambala Bde was split up, the 9th H.H. & the 18th L. being attached to Secbad Bde, who took over from the 176th Infantry Bde on the front GRAND PRIEL WOOD to the TUMULUS just N. of PONTRUET. The Dismounted Regiment, (about 300 strong) under Maj. Corbyn rode as far as VENDELLES & proceeded thence on foot to the valley running N. from LE VERGUIER. 18/Lancers were in Bde reserve in old German trench just W. of PIEUMEL WOOD. Regt. H.Q. at the head of the valley S. of GRAND PRIEL WOOD.	Refmaps. 62c N.E 62c S.E 62b N.W. 62b S.W. 1/20000.

2449 Wt. W14957/M90 750,000 1/16 J.B.C. & A. Forms/C.2118/12.

Instructions regarding War Diaries and Intelligence Summaries are contained in F. S. Regs., Part II. and the Staff Manual respectively. Title Pages will be prepared in manuscript.

Army Form C. 2118.

WAR DIARY or ~~INTELLIGENCE SUMMARY~~

(Erase heading not required.)

18 Lancers. May 1917.

(2)

Place	Date	Hour	Summary of Events and Information	Remarks and references to Appendices
LE VERGUIER	15-5-17.		The relief of the Reserve Regt (18L) was completed by 6.30 pm. The following British officers went up with the Dismounted Regiment. Major Corbyn commanding; Lt Forbes Adjutant. Lt Danby, Signalling; Lt Seagr; Intelligence - A Sqn, Lt Benfield - B Sqn Capt Swatkin - C Sqn Capt Lorimer - D Sqn. Lt Abercrombie. Capt Dening was i/c of "Back Area".	ST QUENTIN SH. 18 - 1/100000 - 62 c. N.E. 62 c. S.E. 62 b. N.W. 62 b. S.W. 1/20000.
	16-5-17.		The wire along the S. side of the old German trench was transferred to the N. side	
	17-5-17.		On the night of the 16/17th B. C. D. Sqns worked on the "BROWN LINE", which is the main line of resistance, & runs (in this sector) on the ridge W edge of GRAND PRIEL wood, along high ground to S.E. exit of LE VERGUIER.	
	18.5.17.		Enemy fired a few shells (shrapnel) on S corner of GRAND PRIEL WOOD, at 5.30 am.	
	19.5.17		Work was continued throughout the day strengthening & deepening the belt of wire transferred on the 16-5-17. 26 H.E. (5.9) fell into LE VERGUIER during the day.	
	20-5-17		On the night 19/20th 50 men A Sqn were employed wiring the support posts of the Poona Horse who were holding the left sector of the Bde front. B Sqn carried up R.E. material from LE VERGUIER to P. Horse Right wing H.Q. by the aerodrome L29. [illegible] 3. (62c NE). The enemy put some 20 5.9 H.E. into LE VERGUIER during the night. An observation post was made just N. of PEAR COPSE, NE. of LE VERGUIER; and from here all movement on the enemy trenches in front of Bde sector was visible, & in some places a good view was obtained well behind the enemy's main HINDENBURG LINE. At some points the wire in front of this line was seen to be 9 belts in depth. The system of the enemys wire is a system of "rays" along the front of which M. Gun fire can be brought to bear —	

2449 Wt. W14957/M90 750,000 1/16 J.B.C. & A. Forms/C.2118/12.

Army Form C. 2118.

Instructions regarding War Diaries and Intelligence Summaries are contained in F. S. Regs., Part II. and the Staff Manual respectively. Title Pages will be prepared in manuscript.

WAR DIARY
or
~~INTELLIGENCE SUMMARY~~
(Erase heading not required.)

18 Lancers. May 1917. (3)

Place	Date	Hour	Summary of Events and Information	Remarks and references to Appendices
LE VERGUIER	21.5.17		On the night 20/21st B Sqn continued carrying R.E. material to P. Horse R. Wing H.Q. A Sqn worked on new support post by above R. Wing H.Q. – C & D. Sqns worked in Sunken road S. of Regtl: H.Q. making new shelters sufficient to hold to 2 Sqns (120 men). Hostile artillery very active during the day. 36 5"9s burst in LE VERGUIER, 32 5.9" burst on N. edge of PIEUMEL WOOD & 67 5"9s on S. edge of GRAND PRIEL WOOD. In the evening C & D Sqns moved out of the old German trench into shelters dug in Sunken road (see above) A & B remained in the German trench, which was not under direct observation by the enemy in this part – C & D. were moved as they were under direct observation – However the whole trench is under observation from balloons, & A & B Sqns, on clear days, could not move about during the day time – Regt H.Q. remained in the same position –	ST QUENTIN SH. 18. 1/100 000 62c N.E. 62c. S.E. 62b. N.W. 62b. S.W. 1/20000.
	22.5.17		On night 21/22nd A & C Sqns carried R.E. material to Right & Left wing H.Q.s respectively of the Deccan Horse, who relieved the Poona Horse on night 20/21. The object of all this "carrying" is to form a forward dump of wire & pickets, so that all the posts may have unlimited wire around them – B Sqn "wired" the front line & Support posts of the Deccan Horse. A Sqn worked on Support posts of 9. H.H. (on right of Deccan Horse) who had relieved 7. D.G.s on night 20/21. Enemy artillery was very quiet during the day, LE VERGUIER only receiving about 15 5.9" H.E.	
		9.30 pm 10.30 pm	An enormous fire was seen burning in ST QUENTIN – some 8 miles S.E.	

2449 Wt. W14957/M90 750,000 1/16 J.B.C. & A. Forms/C.2118/12.

Army Form C. 2118.

Instructions regarding War Diaries and Intelligence Summaries are contained in F. S. Regs., Part II. and the Staff Manual respectively. Title Pages will be prepared in manuscript.

WAR DIARY
or
INTELLIGENCE SUMMARY
(Erase heading not required.)

18 Lancers — May 1917 — (4)

Place	Date	Hour	Summary of Events and Information	Remarks and references to Appendices
LE VERGUIER	23-5-17		A+B Sqns worked (digging wiring) on G.H.H. front & support trenches in vicinity of RED HOUSE. C+D Sqns wired front & support posts of Deccan Horse. All this work is done at night between the hours of 9.30pm & 3.30am —	ST QUENTIN SH. 18 1/100000 62c N.E. 62b N.W. 62c S.E. 62b N.SW. 1/40000
			Artillery on both sides was very active. The enemy put 128 5.9" H.E. into LE VERGUIER. This continual shelling of LE VERGUIER is due to the presence of some 60 pdr guns that are in the W. outskirts.	
			Lieuts PRINSEP (B) WILLIAMS (A) BULLOCK (C) FITZPATRICK (D) joined Dismounted Regiment. The work at night requires a lot of supervision, & the Divn Commander decided that as long as these large working parties were required, more B.O.s should be present.	
	24.5.17		During the night 23/24 work the same as noted yesterday, only A+B & C+D Sqns changed places. 85 more shells fell in LE VERGUIER today.	
	25-5-17		Work the same as on night 23/24. Last night Capt Lorimer & Capt Fowke went & spent the night with the Wing Commanders Deccan Horse, whom we relieve tonight. 10 I.O.s & N.C.O.s per Wing spent the night in the ravine front & support posts, to act as guides this evening when the relief takes place. These N.C.O.s return to Wing H.Q.rs tonight. 37 shells were put into LE VERGUIER during the day. At 4.30pm the enemy put over 12 small shells onto our sunken road — 1 fell & burst in the road. It appears that these are the shells he registers with!	
	26.5.17		The relief was cancelled by the Divn. in view of the fact that we should be relieved on night 27/28 by 4th Divn. Consequently	

2449 Wt. W14957/M90 750,000 1/16 J.B.C. & A. Forms/C.2118/12.

Army Form C. 2118.

Instructions regarding War Diaries and Intelligence Summaries are contained in F. S. Regs., Part II. and the Staff Manual respectively. Title pages will be prepared in manuscript.

WAR DIARY
or
~~INTELLIGENCE SUMMARY.~~
(Erase heading not required.)

18 Lancers. May 1917. (5).

Place	Date	Hour	Summary of Events and Information	Remarks and references to Appendices
LE VERGUIER	26-5-17.		1oc area still in Bde Reserve, & continue supplying working parties - Last night working parties same as night before. LE VERGUIER received normal allotment of shells	ST QUENTIN SH-18 - 1/100000 - 62 c. NE 62 b. N.W. 62 c. SE. 62 b. S.W. 1/40000.
	27-5-17.		A party of 135 men A.B, & D Sqns worked last night under R.E. supervision on new post of 9. H.H. near RED HOUSE. C Sqn carrying material up to Deccan Horse L. Wing H.Q. The enemy put about 30 5.9"s on to the ridge just S. of GRAND PRIEL WOOD & just above Regt. H.Q. - only 13 shells were put into LE VERGUIER.	
	28.5.17		Last night 60 men C & D Sqns worked under RE on post of 9 H.H mentioned yesterday. Another party of 64 men A & B Sqn worked on support posts of Deccan Horse	
TERTRY - CAULAINCOURT		9.30 pm.	The regiment marched on foot to valley S.W. of VENDELLES where horses were met, & dismounted regiment returned to camp, arriving about 5 pm.	
Summary.			During the above period in the trenches the following reliefs took place - Night of 15/16. Sialkot ~~Ambala~~ Bde relieved 176th Bde infantry. In front line. Poona Horse & 7 D.Gs. Support Line Deccan Horse & 9th H.Horse. Reserve 18 Lancers. Night of 20/21 front line regiments & support line regiments changed places. On 28th 9H.Horse & 18/L were withdrawn & rejoined Ambala Bde - Details left behind with the horses included 100 Dismounted Reinforcements - The only training possible was Squadron Staff rides for I.O.s & N.C.O.s - It is most unfortunate that no bombs were available for practice for the details left behind - as when they came in their turn. Bombs & Rifle grenades are	

A5834 Wt. W4973/M687 750,000 8/16 D. D. & L. Ltd. Forms/C.2118/13

Instructions regarding War Diaries and Intelligence Summaries are contained in F. S. Regs., Part II. and the Staff Manual respectively. Title pages will be prepared in manuscript.

WAR DIARY
or
~~INTELLIGENCE SUMMARY.~~
(Erase heading not required.)

18 Lancers. May 1917.

Army Form C. 2118.

(6)

Place	Date	Hour	Summary of Events and Information	Remarks and references to Appendices
TERTRY CAULAINCOURT	31-5-17		handled daily & are a trench store. The necessity of practising night patrolling was most apparent from reports received from the other units. & this is now being done. The Germans, in this front, send out patrols from 20–25 men. Consequently we do the same. "No man's land" opposite this bit of the front varies in width from 600x to 1000x which gives much scope for patrolling. & now that most of the wiring has been completed & the line of forward posts definitely settled, patrol activity, ~~from~~ our side will probably increase.	ST QUENTIN SH. 18 1/100 000
			The German front line – the HARGICOURT SWITCH – opposite the Second Bde Sector ran approximately on the ridge ~~W of~~ VILLERET – BUISSON GAULAINE Fm to ST HELENE –	
	22-5-17		Major Corbyn was promoted to Acting Lt. Col. while Commanding the Regiment dated 20-4-17 vice Tempy Lt. Col. Muspratt, who relinquished the rank of Lt. Col. on 5-4-17 – (evacuated sick.). [List No 135 of appointments of G.H.Q. 12-5-17]	
			Risaldar Lakha Singh & Ressaidar Mohd Inayat were award the Order of British India II class. (5 Cav. Div.) memo A/982 of 14-5-17.	
	26-5-17		Lt. Col. (Tempy Br. Genl) F.A. Maxwell V.C. "mentioned in despatches" – 3rd supplement London Gazette of 15-6-17 p. 4750 –	

[illegible] Lt.

A5834 Wt. W4973/M687 750,000 8/16 D. D. & L. Ltd. Forms/C.2118/13

Army Form C. 2118.

Instructions regarding War Diaries and Intelligence Summaries are contained in F. S. Regs., Part II. and the Staff Manual respectively. Title pages will be prepared in manuscript.

WAR DIARY
or
~~INTELLIGENCE SUMMARY~~. 18th K.G.O. LANCERS.
May 1917.

(Erase heading not required.)

Place	Date	Hour	Summary of Events and Information	Remarks and references to Appendices

Indian Fighting men and Regl Public Followers.	During May 1917		13/11/14 to 31/5/17	
	Men	Followers	Men	Followers
Casualties - To Hospital sick	14	-	377x	11
— do — wounded	-	-	37	-
Killed in action	-	-	7	-
Died of disease	-	-	9	-
Missing in action	-	-	1	-
Prisoner in action ...	-	-	1	-
Transferred to other Units & Followers Surplus to India	-	-	21	5
New formations - Used for new formations	.	-	106	2
Strength of Dismounted Reinforcements on 31/5	.	.	106	5
Reinforcements. From Base or other units	17	-	445	17
Reinforcements. Returned from Hospital	6	.	173	3
Horses and Mules	Horses	Mules	Horses	Mules.
Evacuated lame & sick	7	-	415※	33
Casualties - Used for new formation	.	-	201	62
Transferred Surplus	.	-	48	40
Reinforcements from Base & other units	7	.	585	116

x Includes men evacuated temporarily to I.C.F.A, as well as those to "out of Divisional area".

※ Includes:-
8 wounded in action
4 Killed — do —
3 Missing — do —

[signature] Lt Col.
Comdg 18th Lancers.

31/5/17

A5834 Wt. W4973/M687 750,000 8/16 D. D. & L. Ltd. Forms/C.2118/13

Army Form C. 2118.

Instructions regarding War Diaries and Intelligence Summaries are contained in F. S. Regs., Part II. and the Staff Manual respectively. Title pages will be prepared in manuscript.

War Diary

K Lancers

WAR DIARY or INTELLIGENCE SUMMARY.

(Erase heading not required.)

June 1917

ADJUTANT'S OFFICE No. 29 Date 1/7/17 18th K. G. O. LANCERS

①

Place	Date	Hour	Summary of Events and Information	Remarks and references to Appendices
TERTRY – CAULAINCOURT	1-6-17 4-6-17		Night patrolling & bayonet fighting, in view of the fact that we are due to go into the trenches again on the night 5th/6th. Squadron training however also took place.	ST QUENTIN SH-18 1/100000
			The Dismounted men rejoined at midday from VENDELLES, where they had been working on the Brown Line in the vicinity of LE VERGUIER.	
	5-6-17		Ambala Bde relieved Canadian Bde in the line on the front RED WOOD – SOMERVILLE WOOD – PONTRU. The regiment relieved FORT GARRY HORSE – holding the left half of the Bde sector. 8th Hussars on our right – Secbad: Bde on our left.	62 c. N.E 62 c. S.E. 62 b. N.W. 62 b. S.W. 1/40000.
			Regiment marched from camp at 7.45 pm. via CAULAINCOURT – VERMAND – BIHECOURT. thence dismounted to Regtl H.Q. at COOKERS QUARRY (R.H.C.7.7. 62.c S.E.). B Sqn. took over SOMERVILLE WOOD & DOG'S LEG COPSE (just S. of SOMERVILLE WOOD) with 2 troops (F.32 C & D) 2 troops in support at LONE TREE post (this is Sqn. H.Q.) M.1.b 9.8. D Sqn, on B's left, from N.W. corner of SOMERVILLE WOOD to a point 200x N.W. of N. corner of RED WOOD, with 2 troops. Sqn H.Q. & 2 troops in support, just S. of S. Corner of RED WOOD (M.1.b 3.8.). C Sqn. (counterattack troops) in a post known as HODSONS POST at R.6.a. central. A Sqn. (reserve) in Intermediate or (Brown) Line from R11 b 8.8. to R5 d.2.9.	
			The relief was completed by 1 am. 6.6.17.	
			The system of holding this part of the front is a series of front-line posts & support posts situated from 500x – 1000x in front of Intermediate Line or main Line of resistance.	
			The German front line – (a switch line in front of the HINDENBURG LINE) runs, opposite this sector, from BUISSON-GAULAINE FM – F.27 central – ST HELÈNE –. No man's land was everywhere over 1000x in width, giving large scope for patrolling.	

A5834 Wt. W4973/M687 750,000 8/16 D. D. & L. Ltd. Forms/C.2118/13

Instructions regarding War Diaries and Intelligence Summaries are contained in F. S. Regs., Part II. and the Staff Manual respectively. Title pages will be prepared in manuscript.

WAR DIARY
or
~~INTELLIGENCE SUMMARY.~~
(Erase heading not required.)

18 Lancers — June 1917

Army Form C. 2118.

(2)

Place	Date	Hour	Summary of Events and Information	Remarks and references to Appendices
PONTRU	5-6-17.		The following B.O.s went up with the Dismounted Regt: Col. Corbyn, Comdg. Lt Watson, Adjt. Lt Danby, Signals – Lt Sanger – Intelligence officer – A Sqn – Capt Denning & Lt Williams B Sqn. Capt Watkin & Lt Prinsep – C Sqn. Lt Fulcher & 2/Lt Bullock D Sqn. Capt Frazer Lt Fitzpatrick – Maj. Cormier was left in charge of Back area –	62 C N.E. 62 C S.E. 62 B N.W. 62 B S.W. 1/40000.
	6.6.17.		The wire round our posts was not good & required a lot of improvement – There was no shelling –	
	7.6.17.		Last night was spent in improving the wire, in front of the posts – A Sqn digging Intermediate Line – a small patrol of the enemy was met by a B Sqn patrol – Bombs thrown by both sides.	
	8.6.17.	6am.	enemy put 29 small shells into N.E. edge of RED WOOD – no casualties – SOMERVILLE WOOD (was also shelled – no casualties). a patrol of B Sqn reported MAX WOOD clear of the enemy – RED WOOD was shelled at 7am. 9am 2pm 6pm 7 9.30 pm – 29 shells (H.E) in all – LONE TREE Post got 3 H.E. at 7am. D Sqn H.Q. was also shelled at 1.30 pm. 4 rounds. HODSONS POST at midday 12 rounds H.E – no Casualties –	
	9.6.17.		Last night a patrol from B Sqn under Jem KEHAR SINGH went & inspected wire in front of enemy trench E. of MAX COPSE – wire in good condition – no enemy seen or heard – patrol were fired on by a M.Gun in the bank running N.E. from MAX COPSE – D Sqn sent out no patrols, as this was being effectively done by right regiment of Sectad Bde.	(Max copse is G.33.C Central).
		5.45am	The RHA. O.P at LONE TREE post was blown up by a direct hit – all personnel (RHA) were killed or wounded –	
	10.6.17.		B Sqn reserve post was shelled during the morning – RED WOOD was also shelled – Last night A Sqn relieved B Sqn in SOMERVILLE WOOD – C Sqn relieved D Sqn. Relief started at 10 pm – During this relief at 10.40 pm. the enemy artillery put down a barrage between SOMERVILLE WOOD & LONE TREE POST – also shelled DOGS LEG – and ½ an hour later RED WOOD posts. At 11.15 pm a party of the enemy estimated at 30 – 40 men attacked SOMERVILLE WOOD	

A5834 Wt. W4973/M687 750,000 8/16 D. D. & L. Ltd. Forms/C.2118/13

Army Form C. 2118.

Instructions regarding War Diaries and Intelligence Summaries are contained in F. S. Regs., Part II. and the Staff Manual respectively. Title pages will be prepared in manuscript.

WAR DIARY
or
~~INTELLIGENCE SUMMARY.~~
(Erase heading not required.)

18 Lancers, June 1917 (3)

Place	Date	Hour	Summary of Events and Information	Remarks and references to Appendices
PONTRU area.	10.6.17		The party coming round SE. corner of the wood were held up by M.Gun fire + bombs from Ress. Lakka Singh's right post – Sr Mohd Yan. Mula Singh + 2 other men of B Sqn. The party coming round the N.W. corner of the wood (which was at that moment being taken over by C Sqn from D Sqn) succeeded in getting through the wood + were met by Lt PRINSEP + some men of B Sqn; bombs were thrown by both sides. Lt PRINSEP + his men fired on the enemy, who retired apparently through the wood. It was here that Lt Prinsep + 2 men of B Sqn, were wounded – Our guns now opened fire + by 11.40 pm the wood was clear of the enemy – Our casualties during this raid were 1 B.O. (Prinsep) wounded – 5 O.Rs. wounded + K.D. Surmakh Singh killed – When his body was found his revolver had only 2 rounds left in it – The night was very dark + it was impossible to see what casualties were inflicted on the enemy – The relief was completed by 2.45 am.	62 c. N.E. 62 c. S.E. 62b. N.W. 62b. S.W. 1/40000.
	11.6.17		The day was very quiet – Capt. Gwatkin went to Bde HQ as acting Staff Captain – Last night a patrol from A Sqn, under Jem. Adaulat Khan went out at 9.45 pm. + visited MAX COPSE; they found no enemy – B + D Sqn both supplied wiring parties for work on wire in front of SOMERVILLE WOOD – During the morning enemy artillery very inactive. At 1.15 pm A Sqn reported that a party of the enemy (estimated at) 25 was working in SQUARE COPSE (just W. of enemy wire + 800x N.E. of DOGS LEG) – R.C.H.A. A Bty got on to them at once with good results – Lt BLETSOE arrived from Back area + took over B Sqn from Capt Gwatkin –	
	12.6.17		C Sqn further improved the wire in front of SOMERVILLE WOOD – Hostile artillery again inactive throughout the day, except for	

A5834 Wt. W4973/M687 750,000 8/16 D. D. & L. Ltd. Forms/C.2118/13

Instructions regarding War Diaries and Intelligence Summaries are contained in F. S. Regs., Part II. and the Staff Manual respectively. Title pages will be prepared in manuscript.

18 Lancers.

WAR DIARY
or
INTELLIGENCE SUMMARY. June 1917

(Erase heading not required.)

Army Form C. 2118.

(4)

Place	Date	Hour	Summary of Events and Information	Remarks and references to Appendices
			(926 S. Dullah Khan wounded)	
PONTRU area	12-6-17		an hour from 3-4 pm, when 68 H.E. shells fell round LONE TREE POST - one casualties -	62c N.E.
	13-6-17.		Last night the following reliefs took place - D sqn from HODSONS POST relieved A sqn in SOMERVILLE WOOD + LONE TREE - B sqn from Brown Line relieved C sqn in RED WOOD - C+A sqn were withdrawn to VADENCOURT + came under command of OC 9. H.H. reserve regiment - 2 sqns 9 H.H. went into HODSONS POST + Brown Line respectively - Relief completed by 1 am.	62c S.E. 62b N.W. 62b S.W. 1/40000.
			During the relief a patrol from A sqn under R.D. Mohd Ashraf Khan, went out + searched MAX COPSE + then proceeded to XI Trees (situated G. 33. c. 6.6. about 400x N.E. of MAX COPSE) No enemy was seen or heard at either place - The patrol was however fired on by a M.Gun on the way to XI Trees. M.Gun located above MAX COPSE in main trench - no casualties -	
			D sqn also had out a covering patrol - no enemy appeared -	
			A few shells fell on RED WOOD at 10 am - also on LONE TREE post - no casualties -	
	14.6.17.		enemy artillery very active throughout last night - Capt Drager was wounded (slightly) also Jemadar KEHAR SINGH + 6 O.R.s.x during very heavy shelling of SOMERVILLE WOOD + vicinity of LONE TREE -	X 2829 S. BISHAN SINGH 3823 S. KALUNDA KH. 2488 S. JAGINDA SINGH (C.I.H.) 2581 S. DALEEP SINGH 2756 S. BAGAT SINGH 2761 S. SURAIN SINGH
			a patrol from D sqn visited MAX WOOD + failed to find any enemy -	
	15-6-17.		DRAGOON POST (RED WOOD) was shelled intermittently during the morning -	
			Last night parties of 9 H.H. worked on wire in front of SOMERVILLE WOOD - but were compelled to stop work, owing to hostile shelling from 10 pm. - 2 am. + again heavy shelling on SOMERVILLE WOOD from 3 am - 4 am. 4056 S. BOSTAN KHAN (D) was blown up + Lt FITZPATRICK blown into the air + severely shaken though not wounded - Duff. Mohd Khan (2094 L.D) also had a lucky escape - He did very well during the bombardment -	
			A patrol from D sqn that went out at 11 pm. + came back at 2.30 am. met no enemy -	
			LONE TREE post shelled at midday - no casualties -	
	16-6-17.		Last night following reliefs took place - A sqn 9 H.H. relieved D sqn in SOMERVILLE WOOD - A sqn 9. H.H. relieved B sqn in RED WOOD - B+D sqns to HODSONS POST + Brown Line respectively -	

A5834 Wt. W4973/M687 750,000 8/16 D. D. & L. Ltd. Forms/C.2118/13

Instructions regarding War Diaries and Intelligence Summaries are contained in F. S. Regs., Part II. and the Staff Manual respectively. Title pages will be prepared in manuscript.

Army Form C. 2118.

WAR DIARY
or
INTELLIGENCE SUMMARY.
(*Erase heading not required.*)

18 Lancers. June 1917 (5)

Place	Date	Hour	Summary of Events and Information	Remarks and references to Appendices
PONTRU	16-6-17		During the relief a patrol from D Sqn went out as far as German wire above MAX copse – The night was quiet no shelling – Day quiet.	62 c NE. 62 c SE. 62 b N.W. 62 b S.W. 1/40000
	17-6-17 18-6-17		B & D Sqns supplied working parties for the 2 Sqns 9 H.H. from 10.30 pm – 2 am. this morning –	
	19-6-17		No working parties last night. A patrol of 30 men under Lt Abercrombie went out at 10 pm. to support the flank of a party of the 9 H.H. who were carrying out a raid on ST HELENE Trench (German front line) E. of MAX COPSE. The relief that took place on the night 15/16 was confined to 2 sqns of the 9 H.H. in view of this raid. The other 2 sqns 9 H.H. were practicing. Capt Inges rejoined from Hospital.	
VADENCOURT	20-6-17		B & D sqns in HODSONS POST & Brown Line were relieved last night by 2 sqns 9 H.H. Relief Completed by 9 am. The regiment is now in reserve at VADENCOURT – The weather has broken, after a long spell of fine weather.	
	21-6-17 22-6-17		Working parties were supplied for work on Brown Line – digging & wiring	
CAULAINCOURT	23-6-17		Bde relieved by Secbad Bde – XX D. Horse relieved the regiment, who marched back on foot to camp, arriving at 5.45 pm. Last night a patrol from B Sqn, with Lt Bletsoe & Lt Danby went out to German wire by Max Copse, cut the wire & entered the trench – The enemy post fired on the men cutting the wire & then bolted – No enemy could be found in the trench for 150x either way – The patrol bombed, with incendiary bombs, the dugouts in that part of the line – & then returned without seeing of the enemy.	ST QUENTIN SH. 18.
Summary.	24-6-17 – 30-6-17		Last week of the month was spent in refitting & squadron & troop training. On the 20.6.17 G.O.C. Divn inspected the horses. He expressed himself v. pleased with condition & turn out – Capt. R. Dening was "mentioned" in despatches. II Supplement London Gazette 1-6-17. 1. No. 2480 – Sr Chandan Singh awarded the I. D. S. M. on 13-6-17 – for v. gallant conduct on 9.6.16 helping wounded under shell fire 2. No 2135. A/D. Baz Khan " " " " " " – Remained with Ten Dhunan Khan (wounded) nr High Wood 14-7-16 for 4 hrs under shell fire. till he found a stretcher –	
	17-6-17		Lt E. P. C. Collin joined Base Rouen from leave. He had been on leave (sick) from 29-4-17.	

J.S.

A5834 Wt. W4973/M687 750,000 8/16 D. D. & L. Ltd. Forms/C.2118/13

Instructions regarding War Diaries and Intelligence Summaries are contained in F. S. Regs., Part II. and the Staff Manual respectively. Title pages will be prepared in manuscript.

WAR DIARY
or
~~INTELLIGENCE SUMMARY.~~
(Erase heading not required.)

Army Form C. 2118.

18th K. G. O. Lancers.
June 1917

Place	Date	Hour	Summary of Events and Information					Remarks and references to Appendices
			Indian Fighting Men and Regl Public Followers.	During June 1917		13/11/14 to 30/6/17		
				Men	Followers	Men	Followers	
			Casualties - To Hospital Sick	17	-	394×	11	× Includes men evacuated temporarily to I.C.F.A. as well as those to "out of Divisional area".
			—do— wounded	12	-	49⊗	-	⊗ Includes 2 men wounded at duty.
			Killed in action	3	-	10	-	
			Died of disease	-	-	9	-	
			Missing in action	-	-	1	-	
			Prisoner in action	-	-	1	-	
			Transferred to other units & Followers Surplus to India	-	-	21	5	
			New formations - Used for new formations	-	-	106	2	
			Strength of Dismounted Reinforcements 30/6/17	-	-	95	5	
			Reinforcements. From Base or other units	-	-	445-1	17	
			Reinforcements. Returned from Hospital	17	-	190	3	
			Horses and Mules	Horses	Mules	Horses	Mules	
			Casualties - Evacuated Lame & Sick	3	-	418✱	33	✱ Includes :- 8 wounded in action, 4 Killed —do—, 3 Missing —do—
			Casualties - Used for new formation	-	-	201	62	
			Casualties - Transferred Surplus	-	-	48	40	
			Reinforcements from Base & other units	-	-	585	116	

30/6/17

[signature] Lt Col.
Comdg 18th K.G.O. Lancers

A5834 Wt. W4973/M687 750,000 8/16 D. D. & L. Ltd. Forms/C.2118/13

Instructions regarding War Diaries and Intelligence Summaries are contained in F. S. Regs., Part II. and the Staff Manual respectively. Title pages will be prepared in manuscript.

WAR DIARY
or
INTELLIGENCE SUMMARY.
(Erase heading not required.)

18 Lancers. July 1917.

Army Form C. 2118.

ADJUTANT'S OFFICE No. 30 R Date 1/8/17. 18th K. G. O. LANCERS.

Place	Date	Hour	Summary of Events and Information	Remarks and references to Appendices
TERTRY – CAULAINCOURT	1st–11	7-17.	Squadron & Troop training.	ST QUENTIN SH. 18. 1:100000
	2-7-17.		Lts Royston & Forbes were both gazetted Captains (under the new 4 yrs rule) from 6-7-15 & 22-1-17 respectively. 2094 Dafadar Mohd Khan L.D. was awarded the I.O.M. Class II for great gallantry on the night of 14th–15th of last month. On that night some 200 shells fell in 2 hours of SOMERVILLE WOOD, when this NCO & his party were digging a post. They were compelled to withdraw & moved to take up a position outside the wood – on 2 occasions Mohd Khan returned to the wood to look for missing men, on the 2nd occasion he brought back the body of Sr Bostan Khan D Sqn who had been killed by the shell fire. His party was then relieved, but Mohd Khan remained with the relief till the following night.	
	3-7-17.		G.O.C. Divn inspected transport of the Bde. 18 Lancers transport was specially complimented on this occasion & "left nothing to be desired". Lt Paton I.A.R. is i/c of transport.	
	6-7-17.		Major W.L. rejoined the regiment from Cmdg 17th Cavr. Brigade. He is the first of our regular officers to rejoin in accordance with the latest order that all Indian Army officers serving in France with units other than their own, will rejoin their own units. A very good thing for us, who have been very short of squadron commanders since the departure of Col. Winspratt & Maj. Knightley. Maj. W.L. to D Sqn.	
	7-7-17		Capt Royston rejoined from R.F.C. 35th Squadron, where he had been since March. Posted to B Sqn.	
	11-7-17		Capt Brooke rejoined from 14 M.G. Squadron & posted to C Sqn.	
	12-7-17.		Regiment marched to CURCHILES – arriving 4.15 pm.	
	13-7-17.		Regiment marched to SUZANNE area – starting at 6 am & arriving at 9.15 am. Route via PERONNE.	AMIENS SH 17 1:100000
	14-7-17		Regiment marched to MORLANCOURT – starting at 8 am & arriving at 10.15 am. Via BRAY.	
	15-7-17.		Regiment marched to THIEVRES starting at 6 am & arriving at 10.30 am. Route via VADENCOURT – LEALVILLERS – AUTHIE.	LENS SH. 11. 1:100000.
	16-7-17		Regiment marched to new billeting area ROELLECOURT, starting at 6 am & arriving at 1.30 pm. Route via AMLOY – LUCHEUX – IVERGNY – REBREUVIETTE (watered & fed horses) – BUNEVILLE – TOUFFLIN – RICAMETZ.	
	17-7-17.		& following day spent in cleaning up etc. after the march. Men & horses quite ready for a day's rest.	

A5834 Wt. W4973/M687 750,000 8/16 D. D. & L. Ltd. Forms/C.2118/13

Instructions regarding War Diaries and Intelligence Summaries are contained in F. S. Regs., Part II. and the Staff Manual respectively. Title pages will be prepared in manuscript.

18 Lancers.

WAR DIARY
or
INTELLIGENCE SUMMARY.
(*Erase heading not required.*)

July 1917.

Army Form C. 2118.

Place	Date	Hour	Summary of Events and Information	Remarks and references to Appendices
ROELLECOURT	18.7.17 to 31.7.17		The last fortnight of the month was spent in squadron training as far as roads permitted – it being impossible to go off the roads, as the whole country side here is crops – a great change from the country round CAULAINCOURT, where the movement of squadrons was unrestricted. There has been a regimental & a brigade Tactical Exercise each week. Musketry carried out daily during the last week – ranges however not over 200x – Box Respirator Drills also carried out daily.	LENS SH. 11. 1/100000.
	20.7.17.		The following N.C.O.s were awarded the Indian Meritorious Service Medal for "Devotion to duty in the theatre of War". (5th C.D.O. 1541 of 19.7.17) No 1963 K.D. Mohd Ashraf Khan 4/A. No 1801 Daf: Mohd Khan L/c. No 2200 Daf: Jalak Sher L/D No 1759 Daf: Ali Mardan Khan R/A. No 2059 Daf Nur Khan L/c. & H.Q. Signalling Dafadar.	
	24.7.17		Capt. J. Gwatkin officially appointed Staff Captain. Amb. Bde. DAG. Pt II orders No 55 of 24.7.17.	
	27.7.17		Major C.Q. Risley rejoined the regiment from B/48th Bty R.F.A. posted to B Sqn.	
			Capt. N.M.E. Bray rejoined the regiment from "Special Duty" in Egypt – posted to A Sqn. He left Marseilles on 15th August 1916 for Egypt.	
			The following officers went on leave during the month – "ten days to England" – Lt. J.D.C. Fitzpatrick I.A.R. 14.7.17 – 24.7.17. Lt A.B. Williams I.A.R. 15.7.17 – 25.7.17. Lt R.L. Seager Herts Yeo: & Lt Reason I.M.S. from 19.7.17 – 28.7.17.	
			Maj. L. Lorimer 37th Lancers proceeded to India Office for return to India, on 6.7.17.	
			[signature]	

Instructions regarding War Diaries and Intelligence Summaries are contained in F. S. Regs., Part II. and the Staff Manual respectively. Title pages will be prepared in manuscript.

WAR DIARY
or
~~INTELLIGENCE SUMMARY.~~ 18th K.G.O. Lancers

(Erase heading not required.)

Army Form C. 2118.

July 1917.

Place	Date	Hour	Summary of Events and Information					Remarks and references to Appendices
			Indian Fighting men and Regl Public Followers	During July 17		13/11/14 to 31.7.17		
				Men	Followers	Men	Followers	
			Casualties - To Hospital Sick	10	-	404x	11	× Includes men evacuated temporarily to I.C.F.A as well as those to "out of Divisional area".
			— do — wounded	-	-	49⊗	-	⊗ Includes 2 men wounded at duty.
			Killed in action	-	-	10	-	
			Died of disease	-	-	9	-	
			Missing in action	-	-	1	-	
			Prisoner in action	-	-	1	-	
			Transferred to other units & Followers surplus to India	2	-	23	5	
			New formations - Used for new formation	-	-	106	2	
			Strength of Dismounted Reinforcements 31/7/17	-	-	95	5	
			Reinforcements. From Base or other Units	6	-1	444	16	
			Reinforcements. Returned from Hospital	9	-	199	3	
			Horses and Mules	Horses	Mules	Horses	Mules	
			Casualties. Evacuated Lame + Sick	13	-	431*	33	*. Includes: 8 wounded in action. 4 Killed in action. 3 missing in action.
			Casualties. Used for new formation	1	-	202	62	
			Casualties. Transferred Surplus	1	-	49	40	
			Reinforcements from Base & other units	14	-	599	116	

G. Corbyn Lt Colonel
Comdg 18th Lancers

D/31/7/17

A5834 Wt. W4973/M687 750,000 8/16 D. D. & L. Ltd. Forms/C.2118/13

Instructions regarding War Diaries and Intelligence Summaries are contained in F. S. Regs., Part II. and the Staff Manual respectively. Title pages will be prepared in manuscript.

WAR DIARY
or
INTELLIGENCE SUMMARY.
(Erase heading not required.)

Army Form C. 2118.

ADJUTANT'S OFFICE No. 31 R Date 1/9/17 19th K.G.O. LANCERS

Lancers — August 1917. (1)

Place	Date	Hour	Summary of Events and Information	Remarks and references to Appendices
ROELLECOURT	11.8.17		Maj. C.H. Marsh D.S.O. rejoined the regiment from the Base ROUEN & took up the duties of 2nd in command. He relinquished the rank of Lt. Col. on giving up command of 7th Bn Cameron Highlanders	LENS SH. 11. 1/100000.
	14.8.17		Maj. C.H. Howell joined the regiment & took over command of B Sqn. He has been in Mesopotamia since outbreak of war, with Patiala Lancers.	
	15.8.17		Divisional Horse Show. Regt took 1st prize in H.Qs. Wagons (Mules). 2nd prize. Troop horse. & 2nd prize "Pair of chargers" Lt Frazer.	
	16-8-17 19-8-17		We received 2 Lewis Guns for instructional purposes, the Bde wishing as many men as possible to be "fired" in the Gun. 340 men were so "fired" — The Gun is a much simpler weapon than our Hotchkiss Gun, & would appear to be much more effective. The difficulty of arming cavalry with the Lewis Gun is that it cannot stand the jolting that it would be subjected to at the Gallop etc. Whereas the Hotchkiss Gun is not so delicate a machine —	
	20-8-17		The Bde was inspected by G.O.C. Divn in F.S.M. order. The G.O.C. expressed himself very satisfied with turnout of the regiment —	
	22-8-17.		Major C.G. Risley D.S.O. proceeded to BAILLEUL to organize an Advanced Remount Depot —	
	Summary		Training throughout the month has been greatly curtailed by crops — & during the 1st 3 weeks was confined completely to Sqn tactical schemes along roads — These schemes comprised reconnaissance & inter communication — Towards the end of the month some of the crops were carried, & Sqn & troop drill became possible. There was a Regimental & a Brigade Tactical Exercise every week. During these Bde schemes, inter communication with aeroplanes was invariably practised. The following officers went on "Leave" leave to England during the month. Lt. C Benfield IAR. Lt Fletcher IAR. Lt Dauby IAR. Lt Frazer. Capt Denning. Capt Bray Lt. Col. Corbyn. Risaldar [illegible] awarded Order of B.I. II class Gazette of India 27/7/17 —	

[initials]

A5834 Wt. W4973/M687 750,000 8/16 D. D. & L. Ltd. Forms/C.2118/13

1219+1220

Instructions regarding War Diaries and Intelligence Summaries are contained in F. S. Regs., Part II. and the Staff Manual respectively. Title pages will be prepared in manuscript.

WAR DIARY
or
~~INTELLIGENCE SUMMARY.~~ 18th K.G.O. Lancers

(Erase heading not required.)

Army Form C. 2118.

August 1917.

Place	Date	Hour	Summary of Events and Information	Remarks and references to Appendices

Indian Fighting men and Regl Public Followers.	During Aug 17 Men	During Aug 17 Followers	13/11/14 to 31/8/17 Men	13/11/14 to 31/8/17 Followers
Casualties - To Hospital Sick	4	-	408 ×	11
— do — wounded	-	-	49 ⊗	-
Killed in action	-	-	10	-
Died of disease	-	-	9	-
Prisoner in action	-	-	2	-
Transferred to other Units & Followers Surplus to India	2	-	25	5
New formations. Used for new formations.	-	-	106	2
Strength of Dismounted Reinforcements on 31.8.17	101	4	.	.
Reinforcements. From Base or other Units	11	-	455	16
Reinforcements. Returned from Hospital	3	-	202	3
Horses & mules.	Horses	Mules	Horses	Mules
Casualties. Evacuated Lame & Sick	4	-	435 ※	33
Casualties. Used for new formation	4	-	206	62
Casualties. Transferred Surplus	-	-	49	40
Reinforcements from Base & other Units	6	-	605	116

× Includes men evacuated temporarily to I.C.F.A. as well as those to "out of Divisional Area".

⊗ Includes 2 men wounded at duty.

※ Includes.
8 wounded in action.
4 Killed in action.
3 missing in action.

C H Marsh Major
Comdg 18th Lancers.

31/8/17

A5834 Wt. W4973/M687 750,000 8/16 D. D. & L. Ltd. Forms/C.2118/13

Instructions regarding War Diaries and Intelligence Summaries are contained in F. S. Regs., Part II. and the Staff Manual respectively. Title pages will be prepared in manuscript.

WAR DIARY
or
INTELLIGENCE SUMMARY.
(Erase heading not required.)

18 Lancers   Septr 1917.

Serial No. ~~108~~ 180   Army Form C. 2118.

No. 32 B. Date 1/10/17 18th K. G. O. LANCERS

Place	Date	Hour	Summary of Events and Information	Remarks and references to Appendices
ROELLE-COURT	1.9.17		Cav. Corps Horse Show – Regt took 2nd prize for Limbered G.S. wagon – being the only regt in the Corps represented – all other wagons belonging to Reserve Parks.	LENS 1/100,000
	10.9.17		A draft of 30 men joined regt from Rouen. Same number of men sent to Marseilles in exchange on 14.9.17.	
	12.9.17		Regt rifle meeting 1st event 5 rounds in Box respirators at falling plates – Time 1 minute including putting on respirator. Team of 1 N.C.O. 7 men – won by C Sqn. 2nd event Snapshooting. 1 N.C.O. + 3 men – won by D Sqn – 3rd event. Rapid – 15 rds – 1 minute – Lying. Team of 1 I.O. + 16 O.R. won by B – 4th event Dismounted attack – 1 I.O. 16 men won by B Sqn – MONCHY LE BRETON Range. 5th event Hotchkiss Gun Competition won by B Sqn. Ranges up to 200x. Regt won Section tentpegging at Royal Canadian Dragoons Sports – PIERREMONT.	
	15.9.17		Jem. Alam Sher Khan 17 Cav. to Marseilles for return to 17th at their request. This I.O. has done very good work with regt.	
	16.9.17		Cav. Corps. Commander presented Medal ribbons to Ris. Dost Mohd. Order of B. India 2nd class. I.O.M. 2nd class – 1963 K Daf Mohd Ashraf Khan L/A, 1801 ... 1759 Daf Ali Mardan R/H 2094 Daf Mohd Khan L/D. 2200 Daf Falall Sher Khan L/D, Daf Mohd Khan L/C, 2059 Daf Nur Khan L/C (Signalling Instructor). – Indian Meritorious Service Medal.	
	15.9.17		2Lt H.C. Hodgson, unatt'd List. I.A. & L.M. WYRILL 2Lt joined regt from Rouen (on termination of short leave in England) & posted to A & B Sqns respectively. 2Lt Fitzpatrick slightly injured on range 15.9.17, to Hospital – returned 26.9.17.	
	17.9.17		2Lt. J.R.A. Cruickshank U. List. joined regt from Rouen (on termination short leave in England & posted to C Sqn.	
	22.9.17		British officer of the Day on duty in future, as well as I.O.	
	29.9.17		Inspection of Regt at Foot Drill & Manual Exercises, rifle, sword & lance by G.O.C. Bde. Lt Fraser proceeded on 28.9.17 to Rouen for duty as Instructor	

A5834 Wt. W4973/M687 750,000 8/16 D. D. & L. Ltd. Forms/C.2118/13

Army Form C. 2118.

(2)

Instructions regarding War Diaries and Intelligence Summaries are contained in F. S. Regs., Part II. and the Staff Manual respectively. Title pages will be prepared in manuscript.

WAR DIARY
or
INTELLIGENCE SUMMARY.
(Erase heading not required.)

Place	Date	Hour	Summary of Events and Information	Remarks and references to Appendices
Summary for Sept 1917			During the month, weather remarkably fine & country suited for movement of small bodies – One Bde parade weekly – including intercommunication practise and Route marches during which Box-respirators were worn for periods of about ½ hour. – One regimental day weekly including Tactical Exercises mounted, and practise of dismounted attacks – Squadron training including Riding school. Musketry, individual training mounted & dismounted, wearing of box respirators (up to 1 hour consecutively), by day & night, inspections of kit – Lecture by Medical Officer on preventive measures against lice, Baths once weekly, a German maxim gun allotted to squadrons for 1 day each & some men instructed in how to fire it – At the end of month 22 signallers inspected for classification – Result not yet notified Smeaton Tent-Pegging Cup run off on 30.9.17. won by R/D with 155 points. R/C tied with 153 points – (Teams of 1.0. 3 NCOs 16 OR per ½ sqn – two runs individual, one run section 4 points carry – 2 draw – 1 stand – points deducted for dropping lance, pace & dressing) – On a run off R/C made 47 pts & R/C 39 – Totals were L/C 148, L/A 119, R/A 106, L/D 105, R/B 93, L/B 93. – Officers, sisters & patients of 12 Staty Hospital were present, also 4 American officers – Following officers went to England on leave during month. Capt Reynolds Lt Abercrombie, Lt Bullock — Lt Dandy went to Corps Signals for a short course – Lieuts Blessé & Bullock to Bde & Divl Signals for Signalling Course. Lt Fulcher went to TERTRY (ST QUENTIN 1/100,000 Map) with Jem Khuda Baksh I. & then joined Indian Cav. Pioneer Battn, attd 4 Cav Divn, for purpose of building winter quarters & stables. Mess meeting held 23.9.17 – Decided that Regular officers with Regt pay Rs 4/- p.m. to Depot Mess Fund – All remaining subscns to be collected & used in France – Billiard Fund subscription to cease. Forge fund to continue as heretofore & be sent to Depot. Indian Army Order received during A5834 Wt. W4973/M687 750,000 8/16 D. D. & L. Ltd. Forms/C.2118/13 month granting extra batta as follows. R.H. Risaldars & Ressaidars Rs 20/- p.m., Dfrs & L/Dfrs Rs 8, Jemadars Rs 11/-, Sowars Rs 5/-. G.H.Q. also sanction increase of Establishment in (2 Ressaidars, 3 Jemadars, 12 Dafrs, 9 L Dfrs	France by

(3)

Army Form C. 2118.

Instructions regarding War Diaries and Intelligence Summaries are contained in F. S. Regs., Part II. and the Staff Manual respectively. Title pages will be prepared in manuscript.

WAR DIARY
or
~~INTELLIGENCE SUMMARY.~~
(Erase heading not required.)

18th K.G.O. Lancers
September 1917

Place	Date	Hour	Summary of Events and Information	During Septr 17 Men	During Septr 17 Followers	13/11/14 to 30/9/17 Men	13/11/14 to 30/9/17 Followers	Remarks and references to Appendices
			Indian Fighting men and Regl Public Followers:	Men	Followers	Men	Followers	
			Casualties - To Hospital Sick	6	1	414x	12	x Includes men evacuated temporarily to I.C.F.A. as well as those to "out of Divisional Area"
			— do — wounded	-	-	49⊗	-	⊗ Includes 2 men wounded at duty
			Killed in action	-	-	10	-	
			Died of disease	-	-	9	-	
			Prisoner in action	-	-	2	-	
			Transferred to other Units & Followers Surplus to India	-	-	25	5	
			New formations - Used for new formations	-	-	106	2	
			Strength of Dismounted Reinforcements on 30.9.17	91	4			
			Reinforcements - From Base or other Units	-8	1	447	17	
			Reinforcements - Returned from Hospital	2	-	204	3	
DAG 3rd Schelon ✓			Horses & Mules	Horses	Mules	Horses	Mules	
—			Casualties - Evacuated Lame & Sick	5	-	440x	33	x Includes - 8 wounded in action, 4 Killed — do —, 3 Missing — do —
C.G.S. Simla			Casualties - Used for New formation			206	62	
—			Casualties - Transferred Surplus			49	40	
Depot 18 L.			Reinforcements from Base & other Units	18	1	623	117	

[illegible] Lt Col
Comdg 18th Lancers.

[illegible] 30/9/17

A5834 Wt. W4973/M687 750,000 8/16 D. D. & L. Ltd. Forms/C.2118/13

Instructions regarding War Diaries and Intelligence Summaries are contained in F. S. Regs., Part II. and the Staff Manual respectively. Title pages will be prepared in manuscript.

WAR DIARY or INTELLIGENCE SUMMARY.

(*Erase heading not required.*)

18 Lancers. October.

Army Form C. 2118.

ADJUTANT'S OFFICE No. 33 B Date 1/11/17 18th K. G. O. LANCERS

180

Place	Date	Hour	Summary of Events and Information	Remarks and references to Appendices
RESLLE-COURT	1.10.17		Following officers with HQ & sqns. HQ. Lt Col Corbyn, Major C.H. Marsh, Capt Dening (Adjt) Lt Abercrombie (QrMr) - Lt Watson (R.T.O). Lt Reardon. M.O. A sqn. Capt Bray - Lt Williams, Lt Hodgson B sqn. Maj Howell. Capt Forbes, Lt Brayne, Lt Bletsoe, 2Lt Wyvill. C sqn. Capt Brooke - Lt Fulcher, 2Lt Bullock, Lt Cruikshank D sqn. Maj. Mills, Capt Royston, Lt Fitzpatrick. Lt Seager (Regt Intelligence Officer) - Lt Danby (Sig Offr) at Corps Signals. Major Risley with Cav. Corps Advd Remount Depot. Lt Fulcher with Ind Cav. Pioneer Battn. Lt Bletsoe & Bullock at Divl signals.	1/100,000 LENS
THIENNES	7.10.17	6am	Regt marched to THIENNES via PERNES, LILLERS, ST VENANT, (about 25 miles) - water & feed at 12 noon ~~on~~ on LA BASSEE Canal at HILLANDERIE about 1 mile N of BUSNES - arrived THIENNES about 3pm. Men all under cover. Horses in open fields. Weather very rainy, stormy & cold, high wind	1/100,000 HAZEBROUCK
	8.10.17 to 10.10.17		Billets Thiennes. Weather stormy & rainy. Lt Bullock rejoined from Course at Divl signals on 6.10.17. Lt ~~Da~~ Bletsoe on 10.10.17 on termination of leave. Lt Danby from Corps on 8.10.17 & left regt to become Bde Signalling Officer Ambala Bde on 8.10.17. 2Lt Bullock took over Regimental Signalling Officer the same day.	1/40,000 Sheet 27
	11.10.17	7.30am	March to WATOU area via Hazebrouck & Steenvorde - arrived about 1pm. Men in tents or trench covers. Horses out - with Horse Rugs & blankets. Bivouack in fields at Sheet 27 Belgium & France "K 15 b 38" -	1/100,000 HAZEBROUCK
WATOU (Belgium)	12.10.17 To 13.10.17		Bivouacks as above. Weather very wet, & cold, with a good deal of wind. Divn in readiness under 2nd Army. All infantry operations rendered very difficult owing to mud. Belgian Interpreter joined regt on 13.10.17	
HEURINGHEN	14.10.17	~~8.00am~~ 9am	March West to HEURINGHEM via Steenvorde. Staples - Ebblinghem. Billets for the night. Fine day -	1/100,000 LENS
FAUQUEMBERGUES	15.10.17	10.25am	March to FAUQUEMBERGUES - billets for the night - Fine day	
AUBIN ST VAAST BOUIN	16.10.17	9am	March to AUBIN ST VAAST via FRUGES - FRESSIN - Fine day. HQ Tpt B C & D Sqns in billets at AUBIN ST VAAST - A Sqn at BOUIN. Practically all horses & ~~[illegible]~~ all men under cover.	LENS ABBEVILLE

Instructions regarding War Diaries and Intelligence Summaries are contained in F. S. Regs., Part II. and the Staff Manual respectively. Title pages will be prepared in manuscript.

WAR DIARY
or
INTELLIGENCE SUMMARY.
(Erase heading not required.)

Army Form C. 2118.

(2)

Place	Date	Hour	Summary of Events and Information	Remarks and references to Appendices
AUBIN ST VAAST BOUIN.	17 10/17		Billets – Exercise horses – Cleaning up arms, equipment & saddlery. 2Lt. Hodgson proceeded on 16.10.17 to LETOUQUET for 14 days Hotchkiss Gun Course. Brig. Genl F. MAXWELL. V.C. C.S.I. D.S.O. killed in action on 21.9.17 YPRES neighbourhood. He was in command of 27th Infy Bde & after a successful attack was [illegible] position in the front line, when he was shot through the head by a sniper. Mr SMET – joined the regt as Belgian Interpreter vice the Interpreter who joined on 13.10.17 – (to 8 Hussars)	1/100,000 ABBEVILLE
and ECQUEM-ICOURT	17.10 to 31. 10/17		on 19.10.17 C sqn moved from Aubin to Ecquemicourt to make room for 1 sqn G.H.H. in Aubin. Period occupied in Squadron Training all horses & men under cover. Weather on the whole cold & wet with Bde day once a week. Belgian Interpreter left 25.10.17 Lt Hodgson returned 30.10.17. Major H.A.S. Keighley rejoined from Rouen 22.10.17 & became 2nd in C. Maj. C.H. Marsh – Ress. Sultan Ahmed Khan & 58 men (approx). from 19 10/17 onwards formed part of 5 Cavalry Battalion – under Anzac Corps – then Canadian Corps – Ypres area.	
Summary			Following officers went to England on 10 days leave. Capt Brooke – Lt Bletsoe, Lt Williams, Capt Imbes – Lt Seager. Maj. Hills – Maj Keighley. – Maj Risley. During month. box respirators worn frequently for periods of 1 hour or more. Lt Fulcher reports that work on stables & huts at TERTRY – CAULAINCOURT area proceeding well. – Major Risley in command of Cav. Corps Advd Remount Depot at Bailleul during the whole month.	

Instructions regarding War Diaries and Intelligence Summaries are contained in F. S. Regs., Part II. and the Staff Manual respectively. Title pages will be prepared in manuscript.

WAR DIARY or ~~INTELLIGENCE~~ SUMMARY. 18th K.G.O Lancers.

(Erase heading not required.)

Army Form C. 2118.

October 1917.

Place	Date	Hour	Summary of Events and Information					Remarks and references to Appendices
			Indian Fighting men and Regtl Public Followers	During Oct. 17		13/11/14 to 31/10/17		
				Men	Followers	Men	Followers	
			Casualties - To Hospital Sick	11	.	425 ×	12	× Includes men evacuated temporarily to I.C.F.A. as well as those to "out of Division area"
			— do — wounded	.	.	49 ⊗	-	⊗ Includes 2 men wounded at duty.
			Killed in action	.	.	10	-	
			Died of disease	.	.	9	-	
			Prisoner in action	.	.	2	-	
			Transferred to other units & followers Surplus to India	2	.	27	5	
			New formations. Used for new formations.	.	.	106	2	
			Strength of Dismounted Reinforcements on 31.10.17	101	5			
			Reinforcements from Base or other units	17	2	464	19	
			Reinforcements Returned from Hospital	4	.	208	3	
			Horses and Mules	Horses	Mules	Horses	Mules	
			Casualties - Evacuated lame & Sick	26	3	466 ×	36	× Includes:— 8 wounded in action, 4 Killed — do —, 3 Missing — do —
			Casualties - Used for new formation	4	.	210	62	
			Casualties - Transferred Surplus	-	.	49	40	
			Reinforcements from Base & other units	12	3	635	120	

[Signature] Lt Col.
Comdg 18th Lancers

31/10/17

Instructions regarding War Diaries and Intelligence Summaries are contained in F. S. Regs., Part II. and the Staff Manual respectively. Title pages will be prepared in manuscript.

WAR DIARY or INTELLIGENCE SUMMARY.

(Erase heading not required.)

18 Lancers — November 1917

Army Form C. 2118.

ADJUTANT'S OFFICE No. 34 R Date 8/12/17. 18th K. G. O. LANCERS.

180

Place	Date	Hour	Summary of Events and Information	Remarks and references to Appendices
AUBIN ST VAAST BOUIN ECQUEMICOURT	1.11.17		Following officers with HQ + Sqns - HQ. Lt Col Corbyn - Major Keighley - Capt Dening (Adjt) - Lt Abercrombie (QrMr) Lt Watson (R.T.O) Lt Reardon (M.O.) - 2Lt Mackie (2nd in C) (Sig Offr) - Major C.H. Marsh with 5 Cav Battn (YPRES area) - A sqn Capt Bray, Lt Williams - Lt Hodgson 2Lt Sandeman - B. Major Howell - Maj. Risley. Lt Brayne - 2Lt Wyrill - C. Capt Brooke - Capt Forbes - Lt Cruickshank D Major Mills - Capt Royston - Lt Seager - Lt Fitzpatrick - Lt Bullock + Lt Aletsoe at 5 Cav Divn Signal (R. intelligence offr) squadron. Lt Fulcher with Caulaincourt area with Ind Cav Pioneer Battn building winter quarters.	ABBEVILLE 1/100,000.
	to		2Lts Mackie + Sandeman joined from Base - Rouen on 2.11.17 Major Risley on the closing of Cav Corps advanced Remount Depot on 6.11.17 proceeded on 6 days leave to Paris	
	8.11.17		Weather - Cloudy with a certain amount of rain, but on the whole fine. Divl route march on 3.11.17. Parades. Squadron, Regtl + Bde training. Capt. BRAY mentioned in despatches on 14.9.17 for services in Egypt etc.	LENS 1/100,000
BARLY	9-11-17	8.35 am	Bonnieres to BARLY - where regt Marched via Hesdin - Conchy - sur - Canche - was billeted for the night. Very wet during the beginning portion of the march. 2Lt Bullock proceeded to Base - Rouen.	Amiens 1/100,000.
FRECHENCOURT	10-11-17	9 am	Marched via Doullens - Beauquesne - Toutencourt - Contay to FRECHENCOURT where regt was billeted for night. Day cold + dull - but no actual rain.	
SUZANNE	11-11-17	3pm	Marched via Franvillers - Buire sur L'ancre - Ville - sous - Corbie - Morlancourt - Bray - Suzanne to Camp 17 just N.E. of Suzanne - arrived between 8-9 pm. Dark at 5 p.m. Horses Fine day + night. + men in Govt stables + Adrian huts.	St Quentin 1/100,000
BRUSLE	12-11-17	3.45pm	Marched via Eclusier - Herbecourt - Biaches - Peronne - Doingt - Cartigny to BRUSLE. Regt in huts + Govt stables Thick mist - Arrived about 8pm	

A5834 Wt. W4973 M687 750,000 8/16 D. D. & L. Ltd. Forms/C.2118/13.

Army Form C. 2118.

(2)

Instructions regarding War Diaries and Intelligence Summaries are contained in F. S. Regs., Part II. and the Staff Manual respectively. Title Pages will be prepared in manuscript.

WAR DIARY
or
INTELLIGENCE SUMMARY

(Erase heading not required.)

Place	Date	Hour	Summary of Events and Information	Remarks and references to Appendices
BRUSLE	13.11.17		Misty day – exercise horses & dismounted parades.	
	14.11.17		——— do ——— – Maj. Risley rejoined from leave in Paris	
	15.11.17		Fine day. Exercise horses at dusk to prevent them being seen. Dismounted parades during day	
	16.11.17		Horses exercised at stated hours between 10 am & 2 pm. Dismounted Parades	
	17.11.17		Ress. Sultan Ahmed Khan & 57 men of 5 Cav Battn rejoined & Major Marsh by bus from Ypres area on night 17/18th. – weather cloudy – but no rain.	
	19.11.17		Orders received for Regt to march to FINS area – with a view to operations including the capture of Cambrai. Regt to march at 1.45 am on 20th – Officers as follows. Col Corbyn – Capt Deering (Adjt) Lt Seager (Intelligence) Lt Reardon Capt Forbes (QM?) – Lt Macnie (Signals) (M.O.) Lt Watson (R.T.O.) – A Capt Bray Lt Williams B – Maj Howell – Capt Royston Lt Brown C – Capt Brown Lt Gleeson D Maj Wills – Div Liaison officer Maj Keighley. Bde Galloper Lt Hodgson. Dismtd Men. Major Risley Lt Welt. Maj Marsh & Lt Wynne. On leave in France Lt Fulcher 2Lt Crukshank Lt Sandeman – Ind Cav Pioneer Battn Lt Fitzpatrick. B echelon Lt Abercrombie – also Dismtd Men at Bouzly. A echelon to be Divisionalized. 4 Sqn L.G. & wagons divided into two parts. A.1. Hotchkiss Gun wagon, HQ medical limber – A2, Mess cart – cook cart – watercart – Bicyclists – cook, water & mess carts & cooks under Lt Watson proceeded to N.W. corner of BOIS DESSART so as to have a hot meal ready on Regts arrival.	

2449 Wt. W14957/M90 750,000 1/16 J.B.C. & A. Forms/C.2118/12.

Instructions regarding War Diaries and Intelligence Summaries are contained in F. S. Regs., Part II. and the Staff Manual respectively. Title Pages will be prepared in manuscript.

WAR DIARY
or
INTELLIGENCE SUMMARY
(Erase heading not required.)

18 Lancers.

Army Form C. 2118.

(3)

Place	Date	Hour	Summary of Events and Information	Remarks and references to Appendices
~~20/11~~	20/11/17	1.45 am	Regt marched (in Bde) via BOUCLY – TINCOURT – LONGUAVESNES – LIERAMONT – NURLU – EQUANCOURT – FINS to field N.W. of BOIS DESSART, arriving at 6.24 am – Zero hour was 6.20 am – Tanks, who had previously been concealed in Bois Dessart, are said to have advanced from point 1000x short of enemy's front line at Zero less 10 minutes – no previous bombardment, & the one at Zero hour. 380 tanks said to be taking part. Regt off saddled & watered – was saddled up again & ready to move at 9 a.m. Intention was when infantry took the last German line from ~~Crevecourt~~ – between Rumilly & Masnieres – Escaut Canal W of MARCOING, which they hoped to do by 12 noon – Canadian Bde was to cross at Masnieres – seize high ground Niergnies – Awoingt, thence the high ground Ramillies – Thun, guarding crossing of Escaut Canal N.E. of Cambrai. Secbd Bde was to cross at Marcoing & move in rear of Canadian Cav Bde, pass through it W of Escaut Canal & seize crossings over La Sensee Canal & River between Aubencheul – Paillencourt. Ambala Bde in Divl reserve, to follow Secbd. All railways & roads from SE, E, NE & N towards Cambrai to be cut or blocked, to isolate Cambrai. At 11.50 a.m. 5 Cav Divn were ordered to push patrols out from Dessart Wood & keep touch with infy & act if opportunity offered. At about 12 noon regt was ordered to water – as this was completed orders were received to set	Map St Quentin 1/100,000 Valenciennes 1/100,000

2449 Wt. W14957/M90 750,000 1/16 J.B.C. & A. Forms/C.2118/12.

Instructions regarding War Diaries and Intelligence Summaries are contained in F. S. Regs., Part II. and the Staff Manual respectively. Title Pages will be prepared in manuscript.

WAR DIARY
or
INTELLIGENCE SUMMARY
(Erase heading not required.)

Army Form C. 2118.

(4)

W Lancers

Place	Date	Hour	Summary of Events and Information	Remarks and references to Appendices
E of Bois Couillet	20/10/17		ready at once to move off. Regt moved off about 1.30 pm, (being leading regt of Bde) – in column of troops via B de Gouzeaucourt through Villers-Plouich to E slopes of Villers-Plouich – Marcoing Valley about ½ mile SE of B of BOIS COUILLET – Secbd Bde was in front towards Marcoing. A patrol of 6 (even) under Lt Bletsoe sent on to Marcoing to gain touch with Secbd Bde. This was about 3 pm. Shortly after GOC Bde ordered regt to move up towards Marcoing, but after proceeding about ¼ mile Regt was ordered back by Divl Comdr. Lt Bletsoe returned with information that a portion of 7 DG's were towards NOYELLES, some in Marcoing – remainder of Bde just outside (S.W. of) Marcoing. About 4.15 pm 1 troop D sqn with Capt Royston ordered to find out the situation in front, as Secbd Bde were reported to be moving on NIERGNIES – They returned in about 3/4 hr to report that situation was more or less as Lt Bletsoe had previously reported. It was then dark. The day had been dull & misty. Regt bivouacked for the night where it was (along the Hindenburg ~~Line~~ Line map 1/40,000 57 B square R 2 d.) Night was wet – cold & windy. 1 horse strayed during the night. A echelon Part 1 – which consisted of 4 sqn limbered wagons – 1 H. Gun L.G.S. wagon, under Lt Watson came up evening 20th – A.2 Echelon – Mess, Cook, water carts, oat L.G.S. wagons & HQ L.G.S. wagon came up morning 21st – The men had chupatties etc cooked for them on morning 20th at Bois Dessart – Also had 2 iron rations, one in haversack – one in wallets, & a 3rd iron ration was carried on L.G.S. wagons of squadrons. Horses started with both nosebags full (about 12 lbs) at Bois Dessart. 4½ lbs oats on L.G.S. wagons A1 Echelon per horse.	Valenciennes 1/100,000
	21/11/17			

2449 Wt. W14957/M90 750,000 1/16 J.B.C. & A. Forms/C.2118/12.

Instructions regarding War Diaries and Intelligence Summaries are contained in F. S. Regs., Part II. and the Staff Manual respectively. Title pages will be prepared in manuscript.

WAR DIARY
or
INTELLIGENCE SUMMARY.
(*Erase heading not required.*)

18 Lancers.

Army Form C. 2118.

(5)

Place	Date	Hour	Summary of Events and Information	Remarks and references to Appendices
			6½ lbs per horse on A2 Echelon. – This 8 lbs drawn & put in nosebags on 21st. – also iron ration on A echelon drawn & consumed on 21st. 21st was cold, rainy & misty. No water for horses except from shell holes – & men from water bottles & cart. Horses were saddled up from dawn onwards – but were able to be grazed, on the wet grass. No hostile shelling in the vicinity – About 3.30 p.m. Bde ordered to reinforce & be attached to 1st Cav Divn who were being counter attacked in ~~Cantaing~~ Noyelles – Cantaing – Anneux vicinity. Proceeded in sections along road to MARCOING – Column was not shelled or fired on – probably owing to mist & enemy's attention being on their immediate front line. Marcoing village very little damaged.	1/100,000 Valenciennes
RIBECOURT			~~Horses~~ From Marcoing proceeded to RIBECOURT & bivouacked the night just W of it, in reserve. No opportunity to water horses.	
	22/11/17	8.30 am	Bde ordered to rejoin ~~its~~ 5 Cav Divn. marched 8.30 a.m. via Trescault – Metz-en-Couture to N.W of FINS arrived about 11 am. Horses watered, for 1st time since 12 noon on 20th except for a small amount from shell holes on 21st. One iron ration & 6 lbs oats consumed, leaving one iron ration & 6 lbs per man & horse. Horses & men very well – in spite of cold & wet & shortage of hay for horses & water for horses. At 1.30 pm moved to EQUANCOURT – bivouacked night – Hay & oats & 1 days iron ration for 23rd received.	1/100,000 Lens
	23/11/17	6.30 am.	marched 6.30 am via Etricourt – Moislains – Clery – Maricourt – Bray to billets at CHIPILLY – arriving about 12.30 pm. All horses & men under cover.	Amiens

Instructions regarding War Diaries and Intelligence Summaries are contained in F. S. Regs., Part II. and the Staff Manual respectively. Title pages will be prepared in manuscript.

(6)

Army Form C. 2118.

WAR DIARY
or
INTELLIGENCE SUMMARY.
(Erase heading not required.)

Place	Date	Hour	Summary of Events and Information	Remarks and references to Appendices
CHIPILLY	24/11/17 25/11/17		Billets - Regt on ½ hours notice to move. Since leaving BRUSLE, following total Casualties - Men. 2 evacuated sick. Horses - Strayed at Night 1 (one) Evacuated sick. B echelon rejoined about 6.30 pm on 25th having left BOUCLY at 8.30. a. m. ½ hours notice cancelled evening of 25th.	1/100,000 Amiens St Quentin
	26/11/17		Billets - Lts Abercrombie & Fulcher rejoined from Paris leave. Tem Tapat Singh & Mehir Singh 39th to England on leave - also Lt Cruickshank, Conducting a party of 10s over	
	27/11/17	8.30am	Marched via PROYART - ESTREES - VILLERS CARBONNEL - MONS-EN-CHAUSSEE - TERTRY to lines built for winter quarters just W of Caulaincourt. - These quarters had been previously occupied by another British Cav Divn & then by French troops and were left in a filthy state.	
	28/11/17 29/11/17		occupied in cleaning up huts etc - making wind screens to stables & in improving the quarters - 2Lt Seager proceeded to England for interview with view to a permanent commission in Indian Army, on 29-11-17	
	30/11/17		About 9 am Regt was ordered to get ready to move at once - All A & B echelon waggons were unpacked & there was no idea of any move as Regt had been ordered to take over trenches E of Vadencourt on night 1/2 Decr & arrangements were in progress for this. About 9.30 am orders were received to concentrate as soon as possible at X roads 1000x E of ESTREES - this was done by about 11 am. From that point Regt trotted via Hancourt - Roisel - Villers Faucon to valley just W of Ste Emilie Sugar Factory - There was no walk until reaching Villers-Faucon - which was reached about 12 noon. after a short halt, during which a German aeroplane came over at a low altitude, but did not fire except at a hostile balloon - orders were received for	

A5834 Wt. W4973 M687 750,000 8/16 D. D. & L. Ltd. Forms/C.2118/13.

Instructions regarding War Diaries and Intelligence Summaries are contained in F. S. Regs., Part II. and the Staff Manual respectively. Title pages will be prepared in manuscript.

WAR DIARY
or
INTELLIGENCE SUMMARY. 18 Lancers
(Erase heading not required.)

Army Form C. 2118.

(7)

Place	Date	Hour	Summary of Events and Information	Remarks and references to Appendices
			8th Hussars to move W of EPEHY on Vaucelette Farm – the FM about 1½	1/100,000
			miles due N of PEIZIERES and drive any of the enemy encountered	Valenciennes
			to the N & NE – The enemy had broken through our trench system	
Sunken			and had taken Villers-Guislain, Gonnelieu & Gouzeaucourt – A	
road	30/		Counterattack by the Guards drove them out of Gouzeaucourt today (30th) –	
near	11/		9th H.H. M.G. & 18th were to follow 8th Hrs – It was about 1.15 pm when	
V of	17		Regt moved off from the Ste Emilie valley in rear of H. Guns.	
VILLERS			Moved up to line of PEIZIERE – HEUDICOURT Rlwy – where there was a halt:	
GUISLAIN			8th Hrs were seen galloping over the crest between (Vaucelette) FM & Revelon.	
			9th Horse were sent off to help 8th Hrs & when it got dark about	
		4pm	4pm – 9H & 8th Hrs were holding the sunken road running from	
			Gouzeaucourt through V of Villers Guislain to PEIZIERE, from the V of Villers-	
			Guislain for some 300–400x to the Northwards. The enemy were holding	
			the Gouzeaucourt – Peiziere Rlwy & Gauche Wood in some strength	
		to	& the 8th Hrs were unable to dislodge them. During this time Regt	
			Bde was in reserve in the valley near the FA of SUGAR FACTY, NE of	
			Heudicourt – Between 7–9pm Regt was ordered to move up dismounted	
		7–9pm	and relieve 8th Hrs, who were at the South end of the sunken road, on	
			right of 9H, & to reconnoitre B. GAUCHE with a view to	
		to	attacking it at dawn on 1st Dec., if ordered by Bde to do so.	
			Regt relieved 8th Hrs – B sqn being immediately S of 9th H & D sqn	
		midnight	on their right. 2 MG's of 14th MG sqn were on D's right – some of the	
			Queen's were found on the right rear (or S.W.) of D sqn – A & C sqns & 2 MG's	
			of 14th MG sqn were in reserve, along a bank	
			about 100x W of the sunken road. During the night they dug a shallow	
			communicating trench up to the sunken road.	

(A7092) Wt W12839/M1293 750,000 1/17 D. D. & L., Ltd. Forms/C.2118/14.

Instructions regarding War Diaries and Intelligence Summaries are contained in F. S. Regs., Part II. and the Staff Manual respectively. Title pages will be prepared in manuscript.

Army Form C. 2118. (8)

WAR DIARY
or
~~INTELLIGENCE SUMMARY.~~ 18th K. G. O. Lancers.

(Erase heading not required.)

November 1917.

Place	Date	Hour	Summary of Events and Information	During November 17. Men	During November 17. Followers	13/11/14 to 30/11/17 Men	13/11/14 to 30/11/17 Followers		Remarks and references to Appendices
			Indian fighting men and Regtl Public Followers.	Men	Followers	Men	Followers		
			Casualties. To Hospital sick	9	-	434x	12	x Includes men evacuated temporarily to I. C. F. A as well as those to "out of Division area".	
			— do — wounded	1	-	50⊗	-	⊗ Includes 2 men wounded (at duty). – The man wounded this month was with 5th Cav Battn.	
			Killed in action	-	-	10	-		
			Died of diseases	-	-	9	-		
			Prisoner in action	-	-	2	-		
			Transferred to other units & followers surplus to India.	1 ✱	-	28	5	✱ Divl Gas N.C.O	
			New formations. Used for new formations.	-	-	106	2		
			Strength of dismounted Reinforcements on 30.11.17	89	7	-	-		
			Reinforcements. From Base or other units	-3 ✱	2	461	21	✱ [1 came up, 4 went down]	
			Returned from Hospital.	4	-	212	3		
			Horses & Mules.	Horses	Mules	Horses	Mules		
			Casualties. Evacuated lame & sick	11	-	477✱	36	✱ Includes:— 8 wounded in action, 4 killed — do —, 3 missing — do —, 2 lost during operations.	
			Used for new formation	-	-	210	62		
			Transferred surplus.	-	-	49	40		
			Reinforcements from Base & other units.	15	-	650	120		

V. A. S. Keighley Major
Comdg 18th Lancers.

30.11.17

(A7092) Wt W12839/M1293 75,000 1/17. D. D. & L., Ltd. Forms/C.2118/14.

Instructions regarding War Diaries and Intelligence Summaries are contained in F. S. Regs., Part II. and the Staff Manual respectively. Title pages will be prepared in manuscript.

Army Form C. 2118.

(1)

180.

WAR DIARY or INTELLIGENCE SUMMARY.

(Erase heading not required.)

18 Lancers Dec 1917

Place	Date	Hour	Summary of Events and Information	Remarks and references to Appendices
			Officers were as follows at midnight 30 Nov/1st Dec:– Lt Col Corbyn – 2nd in C. attd to 5 Cav Divn as liaison officer – Major Keighley – Adjt Capt Dening. QrM: Lt Abercrombie Signalling Off. Lt Bleloc – Intelligence officer Lt Sandeman – Regt Transport officer (with A echelon) Lt Watson – A sqn. Capt Bray, Lt Williams. B sqn Maj. Howell. Lt Brague. C sqn. Capt Brooke. Lt Fulcher. D sqn. Maj. Mills. Capt Royston – Lt Yapsill was with A2 Echelon. Maj. Marsh, Capt Forbes with B echelon – Maj Risley with Dismounted Men – {Lts Crookshank & Mackie in England – Lts Scafes} Lt Fitzpatrick with Ind. Cav. Pioneer Batt^n at Brie. Lt Hodgson was with Ambala Bde as galloper.	Sheet 57C 1/40,000.
Sunken road. W 6 c	Midnight 30/1st Dec.		The orders received from Ambala Bde at 7 pm on 30/11/17 were to relieve 8th Hussars in the sunken road, at W 6 c, on the South of G.H.Q. & (a) To reconnoitre Gauche Wood (b) To occupy it, if it was not held (c) To prepare to attack it at dawn on receipt of further orders. – Regt moved up dismounted, about 250 strong from vicinity of W 17 central – Hotchkiss guns, & entrenching tools were taken up on pack animals. 8th Hussars were relieved about midnight. Night was cold dark – with a little rain. Dispositions were then found to be as under. – (a) BOIS GAUCHE & ground between its W edge and Gouzeaucourt / Peiziere railway inclusive held strongly by enemy. whose very lights were falling in the sunken road – (b) Our own troops – a detachment of STRATHCONAS HORSE (Canadian Cav Bde) were some 100 x SW of Chapel Crossing – with whom touch was obtained & maintained by patrols during the night – about W 11 b central was a detachment of the Queens – from between there & W 12 a 38 2 M.G's from 14th M.G. Sqn (attd to 18 Lancers), thence to about W 6 c 96, D & B squadrons 18 Lancers along the sunken road	

(A7092) Wt W12839/M1293 75,000 1/17. D. D. & L., Ltd. Forms/C.2118/14.

Instructions regarding War Diaries and Intelligence Summaries are contained in F. S. Regs., Part II. and the Staff Manual respectively. Title pages will be prepared in manuscript.

WAR DIARY
or
INTELLIGENCE SUMMARY.
(Erase heading not required.)

18 Lancers

(2)

Army Form C. 2118.

Place	Date	Hour	Summary of Events and Information	Remarks and references to Appendices
			road — thence 3 sqdns & 1 troop 9 Horse to about W 6 b 51 — 2 squadrons of 20th Hussars, north of 9 H, then 3 Coys of Middlesex — & Coldstream Guards towards Gouzeaucourt. Regt. had [illegible] A & C Sqns & 2 MG's in support along a bank about 100x W of the sunken road. These two squadrons from about 12.30 to 2 am dug a shallow communicating trench across the exposed portion of ground between this bank & sunken road — Water cart came up about 2 am & men's water bottles were refilled — No rations received, so men were ordered to consume their iron ration on 1st — all animals except 3 signallers horses sent back to led horses in valley about 1000x S.W. of Revelon near Bde H.Q. —	
	1 Dec.	3 am	Orders received from Ambala Bde as follows — 8 Tanks from Revelon will cross the line W12 & 18 not later than 6.30 am this morning to attack Bois Gauche — 6 other Tanks will cross the line further south at same time to attack Villers Guislain & will be supported by Lucknow Cav Bde — Guards Bde from Gouzeaucourt will attack during morning to secure the ridge E of Gouzeaucourt — "A" Bty RCHA will fire on W. edge of Bois Gauche in R26, 31 & 32 from 6.30 am to 6.45 am — 6.45 am to 7 am on E. edge of B. Gauche from 7 am onwards on 22 Ravine. — At 6.45 am 18 Lancers will make a dismounted attack on Gauche Wood which will be occupied and held — 4 M.G. [illegible] will cooperate. — [illegible]	

Instructions regarding War Diaries and Intelligence Summaries are contained in F. S. Regs., Part II. and the Staff Manual respectively. Title pages will be prepared in manuscript.

WAR DIARY or INTELLIGENCE SUMMARY.

(Erase heading not required.)

(3)

Army Form C. 2118.

Place	Date	Hour	Summary of Events and Information	Remarks and references to Appendices
			C.O. decided to attack as under.	

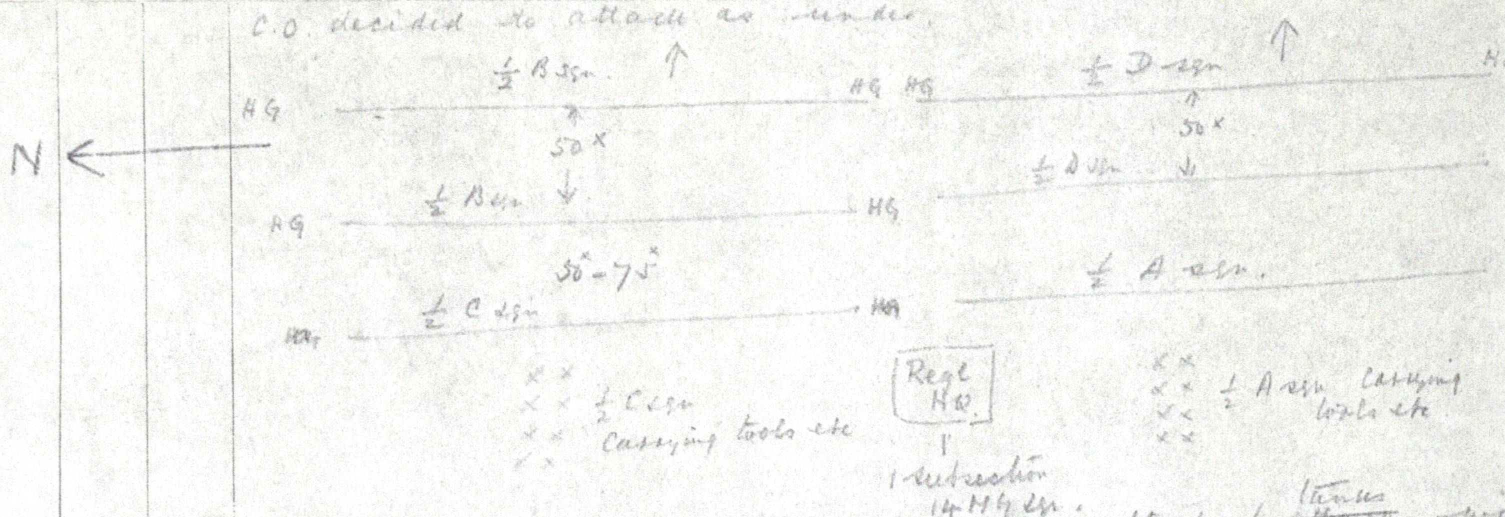

Notes

10 signallers with Regt HQ

3 signallers with 3 horses as relay post 100x W of sunken road near a small spinney, 21, about W6c central

Place	Date	Hour	Summary of Events and Information	Remarks and references to Appendices
	1st	6 am	Message received from Ambala Bde that 6 ~~attacks~~ tanks will attack Gauche Wood 6.30 am – 8 Tanks & Guards attacking Gauche Wood from N at same time.	
		6.40 am	No sign of the tanks – D squadron's column leading wave were lying along the ground some 20–25x E of the sunken road ready to push forward with the tanks – came under heavy rifle & M.G. fire – especially from M.G's at Chapel Crossing – 3 Hotchkiss guns + 12 men, out of 25 & Capt Royston casualties. M.G. officer & man from the subsection on right flank of D sqn killed. As D sqn were absolutely enfiladed from Chapel Crossing – C.O. decided to alter his plan of attack & push forward from B sqn front, in column of ½ squadrons until across the Gouzeaucourt/Peizières railway. This entailed	

(A7092). Wt W12539/M1293 75,000. 1/17. D. D. & L., Ltd. Forms/C.2118/14.

Instructions regarding War Diaries and Intelligence Summaries are contained in F. S. Regs., Part II. and the Staff Manual respectively. Title pages will be prepared in manuscript.

WAR DIARY
or
INTELLIGENCE SUMMARY.
(Erase heading not required.)

Army Form C. 2118.

(4)

Place	Date	Hour	Summary of Events and Information	Remarks and references to Appendices
			entailed D squadron being withdrawn into the sunken road & moved North in rear of B. Meanwhile C & A squadrons had closed up with the sunken road.	
		7.15 AM	Leading Tanks arrived - but seemed uncertain of their direction. Between 7.15 & 7.30 am [illegible] debouched & moved NE towards X 1 central. Between 7.15 & 7.30 am ... B squadron gained the railway line, covered from sunken road - B squadron gained the railway line, covered by fire from D sqn - Right flank was checked by hostile M.G. fire,	
		7.30 am	which action by right flank Hotchkiss Detachment enabled advance to continue. B sqn then advanced E, taking prisoners from direction of X 7 central & then came in touch with the remains of about 2 Coys Grenadiers Guards who had come through the centre of Gauche Wood from Gouzeaucourt. The squadron then moved up to about X 1 d 55 when it was ordered into reserve. In the meanwhile D squadron had moved up on the N flank of B sqn, entered the W edge of Gauche Wood where about 12 M Guns, 4 small trench mortars, some wounded & unwounded prisoners were taken. In the centre of the wood two guardsmen were met, who said that they were held up on E edge of wood, the squadron worked along the northern edge of the wood without opposition & by 8.30 am had taken up a line of trench running N & S in X 2 c 58 commanding 22 Ravine, in which some of the 2nd Grenadiers were found (in the X 2 c 58 trench) C sqn moved in rear of A sqn & eventually prolonged D sqns left in the trench X 2 c 54 - coming up there about 9.10 am - coming into a hostile barrage along the E edge of the wood & suffering some casualties - A squadron in the meantime, who had left the sunken road in rear of D, had been ordered to watch the right or Southern	

Army Form C. 2118.

(5)

No. .... B

Date ....

18th K. G. O. LANCERS

WAR DIARY
or
INTELLIGENCE SUMMARY.
(Erase heading not required.)

18 Lancers

Instructions regarding War Diaries and Intelligence Summaries are contained in F. S. Regs., Part II. and the Staff Manual respectively. Title pages will be prepared in manuscript.

Place	Date	Hour	Summary of Events and Information	Remarks and references to Appendices
			flank & after crossing the railway, when B sqn turned NE, A squadron moved up on their flank, taking some prisoners from the {South SE} + meeting the Grenadier Guards coming out of the wood - the squadron then moved NE into the wood, coming under fire from a hostile aeroplane, but suffering no casualties, + entrenched itself across the SE corner of wood.	
		8.30 am	At 8.30 am the situation was therefore as follows - Guards from about X7 b 55 to the wood at X1 d 81 - thence A squadron to X2 c 32 - Guards + D sqn in trench outside E face of Gauche Wood - both flanks were exposed & no troops were known of on either side -	
		8.40. am	2 HG's 14 MG squadron C squadron moved up on N flank of D - (single front reserve) were sent up to cover the right flank of the Guards about X7 central. Tanks were requested to withdraw from the wood as they were drawing heavy shell fire - officer in command of the Grenadiers was met & arrangements coordinated - the 18th & Guards were very mixed up - Guards only had 2 officers left - several of their parties were taken over by officers of the regt, at O.C. Guards request. Report on dispositions sent to Ambala Bde by runner to the sunken road -	
		8.50 am	Copse. No. 2 where Bde HQ was. thence by mounted signaller to Genin Well. At same time the 2 remaining subsections of 14 MG sqn asked for from sunken road. Casualties up to this point about 30. Shortage of Stretcher bearers was very evident - + Bde informed of this. About 40 prisoners taken, 2 batches sent back, remainder sent in 2's + 3's with wounded men - 8-12 MG's both light + heavy pattern, 4 small trench mortars (Granatenwerfer) taken in	

Instructions regarding War Diaries and Intelligence Summaries are contained in F. S. Regs., Part II. and the Staff Manual respectively. Title pages will be prepared in manuscript.

WAR DIARY
or
INTELLIGENCE SUMMARY.
(*Erase heading not required.*)

Army Form C. 2118.

6

Place	Date	Hour	Summary of Events and Information	Remarks and references to Appendices
			Taken in S.W. of Gauche Wood. — A gun at about X1d 4 9 — of these 2 MG's were brought back on relief at night — Men were too tired to bring any more in the dark. Prisoners were of 145 Infy Regt of 34th Divn (& a few of 30 I R of same divn?) — They referred to the Regt as the "Blue Infantry" presumably owing to our blue Kamarbands. The two M.G's above were later returned to ordnance, marked, & claimed as trophies — A claim was also submitted for 2 of the granatenwerfer but they were not actually brought in.	
			During the advance there was a good deal of shell fire — M.G & rifle fire were chiefly from Villers Guislain & from our S.E. & South.	
		8.50 AM	Regt HQ established in a shell hole about X2c12. B Sqn in reserve about 00 of GAUCHE WOOD — 1 subsection 14 M.G. Sqn came up during the morning & was kept in reserve in shell holes about 50x from Regt HQ.	
		11.30 AM	Message received from C sqn that large parties of enemy were digging in Twenty two Ravine at R32d and X2b, others crossing from Villers Guislain and others appear to be working round between Gonnelieu & Gouzeaucourt.	
		11.35 AM	Bde informed & asked to shell 22 Ravine. Absence of artillery observing officer was much felt throughout the rest of the day. It would not have been difficult to run out a wire from Revelon — A line was run up from Grenadier Battn HQ during the day.	
		[illegible] AM	During the morning the wounded were collected in a little hollow about 100x N of Regt HQ — No S.B's left. Aid post was at Sunken road. Sub Asst Surgeon sent for & came up. Also S.B's from 9 Horse. The wounded were then cleared — but there was a great dearth of Stretchers & S.B's, many Guardsmen being carried down by our S.B's.	

(A7092). Wt W12839/M1293 75,000. 1/17. D.D. & L., Ltd. Forms/C.2118/14.

(7)

Army Form C. 2118.

Instructions regarding War Diaries and Intelligence Summaries are contained in F. S. Regs., Part II, and the Staff Manual respectively. Title pages will be prepared in manuscript.

WAR DIARY
or
INTELLIGENCE SUMMARY.

(*Erase heading not required.*) 18 Lancers

Date	Hour	Hour, Date, Place. / Summary of Events and Information.	Remarks and references to Appendices
	2.30 pm	Heavy shelling with light calibre guns commenced, shell falling about the od of GAUCHE WOOD – recognized as our own shell, falling very short by the direction they came from & their rebound burst.	
	2.50 pm	Message received from Ambala Bde that "4th Cav Divn attack Villers Guislain Ridge at 3 pm from X 17a to X 8 d; with Canadian Cav Bde on their left, with object of seizing ground between S.E. Corner of Gauche Wood & the houses X 8 b 27. Bombardment commences 2.30 pm. Lifts 3 pm".	
	3.0 pm	Enemy snipers very active against S.E. Corner of Gauche Wood. Our barrage lifted to just beyond trench line held by C & D sqns – still very short. Before this, reports had been received that 7 DG's & Coldstreams were on left flank of C sqn & that the left flank was now secure. Ambala Bde asked to send up wire & pickets after dark.	
	4.15 pm	B sqn ordered to relieve D sqn, latter to come into reserve – Gauche Wood heavily shelled chiefly by 5.9s from about 3.45 to 4.45 pm.	
	4.30 pm	Col Corbyn killed, Lt Aletsoe wounded, Lt Sandeman severely shaken by a shell which landed on Regtl H.Q. Maj Howell informed as B sqn were going up & assumed command. Regtl report centre established at X 1 d 44, in a shell-hole.	
	4.15 to 4.45 pm	Men from Strathcona's Horse collecting in S.E. Corner of wood & taken over by C & A sqn – these men came up through S portion of wood, apparently unable to move outside.	
	About 5 pm	D sqn joined reserve on relief by B sqn. – During the day 1 Coy Coldstream Guards & 1 sqn 7 DG's (who dug a trench line occupied by Guards at dusk), came up. Also 1 sqn 9 Horse went on right flank X 7 c central direction – Our squadrons also had consolidated – dispositions & commands were coordinated & all preparations made against a hostile counterattack which would have met with a very warm reception, but no attack was attempted by the enemy. About 3 pm an enemy S.A. Ammn Dump caught fire in Villers Guislain & burnt out. A. B & D sqns were fired on by hostile aeroplanes at different times & the fire was returned – 1 Casualty	

(8)

Army Form C. 2118.

Instructions regarding War Diaries and Intelligence Summaries are contained in F. S. Regs., Part II, and the Staff Manual respectively. Title pages will be prepared in manuscript.

WAR DIARY
or
INTELLIGENCE SUMMARY.

(*Erase heading not required.*) 18 Lancers.

Date	Hour, ~~Date, Place.~~	Summary of Events and Information.	Remarks and references to Appendices
		1 Casualty occurred in D squadron from the aeroplane fire –	
1/12/17	9pm	message received from Ambala Bde that regt would be relieved by 34th & 20th	
		Horse. S.A. Ammn expended on 1.12.17. 3000 rds (16 H Guns & 250 men).	
1/2 12/17	12 midnight to 2am	Relief of regt by 34th H was completed by about 2am & squadrons concentrated at	
		the spinney about W6c central – when pack animals were met & regt marched	
		back to led horses about W22 b99 – Cross roads.	
	4am	arriving there about 4am – about 10am regt moved to Valley W29 a where	
		it remained in readiness throughout the day – the led horses had	
		been shelled on morning of 1st in W17c, a few casualties in horses (2–3).	
		Major Keighley assumed command.	
	3pm	Regt attended the funeral of Col Corbyn at Hendecourt Cemetery.	
		Regt bivouacked the night in W29 a – The weather on 1st & 2nd was	
		bitterly cold & frosty.	
3/12/17	11.30 AM	Regt marched (in Bde) to Sheet 62C. E23 & bivouacked in the Valley	
		W of St Emilie – Casualties on 1st Decr were – killed Lt Col Corbyn. OR1 – 6	
		(A1, C2, D2, HQ1), wounded Capt Royston, Lt Belsoe, Capt Dening slightly at	
		duty, Jem Fateh Ali Khan – OR1 30 (2 slightly) – A6, B5,	
		C3, D14 of which 3 men died of wounds) – horses wounded	
		Killed & missing between 1st & 2nd – 17. Hun evacuated via 1st & 2nd	11 –
		on 3/12/17 Bde was mounted support to troops holding Cav Corps	
		sector & ready to move at short notice & not off saddled. Capt	
		Bray sent up 3.30pm to reconnoitre Sheet 57C W11 central & W5 –	
		central – which regt was to hold in event of being called up –	
		Horses off saddled, with orders to stand to, saddled up fm 8–9.30 am on 4th.	
Lessons		Lessons of 1st Decr appear to be (1) watch your flanks always (2)	
		keep away from tanks in the advance, & send them away the minute the	
		objective is reached – they draw fire (3) A gunner officer should be up	
		(4) Reserve regt – must be asked for stretcher bearers, when attacking dismounted	
		(5) carrying parties should be immediately in rear of & attached to the sqn they are carrying for. (6) Dig in – quick & deep, when you get your objective.	

(9)

Army Form C. 2118.

Instructions regarding War Diaries and Intelligence Summaries are contained in F. S. Regs., Part II. and the Staff Manual respectively. Title pages will be prepared in manuscript.

WAR DIARY
or
INTELLIGENCE SUMMARY.
(Erase heading not required.)

18 Lancers

Place	Date	Hour	Summary of Events and Information	Remarks and references to Appendices
Villers Faucon area.	4/12/17		Hostile observation balloon seen up all day to the East. Regt ordered to march up dismounted & occupy the (215-strong) the Brown line (in support to 2nd Cav Divn) from W11 central to W5 central - by	Map.
		4pm.	4pm. - Order of sqns from the right A C (W5 central to Revelon - Gouzeaucourt Rd)	57C
SW of Gouzeaucourt			B D (up to track W5 central) - 8th Hrs on right - no one on left. Regtl HQ at about W5d20. All 4 squadrons employed during the night deepening & draining the trenches S of the Revelon - Gouzeaucourt Rd. Night & next day bitterly cold many degrees below zero. Trenches only dug the day before - no shelters at all.	1/40,000
	5/12/17		A few small calibre shell during night 4/5th & on 5th in vicinity of trenches. Rations came up during the night & a very welcome box of sundries from the Canteen (Regtl) - which was very popular, especially cigarettes, chocolates & biscuits. Water cart came up - but no use as everything frozen stiff. Water in men's bottles also frozen. About 2-3pm orders received that Regt would be relieved that evening by units of 27th Bde (Gen Maxwell's Cav Bde). Regt was relieved about 7pm & marched back to valley W of St Emilie where horses were, arriving 9-10pm.	Map. 1/40,000 62 C
	6th & 7th 12/17		Bivouack in St Emilie Valley. Bitter frost & cold - Rations not too good. About 10-20 shell each night from E.S.E. - of small calibre - 200-250x being the nearest - no casualties.	

2353 Wt. W2544/1454 700,000 5/15 D. D. & L. A.D.S.S. Forms/C. 2118.

Instructions regarding War Diaries and Intelligence Summaries are contained in F. S. Regs., Part II. and the Staff Manual respectively. Title pages will be prepared in manuscript.

WAR DIARY
or
INTELLIGENCE SUMMARY.
(Erase heading not required.)

Army Form C. 2118.

(16)

Place	Date	Hour	Summary of Events and Information	Remarks and references to Appendices
8/XII/17	8/12/17	12.30 PM	Marched via Roisel & South bank of COLOGNE to Bruile – where Regt was in the old huts & stables occupied just E of Bruile from 13 – 20th Nov.	ST QUENTIN 1/100,000
BRUILE	9–11/12/17		Refitting – cleaning up kits, arms & equipment – Lt Benfield & 47 OR joined from Rouen on 9/12/17. During recent operations – on 1st Dec. Reck & Dismtd Men moved to ATHIES. Echelon joined next in Villers Faucon area on 4/12/17. Major Ridley, Lt Benfield & some 40 OR proceeded to Peiziely on 11th & worked on Corps Line near BIHECOURT. Remainder of D. Men moved from ATHIES to Tertry on 19th. On 8/12/17 Dfr Sant Singh (2242) & Ddfr Kasir Khan & horse 2576 B.C.B.G. [illegible] to Cav. Corps Equitation School (for demonstration purposes). Capt Forbes proceeded to [illegible] school at Cayeux, on 11.12.17. Lt Brown to England on 14 days leave 7/12/17. Went sick in England.	
BRUILE	12–16/12/17		On 15/12/17 M.O. inspected all men's feet. Satisfactory. 15/12/17 2 P.B. men arrived, to run Regt Canteen – [illegible] from leave to England 14/12/17. – Message received from Gen. Sir J. Richardson – Colonel of the Regt "Please tell the British officers & men of the Regt how proud I feel to hear they have done so well." A very complimentary letter also received from G.O.C. Grenadier on 1st in Gauche Wood. Weather very wintry & cold with heavy snow fall & frost. [illegible] for all ranks at Cartigny on 12.12.17.	
	17/18/12/17		On 17/18/12/17 Digging parties 150 strong plus horseholders proceeded mounted to near HERVILLY arriving there at dusk (4pm) – then had 4 hours digging [illegible] about 62 [illegible] – then ride back – started about 2 pm & back by 11–12 pm. Very hard & trying work for the men in the bitter weather – always below zero & thunder over frozen snow. In spite of all precautions men's health & feet suffered to a certain extent. On 18/12/17 Maj Harvell left to start & command 5th Cav Div school & granted rank of Lt Col from 30.12.17.	

2353 Wt. W2534/1454 700,000 5/15 D. D. & L. A.D.S.S. Forms/C. 2118.

Army Form C. 2118.

Instructions regarding War Diaries and Intelligence Summaries are contained in F. S. Regs., Part II. and the Staff Manual respectively. Title pages will be prepared in manuscript.

WAR DIARY or INTELLIGENCE SUMMARY.

(Erase heading not required.)

H Lancers

Place	Date	Hour	Summary of Events and Information	Remarks and references to Appendices
BRUSLE	17-18 12/17		Ressaidar Tawakul Khan & 3 O.R. left for Marseilles for return on leave to India. on 17.12.17 18 12/17 Baths allotted at Cartigny - but impossible owing to all pipes being frozen. Major Risley proceeded to Marseilles for a tour of duty there The following honors granted in connection with the operations at Gauche Wood on Dec 1st Maj. Mills D.S.O. - a bar to D.S.O. - Capt Bray - M.C. - Jemadars Adalat Khan & Mohd Khan (W.H.) & 2870 Sr Indar Singh - the Indian Order of Merit 2nd Class — 1937 Dfr Alla Ditta Khan L/A, 2002 L Dfr Hyat Khan R/C, 2147 Dfr Zahid Khan L/D, 2533 Sr Talib Hussain Khan (Signaller, HQ) 2293 Ghulam Mohd Khan L.A. - 2400 Ward orderly Makhan Khan - all the Indian Distinguished Service Medal Maj. Mills evacuated sick on 20 12/17. Maj Marsh to England - on 21st on 14 days urgent Private affairs. -	
	19 12/17 - 21 12/17		From about 9th to 21st Regt was on short notice to move to reinforce the front or intermediate lines - Regt refitted & general cleaning up ordered, Horses exercised - Country deep in snow & roads covered with ice -	
TERTRY.	22 12/17		Regt marched to winter Quarters about Hesbecourt at TERTRY - HQ, B & R/C at TERTRY - L/C, A & D on East - Meraucourt Road. just N of Tertry - of Meraucourt - & W of Tertry -	
	23 12/17 to 31 12/17		Camp at TERTRY as above - Exercise - Building up of roofs, Nissens put up, 3' high walls round huts & stables commenced stables covered in - which were over to give protection against bombs from aeroplanes - several times by day & night - but did nothing. Snow & frost all the time. All horses & mules shod with frost cogs & nails from 12th Dec onwards - impossible to move without them On 23.12.17 Party of 15 men arrived from base On 25.12.17 Regt Xmas dinner held in HQ Mess (Nissen hut) - the following attended. Major Keighley - Capt Gwatkin, Capt Broome, Capt Bray, Capt Dening, Lts Dandy, Watson, Fulcher, Abercrombie, Fitzpatrick, Williams, Mackie, Hodgson, Wyrill & Cruickshank. Cols Chesney & Ricketts regretted they could not be present.	

Instructions regarding War Diaries and Intelligence Summaries are contained in F. S. Regs., Part II. and the Staff Manual respectively. Title pages will be prepared in manuscript.

WAR DIARY
~~or~~ ~~INTELLIGENCE SUMMARY.~~
(Erase heading not required.)

10 Lancers

(12)

Army Form C. 2118.

No. .... Date .... K.G.O. LANCERS

Place	Date	Hour	Summary of Events and Information	Remarks and references to Appendices
TERTRY.	23–31 12/17		26 12/17 Ris Lakha Singh to Rouen as Instructor. Lt Williams to GHQ Small Arms School Le Touquet for 3 weeks M. Gun Course. Lt Machin & 2 Signalling N.C.O's to Cav. Corps Signal School Flixecourt (between Amiens & Abbeville) for 6 days Power Buzzer Course. Capt Brooke to Pecuilly to command Party of 120 Indian Dismtd Men there – till 31st Dec. Regt very short of officers. 10 left out of 24 – On 26.12.17 Party of 300 men proceeded in 15 lorries to work just E of Templeux le Guerard – only enough tools provided for 150 on arrival – Start 1.45 pm – Return 10–45 pm to 12 midnight – On 29.12.17. 300 men again sent in lorries to Templeux le Guerard – On arrival found only shovels provided & work impossible owing to frost – no picks available – so party returned – No work done! Box respirator practice on 28 12/17. During Decr the weather was practically continuously cold with snow & hard frost. The men suffered a lot of exposure both in operations & in digging parties & stood the test extremely well – in spite of rations not being good. On a great many days the rations were all biscuits & no atta – the absence of atta for any but very limited periods is always much felt by the men, especially when there is no meat either, as in this case. During Nov & Dec the following IO's went for 7 days leave to Paris – Ris Sultan Khan & Ris Gul Mohd Khan – Ris Lakha Singh & Ress. Sultan Ahmed – Ress. Jagat & Amar Singh – Ress Mohd Inayat (from Rouen) – The following went on 10 days leave to England – Jemadars Kehar Singh, Jagat Singh, Khuda Bux II, Shahwali Khan. On 27 12/17 notification of award of Indian Meritorious Service Medal received for 1776 Dfr Hazara Singh R/B, 1625 Dfr Kehar Singh L/B, 1710 K.Dfr Allah Yar Khan R/D, 1696 K Dfr Kishan Singh L/B, 1648 K.Dfr Mirza Khan R/A, 1779 K Dfr Sher Ali Khan L/C, 2400 W.O. Hidhan Khan L/C for Good Service in France.	1/100,000 St Quentin Map

2353 Wt. W2544/1454 700,000 5/15 D. D. & L. A.D.S.S./Forms/C. 2118.

Instructions regarding War Diaries and Intelligence Summaries are contained in F. S. Regs., Part II. and the Staff Manual respectively. Title pages will be prepared in manuscript.

WAR DIARY
or
~~INTELLIGENCE SUMMARY~~. 18th K.G.O. Lancers
(Erase heading not required.)

December 1917

Army Form C. 2118.

(13)

Place	Date	Hour	Summary of Events and Information					Remarks and references to Appendices
			Indian Fighting men and Regtl: Public Followers.	During December 17		13/11/14 to 31/12/1917		× Includes men evacuated temporarily to I.C.F.A as well as those to "out of Divisional area".
				Men	Followers	Men	Followers	
			Casualties. To Hospital sick	30	2	473×	14	
			—do— wounded ..	29*	-	79⊗	-	⊗ Includes 2 men wounded at duty.
			Killed in action	9▣	-	19	-	* Excluding 2 men slightly, at duty of 3 B.O's includes 1 Ind. officer
			Died of disease	-	-	9	-	▣ excluding Lt Col Corbyn
			Prisoner in action	-	-	2	-	
			Transferred to other units + followers surplus to India..	-	-	28	5	
			New formations – Used for new formations ..	-	-	106	2	
			Strength of Dismounted Reinforcements on 31.12.17	87	7	-	-	
			Reinforcements. From Base or other units	65	-	526	21	
			Returned from Hospital	6	1	218	4	
			Horses & mules	Horses	Mules	Horses	Mules	
			Casualties. Evacuated lame + sick	36	3	513*	39	* Includes 5 killed in action. 10 wounded —do— 20 missing —do—
			Used for new formation	-	-	210	62	
			Transferred surplus	-	-	49	40	
			Reinforcements from Base + other units	38	1	688	121	

V. A. S. Keighley Major
Comdg 18th Lancers

31/12/17

2353 Wt. W2544/1454 700,000 5/15 D. D. & L. A.D.S.S./Forms/C. 2118.

Instructions regarding War Diaries and Intelligence Summaries are contained in F. S. Regs., Part II. and the Staff Manual respectively. Title pages will be prepared in manuscript.

January 1918.

WAR DIARY or ~~INTELLIGENCE SUMMARY.~~

(Erase heading not required.)

18 Lancers

ADJUTANT'S OFFICE. No. 36 B Date 1/2/18. 18th K. G. O. LANCERS.

Army Form C. 2118.

(180)

Place	Date	Hour	Summary of Events and Information	Remarks and references to Appendices
	1.1.18		The following officers present with Regt. C.O. Maj. Keighley. Adjt Capt Denning. Qr Mr. Lt Abercrombie. R.T.O. Lt Watson. Sig Offr. Lt Mackie. A Sqn. Capt Bray. Lt Hodgson. B Sqn. Lt Wyrill. C Sqn. Capt Broom. Lt Fulcher. Lt Cruickshank. D Lt Fitzpatrick. H.Q. Lt Reardon. — Maj Marsh on leave in England. Maj Howell at 5 Cav Divn School Buzzy les Daours. Lt Williams on H.G. Course Le Touquet. Capt Forbes at Cav. Corps School. Lt Benfield with Divl Remount Hd Qrs. Previlly. Lt Sandeman with Ind Cav. Pioneer Battn. Bois d'Abbes. Lt Fitzpatrick. Lt Leaper in England on duty since 28.12.17. — Maj Howell mentioned in Despatches. Gazette of 14.8.17 — for services in the East.	
Tertry	1st–5th		Nothing special to report. Weather very severe. General health of the Regt good.	
	6th		1st Scouting Course party consisting of Lt. Cruickshank + Jemadar Mohd Hayat Khan went off, also Daf Hidayat Khan + L.D. Santa Singh.	
	8th		Lt G. W. Fulcher ordered to report to India Office. Struck off the strength from this date.	
	9th		S.A.S. Maganlal proceeded with leave party to England.	
	13th		2nd Scouting Course party left. Jemadar Kehar Singh, Daf [illegible] Khan + L/D Bahadur. Lt [illegible] arrived from [illegible] + went to Divnl Signalling Course. Jemadar Khuda Bakhsh Khan + Jemadar Mohd Hayat Khan to [illegible] on leave.	
	14th		Divnl Order 1711. No 1963 Kot. Dafadar Mohamed Ashraf Khan promoted to Jemadar [illegible] 1917.	
			The following officers were struck off the strength: — Capt. A. W. B. Bray [illegible] to War Office for special duty in Mesopotamia. Resaldar Dost Mohamed Khan I.O.M. ordered to proceed to Marseilles immediately to go with special party to India.	
	15th		Gas Course Resaldars Jagat Singh + Sultan Ahmed, Jemadar Shah [illegible] + 2 N.C.O.s.	

(6

Instructions regarding War Diaries and Intelligence Summaries are contained in F. S. Regs., Part II, and the Staff Manual respectively. Title pages will be prepared in manuscript.

WAR DIARY
or
INTELLIGENCE SUMMARY. 18 Lancers.

(Erase heading not required.)

Army Form C. 2118.

Place	Date	Hour	Summary of Events and Information	Remarks and references to Appendices
E of VADENCOURT & TERTRY	28 1/18		Weather fine. Observation good. Parties of Germans seen on the top of their parapet with hands in their pockets — fired on with H.G's (up to 1700x range) but no visible effect. B sqn relieved A in Lone Tree & C squadron relieved D in Dragoon Post. Reliefs completed by about 10 pm — A party of A squadron put up 150x of food & very necessary wire in front of Lone Tree Post — Communication trenches improved to ~~Dragoon~~ Red Crater Dragoon post — accomodation & shelters in Hudson Post & Dragoon post improved. Casualties NIL	
	29 1/18		Weather as on 28th. Enemy showed himself less owing to our increased artillery activity. Patrol of 1 NCO & 4 men from Dragoon post, to ~~the~~ Angle Bank (E of D. Post).	1/100,000 St Quentin & Amiens
	30 1/18	9.15 am	Regt marched less Trench Party marched via BRIE to BAYONVILLERS arrived about 1.30 pm. All men & horses under cover. Cold day, but no rain.	
	31 1/18	8.30 am	March to VIGNACOURT, water & feed on Somme Canal N of MONTIERES (W of Amiens) — arrived about 3.30 pm. All men & horses under cover.	

A7092). Wt. W12839/M1297 750,000. 1/17. D. D & L., Ltd. Forms/C2118/14.

(2

Instructions regarding War Diaries and Intelligence Summaries are contained in F. S. Regs., Part II. and the Staff Manual respectively. Title pages will be prepared in manuscript.

January 1918

WAR DIARY or INTELLIGENCE SUMMARY.

(*Erase heading not required.*)

18th Lancers

Army Form C. 2118.

Place	Date	Hour	Summary of Events and Information	Remarks and references to Appendices
TERTRY	18.		The following working party worked on a cable trench. Capt Brooke, Lt Mackie & Hodgson with 4 I.Os & 240 diggers. Party paraded at 7.30 AM and returned at about 3.30 pm. 80 men were taken as horseholders. All fatigues & ordinary work has to be suspended [illegible] the large numbers sent.	
	19		Working Party same strength time & place of work. Same officers.	
			The Corps Commander presented the following medals to undermentioned men for Immediate award.	
			Indian Order of Merit: Jemadar Mohamed Khan (I.D.S.M.) Jemadar Adalat Khan	
			Indian D. S. Medal: Daffadar Allah Ditta Khan. A.L.D. Talib Hussain Khan. A.L.D. Makhan Khan. Daf Zahid Khan. L/D Hayat Khan	
	21		The following leave party was despatched for India. Rissaldar Amar Singh. Daffadar [illegible] No 2461 Sowar Nadir Khan. No 2104 Sr Chaman Khan. No 254 Sr Sardar Singh. No 1801 Daf [illegible] Khan was also [illegible] to go with the party & word was sent to [illegible] about him.	
			The work on the cable trench was resumed this time however the work was carried on at night and only 165 diggers were employed. 3 B.Os & 2 Os. 1 B.O. was detailed to stay with the led horses this time. 60 horseholders were [illegible].	
	22		Working party as on 21st.	

2353 Wt. W2544/1454 700,000 5/15 D. D. & L. A.D.S.S./Forms/C. 2118.

Instructions regarding War Diaries and Intelligence Summaries are contained in F. S. Regs., Part II. and the Staff Manual respectively. Title pages will be prepared in manuscript.

WAR DIARY
or
~~INTELLIGENCE SUMMARY.~~
(Erase heading not required.)

Army Form C. 2118.

(3)

January 1918 — 18th Lancers.

Place	Date	Hour	Summary of Events and Information	Remarks and references to Appendices
Testry	23		Capt R Dening rejoined from 14 days leave in England.	
			The following appointments were published in Divisional Orders of date:	
			Major & A S Kingsley M.V.O to be officiating Commandant from 2-12-17	
			Major C H. Marsh D.S.O " " " 2nd in Command " 2-12-17	
			Major C G Risley D.S.O " " " Squadron Commander " 2-12-17	
			Capt A H Brooke " " " 2-12-17 (Should be 23-12-17)	
			Promotion to Indian Officer.	
			No 1648 K.D Firoza Khan RA to be Jemadar vice Jemadar Fateh Ali Khan (wounded) from 7-12-17	
			New Years Honours Indian Distinguished Service Medal. Jemadar Adalat Khan, Jemadar Khuda Bakhsh Khan I, Jemadar Alam Sher Khan 17th Cavalry (now back with his own regiment) No 1937 Dfdr Allah Ditta Khan, No 2461 Sowar Mohd Jan Khan. Owing to the fact that No 1937 Dafdr Allah Ditta Khan had already been gazetted for this medal as an Immediate award before the publication of the New Year Honours, the Cav: Corps decided to convert the Immediate award from I.D.S.M to Bar to I.D.S.M.	
	25th		Advance party of Lt. Benfield, Lt Fitz Patrick + Lt Masters were sent on to take over the A1 sector from the 1st Cav Bde.	

2353 Wt. W2544/1454 700,000 5/15 D. D. & L. A.D.S.S./Forms/C. 2118.

(9)

Army Form C. 2118.

WAR DIARY
or
~~INTELLIGENCE SUMMARY.~~
(Erase heading not required.)

Instructions regarding War Diaries and Intelligence Summaries are contained in F. S. Regs., Part II. and the Staff Manual respectively. Title pages will be prepared in manuscript.

January 1918. 18th Lancers.

Place	Date	Hour	Summary of Events and Information	Remarks and references to Appendices
TEHTRY.	26th		The following party proceeded up to take over the line in the A1 sector. C.O. Major Marsh D.S.O. [illegible] Lt [illegible] Abercrombie Signalling & Intelligence Officer [illegible] A Squadron Lt C W S Benfield & Risaldar [illegible] Khan, B Squadron [illegible] L M [illegible] & Jemadar Jagat Singh, C Squadron Lt H R Watson & Risaldar [illegible] Ahmed Khan, D Squadron Lt J. O.C. FitzPatrick & Risaldar Sultan Khan, H.Q. Jemadar [illegible] & Jemadar [illegible] Singh spare. Squadron strengths [illegible] Total strength [illegible] 12 British. Lt Col Keighley, Capt R Deering & later Capt Forbes were with Ambala	Bde Dismtd HQ
			The weather was very misty and the relief was commenced very early & finished [illegible] without incident. The following dispositions were made.	
				BO	IO	IOR	HS		
		[illegible] from 11th [illegible]	2 Troops & Squadron "A" — [illegible] TREK POST. 1 1 [illegible] ; FORWARD GUN POST. [illegible] ; J.E.S. POST. [illegible]	Same day & night.
		[illegible]	2 Troops Squadron "D" — DRAGON POST [illegible] [illegible] [illegible] [illegible]. Support Squadron "C" — HODSON POST No 2. 1 1 40 2.	[illegible] ; Permanent [illegible] 11081. ; Sends up [illegible] ; [illegible] from DRAGON POST
			Reserve Squadron "B" — Red Crater 1 1 53 4. H.Q. — HODSON POST No 1. 3 2 [illegible]	
		[illegible] midnight	Patrol of 1 N.C.O. & [illegible] men went out from DRAGON POST to reconnoitre [illegible]. Returned [illegible] without having found any trace of the enemy.	

2353 Wt. W2544/1454 700,000 5/15 D. D. & L. A.D.S.S./Forms/C. 2118.

(15)

Army Form C. 2118.

Instructions regarding War Diaries and Intelligence Summaries are contained in F. S. Regs., Part II. and the Staff Manual respectively. Title pages will be prepared in manuscript.

WAR DIARY
or
~~INTELLIGENCE SUMMARY.~~
(Erase heading not required.)

January 1918. 18th Lancers.

Place	Date	Hour	Summary of Events and Information	Remarks and references to Appendices
A 1 Sector. E of VADENCOURT	27th	2 AM	Patrol of 1 N.C.O + 10 men sent out from LONE TREE POST. SOMERVILLE WOOD + DOGS LEG reported clear of the enemy. Patrol returned at about 3.30 AM.	St Quentin 1/100,000 Sheet 62C 1/40,000
			LONE TREE Trench in a very bad state of repair as no revetting has been done or is allowed. Wire weak in front of FORWARD GUN POST. Two very nasty saps out from LEG POST which will have to be properly blocked up. DRAGOON POST communicating trench bad. Sanitary arrangements very primitive. Wire seems good. Paths through the wire in most places are much too well defined + will have to be changed.	
		9 AM	Casualties Nil. Night very quiet. Still very misty and night posts were not withdrawn.	
		8 PM	Working party of 40 men from the 9th H.H. carried pickets up to LONE Tree preparatory to working on the wire in front of FORWARD GUN POST. A covering party of 1 H.G + 11 men was sent forward under Ressaidar Dhumman Khan who placed them in the old No 3 Post on the W edge of SOMERVILLE WOOD and by the side of WATLING ST. They had hardly been in position 10 minutes when a party of the enemy was seen advancing along the tip of the wood from the direction of DOGS LEG. They came to within 250 - 300 yds of the Post + then turned L + moved in the direction of the TUMULUS. H.G + Rifle fire was then opened on them + they retired. Several dropped immediately the firing started and it is thought that some casualties were inflicted as sounds like groans were heard. A patrol sent out at 2.30 AM patrolled SOMERVILLE WOOD + the scene of the fray but without finding any trace of the enemy. The wiring party of the 9th was sent back for fear of hostile retaliation. Night quiet. 3 rounds of T.M into S end of SOMERVILLE WOOD at about 7 pm. Patrol from DRAGOON POST did not go out owing to the brightness of the moon.	
	28th	9 AM	Casualties Nil	

A7092). Wt. W12839/M1293 750,000. 1/17. D. D & L., Ltd. Forms/C2118/14.

(7)

Army Form C. 2118.

Instructions regarding War Diaries and Intelligence Summaries are contained in F. S. Regs., Part II. and the Staff Manual respectively. Title pages will be prepared in manuscript.

WAR DIARY or ~~INTELLIGENCE~~ SUMMARY. 18th K.G.O. Lancers

(Erase heading not required.)

January 1918

Place	Date	Hour	Summary of Events and Information	During January 1918 Men	During January 1918 Followers	13/11/14 to 31/1/1918 Men	13/11/14 to 31/1/1918 Followers	Notes	Remarks and references to Appendices
			Indian Fighting men and Regt: Public Followers.	Men	Followers	Men	Followers		
			Casualties. To Hospital Sick	16	2	489 x	16	x Includes men evacuated transferred to I.C.F.A as well as those to "out of Divisional Area".	
			—do— wounded	-	-	79 ⊗		⊗ Includes 2 men wounded at duty	
			Killed in action	-	-	19			
			Died of disease	-	-	9 ☐		☐ excluding Lt Col Corbyn.	
			Prisoner in action	-	-	2			
			Transferred to other Units + followers surplus to India	-	-	28	5		
			New formations - used for new formations	-	-	106	2		
			Strength of Dismounted Reinforcement on 31.1.18	104	7	-	-		
			Reinforcements. From Base or other Units	30	1	556	22		
1. Ambala Cav Bde			Returned from Hospital	4	1	222	5		
			Horses and Mules.	Horses	Mules	Horses	Mules		
2. C.G.S. Simla			Casualties:- Evacuated lame + sick	9	.	522 x	39	x Includes:- 5 Killed in action. 10 wounded in action 20 Missing —do—	
3. Retained			Used for new formation	.		210	62		
			Transferred surplus	.		49	40		
			Reinforcement from Base + other Units	28	1	716	122		

AH Brooke Capt for Lt Col Commanding 18th K.G.O. Lancers

(A7092). Wt. W12839/M1293. 750,000. 1/17. D. D. & L., Ltd. Forms/C.2118/14.

Ambala

Instructions regarding War Diaries and Intelligence Summaries are contained in F. S. Regs., Part II. and the Staff Manual respectively. Title pages will be prepared in manuscript.

WAR DIARY
or
INTELLIGENCE SUMMARY.
(Erase heading not required.)

18 Lancers   February 1918

Army Form C. 2118.

ADJUTANT'S OFFICE. No. 37 R Date .... 18th K. G. O. LANCERS.

Place	Date	Hour	Summary of Events and Information	Remarks and references to Appendices
			Officers as follows - on 1st - Lt Col Keighley Cmdg Ambala Dismtd Bde in Trenches Capt Denning - Offg. Staff Captain Ambala Bde Back area - Maj. Marsh, Lt Abercrombie (HQ) Lt Watson (C Sqn), Lt Benfield (A Sqn), Lt Wyvill (B Sqn), Capt Fitzpatrick (D Sqn) - Lt Macklin (Signalling Offr) all with Regtl Trench Party - Capt Brooke, Lt Bullock, Lt Hodgson, Lt Williams with Regt in back area - Capt Dobbs A.C. Ambala Dismtd Bde from 26th Jany - Lt Seager Intelligence officer Ambala Dismtd Bde (rejoined Regt 31st Jany & proceed to trenches on 2nd). Lt Sandeman with 2nd Cav Pioneer Battn - Maj. Howell at 5th Cav Divl School Lt Cruickshank on H.G. Course at Le Touquet (from 30.1.18)	Map Amiens 1/100,000 St Quentin Amiens Abbeville Lens
LONG	1/2/18	8.30 am	March via FLEXICOURT to LONG of Regt & led Horses. All horses & men under cover. From 1st to 16th all men in back area occupied in exercising & looking after the horses - Clipping of all horses & general preparations for move to Egypt.	
			TRENCH PARTY	NAUROY Special sheet 1/20,000 parts of 57C SE 57b SW 62C NE SE 62b NW SW.
BELLENGLISE & VADENCOURT neighbourhood	29/1/18		continued from War Diary for January. Patrol from Dragoon Post to Angle Bank was fired on by 3 hostile MG's - 2 of which were approximately located - patrol returned 1.30 am without meeting any enemy - 2nd patrol left Forward Gun Post (just E of Lone Tree Post) at 2.30 am - reconnoitred Dog's Leg, Max Copse, N End of Somerville Wood & returned by Dragoon Post about 4 am. No signs of enemy - a M.G. from Square Copse direction fired into Somerville Wood. ~~Approaches relieved by 9 Horse~~	
	30/1/18		Regt relieved by 9 Horse. Relief complete by 10.30 pm. Regt in the support line Dean Copse - Parker Post - Parker Trench. HQ near Parker Post. A patrol of Capt Fitzpatrick, Risr Sultan Khan, Jem. Shahwali Khan & 45 OR (D-33, A-12) left Hut Post 5.45 pm & lay up in Mad Copse - Capt Fitzpatrick & 4 men crawled to within a few yards of the Eleven Trees - but couldn't proceed any further owing to Hostile Verey lights. Patrol returned 10 pm. No enemy seen or heard.	

A7092). Wt. W12839/M1293 750,000. 1/17. D. D & L., Ltd. Forms/C2118/14.

Army Form C. 2118. (2)

Instructions regarding War Diaries and Intelligence Summaries are contained in F. S. Regs., Part II. and the Staff Manual respectively. Title pages will be prepared in manuscript.

WAR DIARY or INTELLIGENCE SUMMARY.

(Erase heading not required.)

H Lancers — February

Place	Date	Hour	Summary of Events and Information	Remarks and references to Appendices
Vadencourt Vicinity	31/1/18		Quiet day with much mist. Special precautions taken against Gas. Men inspected by M.O. for Vermin & bad feet. Inspection proved very satisfactory. At 6pm Patrol of Lt Wynn, Jem Tofat Singh 22 OR (20 B & 2 C) went out as on 30/1/18 – No enemy seen – Patrol returned about 9 am. Work done in improving trenches nr Soumerville Wood & Dragoon Post. –	
	1/2/18		D Sqn cook evacuated sick – the first man evacuated sick since arrival in the trenches. – On night of 30th Lt Henfield & a working party put up about 150 yds of double apron wire in front of Lone Tree Post. Lt Watson, Ress. Sultan Ahmed & 20 OR C Sqn left Hut Post 11.30pm, went via Max Wood, to Bank East of it and lay up till 3.30 am then returned. No enemy seen or heard.	
	2/2/18		Patrol of Lt Benfield, Lt Mackie, Ress. Dhuman Khan & 20 men A Sqn left Lone Tree Post at 7 pm (a) to gain information about the old gap in the German wire at M3 a 87 (b) to find the track through the German wire from Eleven Trees to about G 33 c 97. Main body of the patrol remained about G 33 d 00 whilst the 2 officers & 2 men crawled to the Eleven Trees, which were unoccupied – they were unable to find the track owing to the frequency of German Very lights one of which almost pitched on them. They then returned to the main body & the whole patrol proceeded to within 50 yds of the wire due West of ST HELENE – they were held up there by Very lights – Talking, coughing & singing could be heard from the direction of the sunken road running NW from ST HELENE. No gap in the wire was found.	
	3/2/18		Regt relieved by 7.30pm by 34th Poona Horse & went into Reserve at VADENCOURT. Working parties of 60 men at Grand Priel Farm & 60 men at Vadencourt during the night	

Instructions regarding War Diaries and Intelligence Summaries are contained in F. S. Regs., Part II. and the Staff Manual respectively. Title pages will be prepared in manuscript.

WAR DIARY
or
INTELLIGENCE SUMMARY.
(Erase heading not required.)

Army Form C. 2118. (3)

18 Lancers — February.

Place	Date	Hour	Summary of Events and Information	Remarks and references to Appendices
Vadencourt vicinity	4/2/18 to 12/2/18		Lt Watson proceeded on leave on 4.2.18. Lt Webster arrived & took over C Sqn (Dismtd) on 5th having joined regt in back area from the base on 3.2.18. All spare men used daily in work on Vadencourt defences. 4 Bos, 4 10s, 100 OR training for raid on German trench line N of ST HELENE. This raid was to be subsidiary to one to be carried out by Canadian Cav Bde to our North and all arrangements had to fit in with theirs. On account of information received the objectives of the raid were changed 2 days before Zero day. It appeared that a relief took place in the German line about the 6th as on the night of 6/7th a patrol of the 7th DG's were fired on from ST HELENE village – whereas previously our patrols had visited ST HELENE nightly & found it unoccupied; & thus the objective of the raid was a portion of trench 400x East of the ST HELENE line. On the night 8/9 a ~~party~~ patrol of 10 men under Lt Benfield with Lt Webster, proceeded to Fisher Crater, thence along the S of the road to within 50x of the wire – they saw 4 men at the junction of the road & wire, & a moment later 3 or 4 men about 50x further South. In the next 20 minutes the two parties of the enemy disappeared and the patrol moved up to the gap which was found open – As the leading men were about to cross the trench the party was fired on, bullets coming close apparently by 3 or 4 men from vicinity of ST HELENE cross-roads. A M.G. apparently from about H3C96 also opened fire but went wide. Very lights were sent up from ST HELENE village & the patrol had to withdraw. The patrol commander was of opinion that there was a standing patrol in St Helene village – On night 9/10 a patrol of 2 Bos, 2 10s & 5 OR left Barrier Post 10 pm. went to H2 d84 thence NE. When 50x from the wire, movement was heard on ST HELENE FISHERS CRATER Road – The patrol approached close to the wire at H3a66 & were fired on by a M. Gun about G33c91 – a party of 20 or 30 men were seen moving about H3C central but at once disappeared. The patrol then returned as numerous very lights were being sent up.	

A7092). Wt. W12839/M1293. 750,000. 1/17. D. D & L., Ltd. Forms/C2118/14.

Instructions regarding War Diaries and Intelligence Summaries are contained in F. S. Regs., Part II. and the Staff Manual respectively. Title pages will be prepared in manuscript.

WAR DIARY
or
INTELLIGENCE SUMMARY.
(Erase heading not required.)

18 Lancers February 1918.

Army Form C. 2118.

(4)

Place	Date	Hour	Summary of Events and Information	Remarks and references to Appendices
Vadencourt.	12/13.		On the night of 12/13th a raid was carried out – the whole object of the raid was (a) to distract attention from a big raid carried out by the Canadian Cav Bde on Lily Trench G27a (2) to secure identifications from the area round ST HELENE – The first object was achieved – The second was frustrated by a German counter barrage – the raid was under taken by Capt Fitzpatrick & 25 men D, Lt Wyrill & 25 men B, Lt Webster & 25 men C, Lt Benfield & 25 men A & one I.O. per Sqn. Lt Mackie & 50 men formed a covering party about Fishers Crater. Casualty 1 man slightly wounded.	
	13th		Regt worked on Vadencourt defences.	
	14th		Lts Benfield & Wyrill proceeded on 5 days leave to England.	
	15th		Regt relieved at Vadencourt by 5 DG's by 3.30 pm. Marched to Q 30 central W of Vermand – Mines by light Rlwy at 6pm to ROISEL where they arrived about 7.30pm. Camped for the night in tents about 400x N of ROISEL station.	
	16th		Left ROISEL by train 12 noon – arrived SALEUX South of Amiens 7pm. By lorry to LONG arrived 10 pm. Capt Forbes Lt Seager rejoined from H.Q. Ambala Cavalry Bde.	
	17th		Capt Denning rejoined from Staff Captain 5th Cavalry Div (7th–16th)	
	"		Col Knightley, Capt Forbes, Lt Abercrombie Capt Brooke 5 days leave to England on 20th Capt Fitzpatrick on 21st –	
	21		All animals being clipped & preparations made for the move to Egypt, but no definite orders received. GOC Divn inspected all animals on 20th & expressed his approval of their condition.	
	22		Orders received for 3 BOs 2 IOs & 52 men to proceed on 23rd, 4 BOs & 2 IOs on 24th to Taranto & thence to Egypt.	

A7092). Wt. W12839/M1293 750,000. 1/17. D. D & L., Ltd. Forms/C2118/14.

Instructions regarding War Diaries and Intelligence Summaries are contained in F. S. Regs., Part II. and the Staff Manual respectively. Title pages will be prepared in manuscript.

WAR DIARY
or
INTELLIGENCE SUMMARY.
(Erase heading not required.)

Army Form C. 2118.

(5)

18 Lancers   Feby 1918.

Place	Date	Hour	Summary of Events and Information	Remarks and references to Appendices
	23/2/18		Lts Watson, Brayne & Cruickshank, Jem. Mohd Ashraf & Kehir Singh & 50 men left in 3 lorries 10am for Saleux (& Toranto). All R.H.A. Drivers left 6pm for base Rouen for transfer to Divl Ammn Column being replaced by sowars. These men have done excellent work for the past 2½ years with the regt in A & B echelons. Lt Benfield & Wyrill rejoined from leave 22nd. Jem Adalat Khan & Jem Alam Sher Khan 17 Cav (since returned to India) Jem Khuda Bakhsh, 2411 L/Dr Mohd Jan awarded Indian DSM, 1937 K/Dfr Alla Ditta Khan Bar to I.D.S.M in the New Years Honors for good services. Capt J Gwatkin, 1892 Dfr Jaimal Singh awarded CROIX DE GUERRE - Belgian on 9-2-18. — 12 L.D. Horses exchanged for mules on 22.2.18	ABBEVILLE 1/100000
	24/2/18		Lt Benfield - Lt Wyrill - Ress Dhuman Khan - Jem Shahwali Khan - ~~Jem Jawala Singh~~ Lt A.B. Wilkinson, Lt R.F. Seager, Jem Sher Ali Khan + 8 ORI, 1ORB left for Saleux + Toranto. 40 horses received from 13th M.G. Sqn. Maj Howell returned from leave. Maj. Marsh proceeded on 5 days leave. His leave is extended pending decision as to whether he gets Command of an Indian Infantry Battalion in India.	
	26-2-18.		The Co, Capt Brooke, Capt Sabes, Lt Abercrombie rejoined from 5 days leave. The Regiment marched to GUISEMICOURT, via PICQUIGNY.	AMIENS 1/100000.
	28.2.18		Capt Denning proceeded on short leave to England.	
	1.3.18.		Remounts. 57 remounts in all have been received since Major General's inspection. These are to bring us up to 10% spare horses. Condition of these horses with 2 or 3 exceptions is distressful - majority from 13th Cav Squadron. [signature]	
	11.2.18		Le Croix de Guerre (Belgian) Capt. J Gwatkin S.C. Ambala Bde 1892 Dafadar JAIMAL SINGH. L/B	

A7092). Wt. W12839/M1293. 750,000. 1/17. D. D & L., Ltd. Forms/C2118/14.

Army Form C. 2118.

Instructions regarding War Diaries and Intelligence Summaries are contained in F. S. Regs., Part II. and the Staff Manual respectively. Title pages will be prepared in manuscript.

WAR DIARY
or
~~INTELLIGENCE SUMMARY.~~
(*Erase heading not required.*)

18th K.G.O. Lancers
February 1918.

Place	Date	Hour	Summary of Events and Information					Remarks and references to Appendices
			Indian Fighting Men and Regl: Public Followers.	During Feby. 18		13/11/14 to 28/2/1918		
				Men	Followers	Men	Followers	
			Casualties – To Hospital Sick	16	1	505×	17	× Includes men evacuated to I.C.F.A as well as those to "out of Divisional area.
			do wounded	1	-	80⊗	-	⊗ Includes 2 men wounded at duty.
			Killed in action	-	-	19	-	
			Died of disease	-	-	9□	-	□ Excluding Lt Col Corbyn.
			Prisoner in action	-	-	2	-	
			Transferred to other Units & followers Surplus to India	-	-	28	5	
			New formations – Used for new formation	-	-	106	2	
			Strength of Dismounted Reinforcements on 28.2.18	66	7	-	-	
			Reinforcements – From Base or other Units	-18	-2	538	20	
			Returned from Hospital	10	1	232	6	
			Horses & Mules	Horses	Mules	Horses	Mules	
			Casualties – Evacuated lame & sick	37	4	559*	43 ∦	* Includes:- 5 Killed in action. 10 Wounded in " 20 Missing " "
			Used for new formation	-	-	210	62	
			Transfd: Surplus	1	-	~~49~~ 50	40	∦ Includes 2 L.D. Mules missing in action during Feby. 1918.
			Reinforcements from Base & other Units	61	-	777	122	

[signature] Capt
for Lt Col.
Commanding 18th Lancers

D/1-3-18

A7092). Wt. W12839/M1293. 750,000. 1/17. D. D & L., Ltd. Forms/C2118/14.

Instructions regarding War Diaries and Intelligence Summaries are contained in F. S. Regs., Part II. and the Staff Manual respectively. Title pages will be prepared in manuscript.

WAR DIARY or ~~INTELLIGENCE SUMMARY.~~

(Erase heading not required.)

18th Lancers. March.

Army Form C. 2118.

ADJUTANT'S OFFICE No. 38 B Date .... 18th K. G. O. LANCERS.

(1)

Place	Date	Hour	Summary of Events and Information	Remarks and references to Appendices
1.3.18 GUISEMICOURT			Officers with the regiment. C.O. Lt.Col. Keighley – Adjt (acting) Capt Inbes – Qrmr. Lt Abercrombie – A sqn Lt. Bullock. B sqn – Maj. Howell – C sqn Capt Brooke D sqn – a/Capt Fitzpatrick – M.O. Lt Reardon. On leave – Lt. Webster Lt. Mackie + Capt Dening – Proceeded with D.M. by rail to TARANTO Lts Watson, Brayne, Cruikshank, Benfield, Wyrill, Williams, + Sandeman.	AMIENS 1/100,000
	1.3.18	12 noon.	At midday Capt Fitzpatrick, Lt Bullock, Jemadars Khuda Bux, Jowala Singh + Ahahyar Khan and + 92 O.R. entrained at SALEUX for TARANTO.	
		11.30pm	The following commenced entraining at SALEUX for MARSEILLES. 4 B.O.s 5 I.O.s 150 O.R. + followers 232 animals + all transport, consisting of 6. G.S. wagons 6 L.G.S. wagons, water-cart + mess cart. The officers were the C.O. + Capt Inbes, Lt Abercrombie + the M.O. Woordie Major + Jem. Moh'd Amir (H.Q.) and Ress. Moh'd Inayat + Jemadar Adalat Khan both A sqn. + Jemadar Sultan Mahmud (Tpt). Animals were H.Q. Tpt + most of A sqn. Entraining took place in the snow.	
	2.3.18	5.30am	The following commenced entraining as above 1 B.O. 5 I.Os 159 O.R. + followers 253 animals of C + D squadrons. Officers were Capt Brooke Ris. Sultan Khan. Ress. Sultan Ahmed Ress Moh'd Raza Khan. Jemadar Khuda Bux (1), Jemadar Sultan Khan.	
	2-4.3.18		The journey to Marseilles occupied 3 days – arrangements for watering horses + for hot water for men at the HALTE REPAS along the line were excellent.	
	4.3.18		The first of the 2 trains arrived at 10.30 pm. at ARENC STA. Marseilles in a thunderstorm. Regtl Transport was taken direct from Station to the Docks after kits had all been unloaded in the rain. Kit sent to camp in lorries. Details of the 1st train marched through Marseilles to Camp No. 8. 6 miles from the station, reaching camp at 3.45 am. wet through. The lines	
	5.3.18		were the horses were picketted during the night were actually 6" under water – + the tents for the men flooded out. Details from 2nd train arrived in camp at 5.30 am.	

A7092). Wt. W12839/M1293 750,000 1/17. D. D & L., Ltd. Forms/C2118/14.

Instructions regarding War Diaries and Intelligence Summaries are contained in F. S. Regs., Part II. and the Staff Manual respectively. Title pages will be prepared in manuscript.

WAR DIARY
or
INTELLIGENCE SUMMARY.

(Erase heading not required.)

Army Form C. 2118.

18th Lancers — March 1918 — (2)

Place	Date	Hour	Summary of Events and Information	Remarks and references to Appendices
MARSEILLES	5.3.18		The remainder of the regiment - 1 B.O. (Maj Howell) 2 I.O.s Ressaidar Jagat Singh, Jemadar Jagat Singh, Jemadar Shah Wali Khan 15AS 130 O.R.s & 176 animals - (includes whole of B Squadron) were left behind at CHAIRY under command of Maj Howell - Lt Webster is expected to rejoin regiment at CHAIRY. These comprise Group B. All R.H.A. personnel who had been with regiment since 3½ years, were recalled at the end of last month & despatched to ROUEN, for duty with Divisional Ammunition Columns in France. During the afternoon kits & baggage of parties embarking on the 6th instant were loaded on the H.T. "ELLENGA" (B.I.S.N.C) & H.T. City of BENARES. (Docks No 8).	
	6.3.18		The following parties of the regiment embarked - 1st party - commenced embarking on H.T. CITY of BENARES at 8 am. Lt Abercrombie - Ressaidar Mohd Inayat Khan Jemadar Sultan Mahmud Khan - 70 O.R.s. and 195 animals - including all transport & nearly the whole of A Sqn & a few details of H.Q. All regimental transport was also [illegible] loaded on this ship - 2nd party - commenced embarking on H.T. "ELLENGA" at 9 am. The C.O. & Capt Forbes - Jemadar Mohd Khan (W.M) Jem. Mohd Amir - Jemadar Adalat Khan & Ressaldar Sultan Khan. & 136 O.R. No horses were on this boat. The C.O. commanded all troops on this ship. The remainder of those who detrained at Marseilles on morning of 5th inst remained behind in camp in Marseilles under Capt Brooke - 2 B.O.s (includes M.O.) 4 I.O.s Risaldar Sultan Ahmad, Ressaidar Mohd Raza Khan & Jemadar Sultan Khan - & Jemadar Khuda Bux (1) - 103 O.R. & 287 animals (C & D). The convoy moved out from the docks in the evening but did not sail from Marseilles till 10 am 7th inst. On the evening of the 6th a minefield was reported	
	7.3.18			

Instructions regarding War Diaries and Intelligence Summaries are contained in F. S. Regs., Part II. and the Staff Manual respectively. Title pages will be prepared in manuscript.

WAR DIARY
~~or~~
~~INTELLIGENCE SUMMARY.~~
(Erase heading not required.)

Army Form C. 2118.

18th Lancers — March 1918. (3)

Place	Date	Hour	Summary of Events and Information	Remarks and references to Appendices
MARSEILLES	7-3-18		just outside the harbour. This was swept before we sailed.	
MALTA	10-3-18		Arrived MALTA & sailed again night of 11th inst.	
ALEXANDRIA	15-3-18		Arrived ALEXANDRIA in the afternoon. The Convoy was escorted to MALTA by 2 British & 2 Japanese destroyers – from there onwards by 4 Japs	
	16-3-18		Disembarked horses, men slept on board.	
	17-3-18.		Entrained for TEL-EL-KEBIR arriving at 2.45 pm. a great contrast to France. No casualties on the voyage & no horses lost. On arrival found the parties that left LONG on 23rd & 24th February had arrived on the 16th. No men were evacuated sick at TARANTO – otherwise no casualties. The remainder of the month was spent in gradually conditioning horses of A Sqn & H.Q. & transport animals. Horses rations changed from oats & hay (France) to Grain, barley & bran, and very coarse hay supplemented with Bhusa – It is hardly expected that they will keep the same condition as in France – Weather very fine & dry & miles of desert for squadron training next month.	
	30-3-18		Capt. Frazer rejoined the Regiment from Sick leave in ~~Ire~~ England.	
	25-3-18.		The Duke of Connaught visited TEL-EL-KEBIR & was met at the station by the C.O. & Risaldar Sultan Khan (R/D) Sirdar I.D. present with regiment, and Risaldar Major Ahmadyar Khan from the Base Depot – also at this place – H.R.H. had not time to visit units lines.	
	21-3-18.		The party that left SALEUX under Capt Fitzpatrick arrived – no casualties.	

[illegible signature]

A7092). Wt. W12839/M1293 750,000. 1/17. D. D & L., Ltd. Forms/C2118/14.

Instructions regarding War Diaries and Intelligence Summaries are contained in F. S. Regs., Part II. and the Staff Manual respectively. Title pages will be prepared in manuscript.

WAR DIARY
or
~~INTELLIGENCE SUMMARY.~~
(Erase heading not required.)

Army Form C. 2118.

18th K.G.O. Lancers

March 1918

Place	Date	Hour	Summary of Events and Information					Remarks and references to Appendices
			Indian Fighting Men and Regl Public Followers.	During March 18		13/11/14 to 31/3/1918		
				Men	Followers	Men	Followers	
			Casualties – In Hospital Sick	10	–	515x	17	x Includes men evacuated to I.C.F.A as well as those to "out of Divisional area".
			—do— wounded	–	–	80⊗	–	
			Killed in action	–	–	19□	–	⊗ Includes 27 men wounded at duty.
			Died of disease	–	–	9	–	
			Prisoner in action	–	–	2	–	□ Excluding Lt Col Corbyn.
			Transferred to other Units & followers Surplus to India	–	–	28	5	
			New formations – Used for new formation	–	–	106	2	
			Strength of Dismounted Reinforcements on 31.3.18	61	7	–	–	
			Reinforcements – From Base or other units	5	2	543	22	
			Returned from Hospital	–	–	232	6	
			Horses & Mules	Horses	Mules	Horses	Mules	
			Evacuated lame & sick	75	–	634x	43	x Includes:– 5 Killed in action; 10 wounded —do—; 20 missing —do—
			Casualties – Used for new formation	–	–	210	62	
			Transfd. Surplus			50	40	
			Reinforcements from Base & other units	–	–	777	122	

V. A. S. Keighley
Colonel
Comdg 18th K.G.O. Lancers

2/4/1918

A7092). Wt. W12839/M1293 750,000. 1/17. D. D & L., Ltd. Forms/C2118/14.

1917-1918
5TH CAVALRY DIVISION
AMBALA CAVALRY BDE

MACHINE GUN SQUADRON

JAN 1917 - ~~JAN~~ FEB 1918

SERIAL NO. 325

Confidential

War Diary

of

MACHINE GUN SQUADRON, AMBALA CAVALRY BRIGADE.

FROM 1st January 1917 191[?] TO 31st January 191

Instructions regarding War Diaries and Intelligence Summaries are contained in F. S. Regs., Part II. and the Staff Manual respectively. Title Pages will be prepared in manuscript.

WAR DIARY
or
INTELLIGENCE SUMMARY
(Erase heading not required.)

Ambala M. G. Sqdn. Army Form C. 2118.
Vol V

Place	Date	Hour	Summary of Events and Information	Remarks and references to Appendices
	Jany.			
TILLOY.	1		New Years Day. Holiday.	
	2	9 a.m.	Head Quarters & Transport, Marching Order Parade. A. B. & C. Troops Drill under Troop Leaders. Afternoon Gun & Rifle Drill & Judging distance.	
	3	9 a.m.	"A" Troop Marching Order Parade. Remainder Drill under Troop Leaders.	
		2 p.m.	Afternoon. Gun & Rifle Drill and Football.	
	4	9 a.m.	"B" Troop Marching Order Parade. Remainder Drill under Troop Leaders.	
		2 p.m.	Afternoon. Gun & Rifle drill and Football.	
	5	9 a.m.	"C" Troop Marching Order Parade. Remainder Drill under Troop Leaders.	
		2 p.m.	Afternoon. Gun and Rifle Drill, and Football.	
	6	9 a.m.	Exercise and Inspections. Afternoon. Football.	
	7	11a.m.	Church Parade.	
	8	9 a.m.	Troop and Section Drill. Afternoon. Practise Part 1 Table C, G.M.G. Course Practise Bombing.	
	9	9 a.m.	Squadron Marching Order Parade. Afternoon. -do- -do- -do-	
	10	9 a.m.	Exercise. Cleaning and repairing billets afterwards.	
	11	9.30	Horse Inspection by A. V. O. Afternoon General Fatigue.	
	12	9 a.m.	Exercise. Cleaning and Repairing Billets.	
	13	do.	Exercise and Inspections.	
	14		Holiday.	
	15	9.15	Squadron Drill. Afternoon. General Fatigue.	
	16	9 a.m.	Squadron Route March via HINTRAY, TRANSLAY, MARTAINNEVILLE & VISMES.	
		2 p.m.	Afternoon. General Fatigue.	
	17	9.15	Squadron Drill. Afternoon General Fatigue.	
	18	9.0	Exercise. Afternoon. General Fatigue.	
	19	9.0	-do- -do- -do-	
	20	9.0	Exercise and Inspections. Afternoon Football.	
	21	11 a.m.	Church Parade.	
	22	9.0	3 Section Equitation. 3 Sections Squadron Duties.	
		2 p.m.	Afternoon. 3 Sections Squadron Training. 3 Sections Squadron Duties.	
	23	9.0	3 Sections Equitation. 3 Sections Squadron Duties.	
		2 p.m.	Afternoon. 3 Sections Squadron Training. 3 Sections Squadron Duties.	
	24	9 a.m.	3 Sections Squadron Training. 3 Sections Squadron Duties.	
		2 p.m.	Afternoon. 3 Sections Squadron Training. 3 Sections Squadron Duties.	

2449 Wt. W14957/M90 750,000 1/16 J.B.C. & A. Forms/C.2118/12.

Instructions regarding War Diaries and Intelligence Summaries are contained in F. S. Regs., Part II. and the Staff Manual respectively. Title Pages will be prepared in manuscript.

WAR DIARY
or
INTELLIGENCE SUMMARY
(Erase heading not required.)

Army Form C. 2118.

Place	Date	Hour	Summary of Events and Information	Remarks and references to Appendices
	1917 [illegible]			
[illegible]	26	7 a.m.	Exercise	
		9 a.m.	Drill. Description and Mechanism.	
		2 p.m.	Afternoon. Squadron Training.	
	[illegible]	7 a.m.	Exercise	
		9 a.m.	Drill. Description and Mechanism.	
		2 p.m.	Afternoon. Squadron Training.	
	[illegible]	7 a.m.	Exercise	
		9 a.m.	Drill, Description and Mechanism.	
		2 p.m.	Afternoon. Squadron Training.	
	[illegible]	9.30 a.m.	Inspection Gas Helmets. Remainder of day Holiday.	
	[illegible]	7 a.m.	Exercise.	
		9 a.m.	Drill. Description and Mechanism.	
		2 p.m.	Afternoon. Squadron Training.	
	30	9 a.m.	Squadron Parade.	
		2 p.m.	Afternoon. Squadron Training.	
	31	[illegible]	[illegible]	
		9 a.m.	Squadron Parade. [illegible]	
		2 p.m.	Afternoon. Squadron Training.	

[signature] [illegible]

Commanding [illegible]

31 / [illegible] / 17.

2449 Wt. W14957/M90 750,000 1/16 J.B.C. & A. Forms/C.2118/12.

Instructions regarding War Diaries and Intelligence Summaries are contained in F. S. Regs., Part II. and the Staff Manual respectively. Title Pages will be prepared in manuscript.

WAR DIARY

~~or~~

~~INTELLIGENCE SUMMARY~~

(Erase heading not required.)

14 Sqdn M.G.C. (Cav)

Vol. VI

Army Form C. 2118.

Place	Date 1917	Hour	Summary of Events and Information	Remarks and references to Appendices
	Feby.	a.m.		
TILLOY FLORIVILLE	1	9	Route March. Afternoon. Rifle Exercises, Revolver & Bombing	
	2	9	Route March. 2.0. p.m. do do Practices	
	3	9	Route March. Football.	
	4	11.30	Church Parade 11.30 a.m.	
	5	9	Equitation Rifle Exercises, Revolver & Bombing	
	6	6.45	Exercise. 11.0 a.m. G.O.C's inspection of Stables and Billets Practices	
	7	9	Route March. Afternoon. Rifle Exercises, Revolver & Bombing Practices	
	8	9	Route March 2.0. p.m. Rifle & Bombing Practices, Revolver firing.	
	9	9	Route March do do	
	10	9	Route March Football.	
	11		Holiday.	
	12	9	Equitation Rifle Exercises, Bombing Practice and Revolver Firing.	
	13	9	Equitation do do	
	14	9	Equitation do do	
	15	9	Equitation do Bombing Practice.	
	16	9	Equitation do. do	
	17	6.45	Exercise, Inspections. Football.	
	18	11	Church Parade.	
	19	9	Equitation Musketry Course.	
	20	9	Equitation do	
	21	9	Equitation do.	
	22	9	Equitation do.	
	23	9	Equitation do.	
	24	6.45	Exercise. Inspections Football.	
	25	9	Range Practices.	
	26	9	Equitation Musketry Course	
	27	9	Equitation Musketry Course	
	28	9	Equitation Football.	

[signature] Major.
Commdg. No. 14 Sqdn. M.G.C. (Cavalry).

2449 Wt. W14957/M90 750,000 1/16 J.B.C. & A. Forms/C.2118/12.

Instructions regarding War Diaries and Intelligence Summaries are contained in F. S. Regs., Part II. and the Staff Manual respectively. Title Pages will be prepared in manuscript.

WAR DIARY
or
INTELLIGENCE SUMMARY
(Erase heading not required.)

1st Sqdn M. G. C. (Cav) Army Form C. 2118.

Vol VII

Place	Date	Hour	Summary of Events and Information	Remarks and references to Appendices
Field	1/3/17	am 9.0	Drill — Afternoon 2pm Range Practices.	
	2/3/17	9.0	do — 2pm — do —	
	3/3/17	6.45	Exercise. Inspection of Billets &c Afternoon Football	
	4/3/17	11.30	Church Parade	
	5/3/17	9.0	Drill & Action — Afternoon 2pm Rapid firing, Bombing & M G drill	
	6/3/17	9.0	2 Troops drill 1 Troop Field firing Scheme. Afternoon — do —	
	7/3/17	5.45	Sqdn Parade for Decoration Parade GAMACHES Afternoon Football	
	8/3/17	9.0	Drill — Afternoon Drill dismounted.	
	9/3/17	10.0	Inspection by Corps Machine Gun Officer. Marching Order. Afternoon Rapid firing Bombing & M.G. Drill	
	10/3/17	6.45	Exercise. Inspection of Billets &c Afternoon Football	
	11/3/17	9.0	Inspection of Equipment Afternoon Holiday	
	12/3/17	8.30	Drill — Afternoon Rapid firing Bombing M.G. Drill	
	13/3/17	8.30	2 Troops drill, 1 Troop Scheme Afternoon Rapid firing, Bombing & M G drill	
	14/3/17	8.30	— do — do — Afternoon Football	
	15/3/17	8.30	Drill. — Afternoon Rapid firing, Bombing & M.G. drill	
	16/3/17	6.30	Exercise. Inspection by Medical Officer Afternoon — do —	

2449 Wt. W14957/M90 750,000 1/16 J.B.C. & A. Forms/C.2118/12.

Instructions regarding War Diaries and Intelligence Summaries are contained in F. S. Regs., Part II. and the Staff Manual respectively. Title Pages will be prepared in manuscript.

WAR DIARY
or
INTELLIGENCE SUMMARY
(Erase heading not required.)

Army Form C. 2118.

Place	Date	Hour	Summary of Events and Information	Remarks and references to Appendices
Field	17·3·17	6·30	Exercise Inspection of Billets &c Afternoon Football	
	18·3·17	11·30	Church Parade	
	19·3·17		Preparations for moving to forward area.	
	20·3·17	10·23	Brigade rendezvous BOUTTENCOURT. Marched to Billets BROCOURT.	
	21·3·17	8·35	" " BROCOURT " " " CONTY	
	22·3·17		" " ROSSIGNOL " " " CAIX.	
	23·3·17		" " HARBONNIERS " " Bivouac BOIS DE MEREAUCOURT.	
	24·3·17		Brigade took up an outpost line BEAUVOIS · VILLEQUE · CAULAINCOURT POEUILLY · BERNES MARQUAIX	
			1 Section attached 9th Hodson Horse was kept in reserve at MONCHLY LAGACHE	
			18th Lancers took up a position covering N.E. of BERNES	
			Remaining Sections marched to Bivouacs in DEVISE	
	25/3/17		Section att: 9th H Horse sent up at 9·0 am to VILLEVEQUE covering high ground to the East	
			Section att 18th Lancers moved to MARQUAIX being shelled on route a position was taken up covering the Rly to ROISEL.	
			An enemy M. G. was fired on between MARQUAIX + ROISEL which immediately ceased fire. Enemy mounted patrols were fired on on the high ground N of MARQUAIX	

Instructions regarding War Diaries and Intelligence Summaries are contained in F. S. Regs., Part II. and the Staff Manual respectively. Title Pages will be prepared in manuscript.

WAR DIARY
or
INTELLIGENCE SUMMARY
(Erase heading not required.)

Army Form C. 2118.

Place	Date	Hour	Summary of Events and Information	Remarks and references to Appendices
Field	25/3/17		The Cavalry were withdrawn during the night replaced by Infantry. The Section remained in their positions	
	26/3/17		Early the previous evening the Section att 9th H Horse moved to POEUILLY & took up a position covering the ground between POEUILLY and SOYECOURT, & were heavily shelled all day & that night. A number of enemy mounted & infantry patrols were seen but not fired on, Orders having been received not to fire unless attacked Section att 18th Lancers remained at MARQUAIX & came under shell & M G fire continuously all day: the infantry attacked ROISEL at 10-0 am. The section covered the advance with flanking fire. The infantry occupied ROISEL at 11-30 am. Cavalry came up on left ~~the~~ about 11-0 am. The fire of the Section was directed across the high ground N.E. of MARQUAIX in order to support this advance	
	27.3.17		Section att 9th H Horse was withdrawn in reserve at MERANCOURT & remained there all day. Section att 18th Lancers was withdrawn to HANCOURT & remained there all day	

2449 Wt. W14957/M90 750,000 1/16 J.B.C. & A. Forms/C.2118/12.

Instructions regarding War Diaries and Intelligence Summaries are contained in F. S. Regs., Part II. and the Staff Manual respectively. Title Pages will be prepared in manuscript.

WAR DIARY
or
INTELLIGENCE SUMMARY
(Erase heading not required.)

Army Form C. 2118.

Place	Date	Hour	Summary of Events and Information	Remarks and references to Appendices
Field	27/3/17		8th Hrs were detailed to make an attack on VILLIERS-FAUCON. No orders were received for M G Section to accompany this Regt. Permission was however obtained from HQ for 1 section to accompany the Regt. At 4-30 Artillery preparation was made at 5 pm the Cavalry advanced across the open ground S.W. of VILLIERS FAUCON. M.G. Section covering left flank. Section came into action in wood SW of VILLIERS FAUCON & supported the mounted attack on the village with overhead fire. After the Cavalry had entered the village M.G. Section advanced through the village & took up a position N.W. corner covering ground between SAULCOURT & Sugar factory & got into touch with Canadian Cavalry on left at 1-0 pm. ~~on~~ a message arrived from Bde HQ for a M.G. Section to be sent up & report at Bde HQ in TINCOURT WOOD. At 6 pm orders were received for this Section to report at HQ. 8th Hrs., & take part in the consolidation of the village. The Section reached VILLIERS after dark. One gun was placed in position covering the road from VILLIERSFOUCAN - St EMILIE. The other gun was pushed forward & placed in position in NW corner of the village operating in conjunction with the section already	

2449 Wt. W14957/M90 750,000 1/16 J.B.C. & A. Forms/C.2118/12.

Army Form C. 2118.

WAR DIARY
or
INTELLIGENCE SUMMARY
(Erase heading not required.)

Instructions regarding War Diaries and Intelligence Summaries are contained in F. S. Regs., Part II. and the Staff Manual respectively. Title Pages will be prepared in manuscript.

Place	Date	Hour	Summary of Events and Information	Remarks and references to Appendices
Field	27.3.17		in position. Both sections were shelled during the night & next day. At daylight enemy mounted infantry patrols were fired on. The Cavalry with both sections were withdrawn at about 11-30 am & were relieved by the infantry & a Sqdn of the 18th Lancers.	
			Both section marched back to DEVISE & remained in bivouacs the next day.	
	28.3.17		Sections att 9th H Horse & 18th Lancers remained with their HQ in reserve. Remainder of sqdn remained in bivouacs at DEVISE.	
	29.3.17		Brigade rendezvous 1-5 pm at DOINGT & marched to bivouacs in BOIS DE MEREAUCOURT. 2 Sections att: 9th H Horse & 18th Lancers marched to Brigade rendezvous with the Regts to which they were attached	
	30.3.17		Brigade rendezvous BOIS DE MEREAUCOURT, marched to Billets in LAMOTTE-EN-SANTERRE	
	31.3.17		In billets LAMOTTE-EN-SANTERRE.	

A H Brooke Major
Comdg No 14 Signal Sqdn (Cavalry)

Copy.   Ambala Brigade Operation Order No. 1.
19 / 3 / 17.

Reference Map Sheets 14 and 11.

1. The Brigade will march tomorrow to the Liomer Area via Senarpont - Lequesne as per attached march table.

2 Echelon A. will accompany Units.

3. Echelon B. will accompany Units to the Starting point where it will be Brigaded and continue the march under the B.T.O. Order as per march table.

4. Billeting Parties will rendezvous at starting point at 8.0. am and proceed to new billeting area under the senior Officer.

5. All cyclists will be Brigaded at road junction South of 1st. U. in BOUTTENCOURT and will follow A Echelon, M.G. Sqdn. under a N.C.O. to be detailed by 8th. Hussars.

(Signed) A. Graham Captain,
Brigade Major, Ambala Brigade.

MARCH TIME TABLE.

B.H.Q.	Cross Roads B. of Bouttencourt	9.55 a.m.	Liomer.
8th. Hrs.	-------------do-----------	10.0. a.m.	Hornoy.
9th.H.H.	Road junction South of U of BOUTTENCOURT	10.8 a.m.	Selincourt Boisrault.
18th.Lcrs.	-------------do-----------	10.15 a.m.	Bromesnil Villers Campsart
M.G.Sqdn.	Cross Roads B. of Bouttencourt	10.23 a.m.	Brocourt.

COPY Ambala Brigade Operation Order No. 2.
20 / 3 / 17.

Reference Maps Amiens Sheet.

1. The Brigad will move to CONTY Billeting area tomorrow in accordance with the attached march table.

2. A. Echelon will march with units.

3. (a) B. Echelon 8th. Hussras, "X" Batty, 9th. H.H. 18th. Lcrs. will accompany units to starting point where it will be brigaded and continue the march under the B.T.O.

(b) B. Echelon M.G. Sqdn., B.H.Q., and M.V.S. will rendezvous at Farm 500 yds N.E. of T. in Brocourt and will proceed to rejoin its Units in the new billeting area under Sgt. Plowman.

4. All cyclists will be brigaded at THIEVLLOY L'ABBAYE and continue the march in rear of A. Chelon under the comm nd of a N.C.O to be detailed by the 8th. Hussars.

5. Billeting parties will proceed early to the new billeting area

(Signed) A. Graham Captain,
Brigade Major, Ambala Brigade.

8th. Hrs.	Cross roads 1st.L of THIEVLLOY L'ABBAYE.	9.35 a.m.	POIX FREMONTIERS	LOVEILLY WAILLY.
X.Batty.	--------do--------	9.45 a.m.	-----do----	TILLOY
9th.H.H.	Road Junction ½ Mile S.E. of BOISHAULT	9.20 a.m.	-----do----	FLUERY COETRE
18thLcrs	--------do--------	9.30 a.m.	-----do----	VALENNES
M.G.Sqdn B.H.Q. M.V.S.	500 yds. N.E. of T.in Brocourt	8.35 a.m.		CONTY

Ambala Brigade Operation order No. 3.
21 / 3 / 17.

Reference Map Sheet AMIENS

1. The Brigade will march to the Cayeux area tomorrow as per attached march table.

2. Billeting parties will be sent on ahead.

3. A. Echelon will march with Units

4. B. Echelon under the B.T.O. will march in rear of the Brigade.

5. Cyclists will march in rear of M.V.S.

(Signed) T. W. Corbett Captain,
For Brigade Major, Ambala Brigade.

B.H.Q. Sig.Tp. M.G.Sqdn.	Cross Roads at ROSSIGNOL	9.0. a.m.	CAIX
X. Batt.	-----do----	9.10 a.m.	CAIX
8th.Hrs.	JUMEL	10.10 a.m.	CAYEUX IGNAUCOURT
9.HH.	Cross Roads at ROSSIGNOL	9.20 a.m.	COURCELLES
18.Lcrs	In rear of 9th. H.H.		DEMUIN
M.V.S.	In rear of 18th. Lancers.		CAIX
B. Echelon	Cross Roads at ROSSIGNOL	9.40 a.m.	

Ambala Brigade. Operation Order No. 4.

The Brigade will continue the march today 23rd. under orders of Lt. Col. F. W. Mussenden, 8th. Hussars to BOIS DE MEREAUCOURT via Proyart - S of FRUISSY-CAPPY as follows :- 9th H. H. starting point Harbonniers 10.0. a.m. (via Marcel-Cave) 18th. Lancers will follow, 9th. H.H. 8th. Hussars starting point Harbonnieres 10.15 a.m. (via CAIX) M.G. Sqdn., X. Batty, B.H.Q., M.V.S. follow 8th. Hussars in that order. Mhow Field Ambulance will reach cross 1 mile S.W. of PROYART at 10.50 a.m. Echelon A. will accompany Units to starting point where it will be brigaded and continue the march under Capt. Houston, 8th. Hussars. B. Echelon will be brigaded at Harbonniers under B.T.O. as soon as possible. Rug wagons will join brigade in new area. Other wagons will be Divisionalised at Herbecourt and come under orders of Senior Officer present.
Sergeant detailed by X. Batty R.H.A. will be in charge and units will detail 1 o.r. to accompany each wagon
1 Officer each from 9th. H.H. and 18th. Lancers will report at B.H.Q. 9.0 a.m. to be directed as special reconnaissance of Peronne and crossing over Somme river. Staff Captain will reconnoitre route to new area early and drop guides. Usual clearing up parties.
Following parties will report to B. I. Officer at 11 a.m. tomorrow B.H.Q. CAIX to takeover maps
Billeting parties will report to the Staff Captain at the Southern entrance to BOIS de MEREAUCOURT at 11 a.m.

(Signed) A. Graham Captain,
Brigade Major, Ambala Brigade.

Ambala Brigade Operation Order No. 5.

1. Information is already given verbally.
2. The task of the 5th. Cavalry Division is
   (a) To ascertain the dispositions of the advanced hostile detachments
   (b) To ascertain the enemy's dfences and strength.
   (c) To pick at the enemy so as to prevent his advancing and so to give instant information of any withdrawal.
   (d) To be ready to follow up the enemy if he withdraws
3. The Ambala Brigade (and attached troops) inconjunction with XIV French Corp Cavalry (H.Q. Ham) on its right and Canadian Brigade on its left will carry out the above task as follows
   (a) Right Sector detachment. (strength as under) will cross the Somme River at St. Christ Briost and will reach the line approx Canchy - Tertry with detachments on the line GERMAIN -BEAUVOIS -POEUILLY 11.15 a.m.
   Commander Lt. Col. Beatty 9th.H.H., 9.th. H. H. 1 Sect. 14 Sqdn. M.G.C. 2 Platoons 14th. Corps Cyclists Echelon A.

   Left Sector Detachment. (Strength as under). willmarch at 8.15 from Bivouac in Biaches - Faubourc de Paris - Peronne - Peronne station - Cross Roads 1 mile S.W. of Cartigny to reach the line BEAUERTZ-BOUVINCOURT with d tachments on the line FLECHIN-BERNES- MARQUAIX at 11.15 a.m.
   Commander Lt. Col. Muspratt, 18th. Lcrs., 1 Sect. M.G.Sqdn 2 platoons 3rd. Corps Cyclists.
   (c) Remainder of the Brigade order as per table will pass road junction North of FLAUCOURT at 8.45 a.m. and will move in rear of Col. Muspratt's detachment to Mons-en-Chausee
   B.H.Q., Field Troop R.E., 2 Sects. M.G. Sqdn. 8th. Hussars X. Batty, A. Echelon Mhow F. Ambulance.
   (Less A. Echelon. Left Sector detachment) willbe brigaded under Capt. Houston 8th. Hussars at cross roads North of X T in Harbecourt at 8.45 a.m.
   (d) One company 3rd. Corps Cyclists (less 2 platoons) will come under orders G.O.C. Ambala Brigade at Mons en Chausee at 11a.m.
4. Boundary lines between sectors
   (a) Between right sector and 14 French Corps VIEFVILLE (inc) VILLERS St. CHRISTOPH - DOUCHY - ROUPY - St. QUENTIN (exclusive to Right sector)

(b) Between right and left sector.
BRIE-VERNAND Road (inclusive to Right sector)

(c) Between right sector and Canadian Brigade
AIZECOURT LE HAUT - TEMPLUX - LONGAUBENS - APENY - MONNECOURT
(all exclusive to left sector.

5 Touch will be obtained as early as possible between sectors and between sectors and advanced detachments of formations on either flank. Touch gained will be reported to Brigade report centre.

6. The following Liaison Officers will report to B.H.Q. at Road Junction North of FLAUCOURT at 8.45 a.m. tomorrow.

Ambala Brigade Operation Order No. 6.
28 / 3 / 17.

The Division is being withdrawn tomorrow to a position of assembly West of Peronne.

The Ambala Cavalry Brigade and attached Troops will march to the Bois de Mereaucourt via Peronne-Halle-Biaches-Herbecourt- as follows.
Starting point Doingt.

B.H.Q. Sig. Troop. Field Sqdn, R.E. (less 1 Troop.)	1.0. p.m.
14th. M.G. Sqdn.	1.5. p.m.
X. Batty. light Sec. A. Col	1.15 p.m.
18th. Lancers	1.25 p.m.
8th. Hussars	1.35 p.m.
9th. H. Horse	1.45 p.m.
Mhow Fd. Amb.	1.55 p.m.

Each Unit on arrival will re-occupy its original bivouac area.

3. O.C. Field Troop R.E. attached Ambala Brigade will detail 1 troop which will leave the Brigade at Herbecourt and proceed to Camp 56 North of Cappy where it will come under orders of G.O.C. Sec' Brigade . The A. Echelon ofthe troop will accompany it on the march

4. The Co. 14th. Corps Cyclists at VAUX will rejoin its Batt. at MONT St. QUENTIN at 10. 0.a.m. tomorrow.
Thence the Batt. will march independently to report for orders to O.C. 14th. Corps Mounted Troops at LE Mesnil en Arrouaisne.

5. A. Echelon (less that of Field Troop) will rendezvous at cross roads P. of PRUSLE at 1.0. p.m. It will be Brigaded and follow the Brigade to Bivouac under Capt. Houston 8th. Hussars.

6 Intervals of 100 yds. will be maintained between Sqdns. or equivalent units.

7. Brigade Report centre will close at ESTREES at 12 noon and will open at BOIS DE MEREAUCOURT at 3.0. p.m.

(Signed) A. Graham Captain,
Brigade Major, Ambala Brigade.

30 / 5 / 17.

The Brigade will move to WARFUSEE-ABBINCOURT today as follows

B.H.Q. Sig. Troop.	Western end of Bois de Mereaucourt in FEUILLERS-FRISE Rd.	10.30 a.m
8th. Hrs.		10.30
9th. H. H.		10.40
18th. Lcrs.		10.50
14 Sqdn.M.G.C.		11.0.
5th. Field Sqdn.		11.5 a.m.
X. Batty		11.15
Mhow Fd. Amb.		11.15

Echelon A. will be ~~XXXXXXXXX~~ brigaded South of above road and east of MEREAUCOURT Wood by 11.0. a.m. and will follow the Brigade under Capt. Houston 8th. Hussars.

Billeting parties will meet the Staff Captain at the Church at Warfusee at 11.30 a.m.

Echelon B. will remain at Cappy Echelon B. Kits will be dumped under two men per Unit by side of theFEUILLERS-FRISE Road where it will be collected by lorry.

Brigade report Centre will close at Bois de Mereaucourt at 10.30 a.m. and will open at Warfusee -Abbincourt at 1.0. p.m.

Instructions regarding War Diaries and Intelligence Summaries are contained in F. S. Regs., Part II. and the Staff Manual respectively. Title Pages will be prepared in manuscript.

WAR DIARY
or
INTELLIGENCE SUMMARY
(Erase heading not required.)

Army Form C. 2118.

VM.8

Place	Date 1917	Hour	Summary of Events and Information	Remarks and references to Appendices
	April			
LAMOTTE	1st.	8.30	Exercise. Inspections.	
	2nd	8.30	do. do.	
	3rd.	8.30	do. 3.0. p.m. Sqdn moved from Billets in LAMOTTE to Huts in BOIS D'ARQUAIRE	
BOIS D' ARQUAIRE.	4th.			
	4th.	8.30	do. Afternoon. 2.0. p.m. M.G. Drill, Mapreading and Rangetaking	
	5th	8.30	do. ----------------do----------------	
	6th.	8.30	Section drill. ----------------do----------------	
	7th.	9.0	Exercise ----------------do----------------	
	8th.	9.0	Exercise.	
	9th.	8.30	Exercise ----------------do----------------	
	10th.	6.0	Exercise ----------------do----------------	
	10th.	9.45	Box respirator fitting and drill.	
	11th.	9.0	1 Sect. Drill, 2 Sects. Exercise. 2.0. p.m. Map reading and range practices	
	12th.	2.30	Brigade Route March	
	13th.	9.0	Section Drill. Afternoon.2.0. p.m. M.G.Drill, Mapreading and Rangetaking.	
	14th	8.45	The Brigade marched to CAULAINCOURT and POEUILLY WOOD W. of TERTRY area via BRIE and ESTREES-en-CHAUSSEE.	
CAULAINCOURT	15th	8.30	Exercise Arms and ammunition in pection.	
	16th.	8.30	Section drill. Officers and N.C.O.s observation and reconnaissance of country.	
	17th.	8.30	do. ----------------do---------------- Remainder M. G. Drill and Box Respirator drill.	
	18th.	8.30	do. ----------------do----------------	
	19th.	10.15	Marching order Inspection by Brigadier General.	
	20th.	8.30	Section drill. Signallers visual signalling. Afternoon. M.G. Drill	
	21st	8.30	do. ----------------do----------------	
	22nd	10.0	Church Parade.	
	23rd.	10.30	Marching Order inspection by Major General.	
	24th.	8.15	Squadron took part in Brigade Tactical Exercise.	
	25th.	8.30	Section Drill. Afternoon. Improving camp and horse lines.	
	26th.	8.30	2 Sections Range Practices. 1 Section with 6th. H. Horse for scheme.	

2449 Wt. W14957/M90 750,000 1/16 J.B.C. & A. Forms/C.2118/12.

Army Form C. 2118.

Instructions regarding War Diaries and Intelligence Summaries are contained in F. S. Regs., Part II. and the Staff Manual respectively. Title Pages will be prepared in manuscript.

WAR DIARY
or
INTELLIGENCE SUMMARY
(Erase heading not required.)

Place	Date	Hour	Summary of Events and Information	Remarks and references to Appendices
	1917. April	a.m.		
CAULAINCOURT	7th.	8.30	Section drill. Afternoon. M. G. Drill,	
		6.0	Exercise Inspections.	
		10.0	Church Parade.	
		8.30	Squadron drill. M. G. Instruction.	

Field
30/4/17.

[illegible] Major
Commdg No 14 Sqdn M G C Cav

2449 Wt. W14957/M90 750,000 1/16 J.B.C. & A. Forms/C.2118/12.

OPERATION ORDERS No. 8. Copy No. 5.

Reference Maps 1/100.000 Sheets 17 & 18. 18 / 4 / 17.

1. The Brigade and attached troops will move to CAULAINCOURT - POEUILLY WOOD W. of TERTRY area tomorrow via BRIE and ESTREES -en-CHAUSEE as follows :-

(A)

Unit.	S.P.	Time.	
Bde. HQ.) SignTp.)	Road Junction N. of 1st E. in LAMOTTE en S.	9.35	a.m.
8th. Hrs	do	9.35	a.m.
18th. Lcrs	do	9.45	a.m.
9th. H.H.	Do.	9.55	a.m.
M.G.Sqdn	do.	10.5	a.m.
"X" Batty	do	10.10	a.m.

(b) Echelon A. and M.V.S. will be Brigaded at above starting point and continue the march in rear of the Brigade under orders of Lt. Williams, 8th. Hussars.

(c) Mhow Field A. will march in rear of Echelon A.

(d) Echelon B. will be Brigaded east of above S.P. by 7.55 a.m. and will move at 8.0. a.m. independently to new area via BRIE and ESTREES-en-CHAUSEE under orders of Lt. Cussell, A.S.C. crossing the SOMME river at BRIE between 12.40 p.m. and 1.30 p.m.

2. The Brigade will cross the SOMME river at BRIE between12.40 and 1.20 p.m. and if necessary after 1.40 p.m.

3. (a) East of strating point an interval of 100 yds will be maintained between each Squadron or equivalent body and an interval of 25 yds between each Section of Guns or group of 5 Limbered G.S. Wagons.
(b) The column will close up when the head reaches BRIE crossing.
(c) In the event of delay at BRIE crossing Units will clear the Road.

4. Cleaning up parties left behind by each Unit, will be Brigaded at above starting point at 12.0. noon, and will move to the new area under the Senior Officer.

5. 18th. Lancers will detail a rearguard of 1 Officer and 2 Regl. Police to collect and Brigade stragglers.

6. All cyclists will be brigaded at the starting point and proceed to the new area in rear of Mhow F.A. under orders of a N.C.O. to be detailed by 8th. Hussars.

7. (a) Units will take special care to make every use of cover from view in the new area, both as regards horse lines and tent positions.
(b) Bivouac areas are allotted in every case exclusive of accommodation and ground at present occupied by other troops.

8. Liaison Officers and Gallopers will report at Divl. H.Q. at GUIZANCOURT by4.0. p.m., They will proceed with the Staff Capt. from Brigade.H.Q. at 7.0. a.m.

9. Tent and Dismounted parties will move under instructions by the Staff Captain attached.

10. Brigade report centre will close at LAMOTTE at 9.0. a.m. and will open at CAULAINCOURT at 2.0. p.m.

11. Acknowledge.

(Signed) A. Graham Captain.
Brigad Major Ambala Cavalry Bde.

Army Form C. 2118.

Instructions regarding War Diaries and Intelligence Summaries are contained in F. S. Regs., Part II. and the Staff Manual respectively. Title Pages will be prepared in manuscript.

WAR DIARY
or
INTELLIGENCE SUMMARY
(Erase heading not required.)

Vol IX

Place	Date	Hour	Summary of Events and Information	Remarks and references to Appendices
	May 1917.	a.m.		
CAULAINCOURT.	1	8.15	Squadron Drill. 2.0 p.m. M.G.Instn. Signalling, Rangetaking, Grazing.	
	2	8.15	do do 1 section with 8th.Hussars Tactical Exercise. 3.0 p.m. Inspection by Div.Commdr. "A"&"B"Echelon.	
	3	8.30	Range Practices. 1 section with 9th.Horse, Tactical Exercise. 2.0 p.m. Rangetaking, M.G.Instn. Signalling.	
	4	8.30	Brigade Tactical Exercise.	
	5	8.30	Exercise. Weekly Inspections.	
	6	6.0	Exercise. 2.0 p.m. Grazing.	
	7	10.0	Squadron Drill. 2.0 p.m. Grazing, Rangetaking, M.G.Instn. Signalling, Grazing.	
	8	10.0	do do do do do do do Map Reading, Grazing.	
	9	10.0	do do do do do do do do do	
	10	10.0	dd do do Inspection of all box respirators by Brigade Gas N.C.O.	
	11	9.0	do do do Bathing.	
	12	6.0	Exercise. 8.0 a.m. Medical Inspection. 10.30 a.m. Saddle & Harness Inspection. 2.0 p.m. Arms Inspection.	
	13	10.30	Inspection by G.O.C. Dismounted Squadron.	
	14	9.0	Squadron Drill. Signallers under Bde.Sig.Sergt. 2.0 p.m. M.G.Instn. Rangetaking, Map Reading, Grazing.	
	15 to 31st		Horse grazing in back area	

2449 Wt. W14957/M90 750,000 1/16 J.B.C. & A. Forms/C.2118/12.

14th Contd OVER----

Plan of Defence. (a) The outpost line is the line of the most advanced posts.
(b) The Main Line of Resistance is what is now known as the Brown Line.
(c) The Second Line is not yet settled.

General Policy. Brigadiers are responsible for all defence work in and in front of the present front trenches of the Brown Line.

May 14th. 1917.
14th.M.G.Squadron. On 14th. May 1917 O.C. 14th.Sqdn. accompanied by Section Officers proceeded in advance to inspect positions and make arrange ments for relieving 177th. M.G.Coy.

May 15th.1917. On night 15/16th. May 1917, 14th. M.G.Squadron composed of 3 dismounted sections as below, marched from their Base at CAULAINCOURT at 8.15 p.m. and duly relieved 177th. M.G.Coy. "A" Section under Lieut. C. Grant with 4 Vickers guns to Support Line.-"B" Section under Lieut. B. C. King to Main Line with 4 Vickers guns.- "C"Section under Lieut. M. S. H. Jones with 4 Vickers guns in Reserve to H.Q's. situated at ODINS COPSE vide 1/20.000 Map,reference R.3.b.8.7. South of"V" in LEVERGUIER.

Composition. Head Quarters.
Major A. H. Brooke.
Captain W. F. Martin.
S. S. M. F. Flight.
12 O.R. including 6 Signallers.

"A" Section.
Lieut. C. Grant.)
1 Sergeant.) 4 Vickers Guns.
29 O.R.) Ammn. 16.000 rds.

Situation.
1/20.000.
1 Gun R.5.b.51.
1 Gun R.5.b.47.
1 Gun L.35.c.48.
1 Gun L.35.d.32.

"B" Section.
Lieut. B.C.King.)
1 Sergeant.) 4 Vickers Guns.
28 O.R.) Ammn. 16.000.rds.

Situation.
1/20.000. 4 Guns behind in main trench held by 9th. Hodsons Horse.

"C" Section.
Lieut.M.S.H.Jones.)
1 Sergeant.) 4 Vickers Guns.
27 O.R.) Ammn. 16.000 rds

Situation. With H.Q's. in Reserve.

Total Strength.

Officers.	5
Warrant Officers.	1
N. C. O's.	24
O. R's.	79(incldg.4 drivers attd. R.E's.)
	109.
Mules.	- 8.

Back Party. At CAULAINCOURT.(14th.M.G.Sqdn.Base.) consisted of :-
Capt. E.W.McArthur.) Remained in
2nd.Lieut.T.N.Jones.) charge of the
S.Q.M.S.Dray.) horses etc.
162 O.R's.)

May 16th. A telephone wire was laid to Brigade forward station, JEANCOURT, and also to H.Q's. of Sections in forward positions situated in Quarry at R.5.b.4.2. 1/40.000.

May 17th. All quiet along our front.

May 18th. All reported quiet. Intermittent shelling.

May 19th. After "Stand To" 9.30pm. "C" Section (in Reserve) under Lt.M.S.H.Jones relieved "B" Section under Lt.B.C.King and "B" Section relieved "A" Section under Lt.C.Grant. "A" Section as Reserve to H.Q's. Reliefs reported complete by telephone at 11pm.

May 20th. Intermittent shelling throughout day of PURPLE COPSE--ASCENSION FARM-LE VERGUIER-GRAND PRIEL FARM. 9.30pm.- 3.0am. Digging party from our reserve Section, in 2 reliefs, each under 1 Officer, sent to dig new gun emplacements in R.5.b.4.2.

May 21st. 7 shells in the afternoon dropped in valley where H.Q's. are situated, 1 about 70 yds. from Orderly Room. At 2.45pm. about 35 shells were fired from the direction of the Aerodrome straight over the position of 2 left guns. They seemed to be directed at the high ground N.E. of LE VERGUIER. 2 shrapnel and 5 H.E. shells burst about 150 yds. behind the gun positions. The remainder fell far behind on the high ground. Firing ceased at 3.25pm. At 4.0pm. about 10 more shells were fired in the same direction and further hostile shelling took place from 5.15pm. to 5.40pm. The shells fired were 77mm. Further work was done in the erection of M.G. emplacements and digging trenches etc. during the night.

May 22nd. 20 men 7th.D.Gds. and "B" & "C" Sections at night improving dug outs, No.1 position emplacements and digging new trench (communication).

May 23rd. LE VERGUIER shelled during the day. 20 men 7th. D.Gds. at night digging trench to new emplacement etc. as night previous.

"A" Section relieved "C" Section.) Reliefs took place
"C" Section relieved "B" Section.) after "Stand To" and
"B" Section to Reserve.) completed at 11pm.

May 24th. Aerial activity. All quiet along front during day.

May 25th. Aerial activity. Enemy artillery considerably below normal. LE VERGUIER, ASCENSION FARM lightly shelled. Of 13 shells fired on LE VERGUIER 6 were blind. Previous night a working party of our men and some tunnellers engaged in digging new emplacements and dug outs.

May 26th. Same working party at night. This work continued during the day under screens of brushwood on No.3 & 4 gun emplacements. Corps M.G. Officer, Col. Codrington, visited Squadron H.Q's. in the field.

May 27th. Enemy artillery normal during day, above normal during night. the area in and around LE VERGUIER, GRAND PRIEL FARM, ASCENSION FARM, and RED WOOD.

May 28th. "B" Section, under Lt.B.C.King, relieved "C". "C" Section, under Lt.M.S.H.Jones, came in reserve and "A" Section, under Lt.C.Grant, returned to bivouacs at CAULAINCOURT. Reliefs completed after "Stand To". Artillery activity below normal. A few shrapnel at ASCENSION FARM during the day and about 20 during the night. A few 5.9 fell in LE VERGUIER during the day. On night of 28th. 2nd.Lt. Kernick and 2nd.Lt. Chase arrived at Forward H.Q's. from CAULAINCOURT. 2nd.Lt. Kernick to "C" Section and 2nd.Lt.Chase to "B" Section.

May

1917. In Back Area No.47309 Pte. E. Stoneman was killed by a shell whilst on Police Duty at CAULAINCOURT.

May 29th. vide Secunderabad Cav. Bde. Operation Order No.40/d/27/5/17. The 4th. Cavalry Division and the Canadian Cavalry Brigade. on taking over part of sub-sector A.2 on the night 28/29th. May. The Ambala Cavalry Bde. Troops(less H.Q's. and 2 Sections 14th.M.G.Squadron) will return to back area on 28/29th. May.as follows :-

(a) The 14th. M.G.Squadron(less 1 Section) will remain in its present location.
(b) 18th.Lcrs. and Transport will march to etc.etc.
(c) 9th. H.Horse and Transport will march to etc.etc.
(d) 1 Section 14th.M.G.Squadron will move independently after 9.30pm.

Reliefs by Secunderabad Bde. Troops will be reported by code word "PARIS".

Consequent on these reliefs and changes, the front of A.2 sub-sector held by the Secunderabad Cavalry Bde. will be :-

Northern Boundary.
G.20 Central - GRAND PRIEL FARM - N. side of PIEUMEL WOOD L.27.6.9.5.

Southern Boundary.
G.27 Central - ASCENSION FARM - MILL SPINNEY.(all inclusive to A.2.L.)

14th.M.G.Squadron now have 4 guns in support line in positions
1. R.5.b.5.1.
2. R.5.b.4.7.
3. L.35.c.4.8.
4. L.35.a.3.2.

and 4 guns in reserve at H.Q's. ODINS COPSE. viz. "B"Section under Lt.King and 2nd.Lt.Chase, "C"Section under Lt. Jones and 2nd.Lt.Kernick.

Preparation of 8 new gun emplacements, in place of present gun positions, is proceeding day and night, under the direction of a section of R.E.tunnellers aided by 7 skilled workmen from this Squadron, at positions :-
1. R.5.b.8.1.
2. R.5.a.6.5.
3. R.5.a.8.7.
4. L.35.c.5.1.
5. L.34.d.4.8.
6. L.35.c.4.9.

Work continued on new gun emplacements under R.E's super--vision. Artillery below normal. Odd shell or two-LE VERGUIER and ASCENSION FARM shelled during evening and night, about 30 in all.

May 30th. Work continued on new gun emplacements. Artillery very quiet.

May 31st. Work on new emplacements etc. under supervision of R.E. further carried on.

E.L. McArthur Capt.
for Major,
Commanding No.14 Squadron, M.G.C.(Cavalry)

Field.
1.6.17.

COPY.   Copy No.10.

Ambala Cavalry Brigade Operation Order No.11.

Ref.Map. 1/40.000.   27th.May 1917.
62.c.

1. Units of the Ambala Cavalry Brigade, less H.Q. & 2 Sections 14th. M.G.Sqdn. and the personnel and transport detailed in para 3 will be withdrawn to-morrow from the line under orders of Sec' bad and Canadian Cavalry Brigades.

2. (a) Led horses will be provided as follows on the 28th. inst.

UNIT.	PLACE.	TIME.	REMARKS.
18th.Lcrs.	Q.12 Central.	3.30pm.	Will keep on the march 450 yds.distance between troops
9th.H.H.	L.25.d. Central.	10.0pm.	(a) Will not cross the VERMELLES-BERNES Ridge before 9.30pm. (b) Will march 130 yds. distance between troops.

(b) 8th. Hussars will return to the Back Area on foot reaching VERMAND at 9.45pm.(as ordered by Canadian Cav. Bde.)

(c) 1 Section 14th.M.G.Sqdn. will return to Back Area to-morrow night under orders of O.C. 14th. M.G.Sqdn.

3. The following personnel and transport will be left under the orders of the Sec'bad and Canadian Cavalry Bdes. respectively.
(a) 18th.Lcrs. - 2 Officers, 100 O.R's. 1 L.G.S.
9th.H.H. Major Dyce, 1 Officer, 27 O.R's. 1.L.G.S.
8th.Hsrs. 2 Officers, 27 O.R's. 1 L.G.S.

(b) Major Dyce will be in command,until further orders, of above details 9th.H.H. & 18th.Lcrs.and of 8th.Hussars when they join up.

4. Water Cart from the M'how F.A. will remain in the forward area to supply the 9th.H.H. and 18th.Lcrs., dismonted men,and eventually the 8th.Hussars party when it joins up. 8th.Hussars dismounted party will be supplied with water by the Canadian Cav. Bde. for the present.

5. Personnel mentioned in above para form the equivalent of Dis--mounted reinforcements and will be used by the 5th. Cav. Div. to provide Digging Parties.

It will not be returned to its units probably until just before the Brigade returns to the trenches as a complete unit.

Commanding Officers therefore wishing to make exchanges in personnel of Back and Forward Areas can arrange to do so after the 29th. inst. through this office.

6. ACKNOWLEDGE.

(signed) A. Graham. Captain.
Brigade Major, Ambala Cavalry Brigade.

WAR DIARY.

14th. Squadron, M.G.C.(Cavalry) attached to
Secunderabad Cavalry Bde. 5th. Cav. Division.

Secunderabad Cav. Bde. Operation Order No.37.

Secunderabad Cav. Bde. Operation Order No.37.14/5/17
Reference Map. Sheets 62C. N.E.& 62C. S.E. 1/20.000

1. The Secunderabad Cav. Bde. with 9th. Hodsons Horse, 18th.Lancers, 14th.Squadron, M.G.C.(Cav.) and 1 Field Troop attached(from Ambala Cav. Bde.) will take over the line from the 177th.Infantry Bde. on May 15th. & night May 15/16th. in accordance with attached Table.

2. The Brigade Frontage will be L.22.a. to R.5.d.35. divided into 2 sub-sections, the dividing line between sub-sections being South end of PIEUMEL WOOD(L.28.c.9. 7.) - L.30.6.8.8.- road junction G.20.d.6.5.

3. The Brigade will be disposed as follows :-

Right Sub-Section.

Advanced troops. 7 Dragoon Guards relieving 4 Coys. 4/Lincolns.

Support. 9th. Hodsons Horse releiving 4 Coys 4/Lincolns.

Left Sub-Section.

Advanced Troops. Poona Horse relieving 4th.Leicesters

Support Troops. Deccan Horse relieving 5th. do.

Brig ade Reserve. 18th. Lancers

Brig ade H. Q. MONTIGNY FARM.

Advanced H. Q. & Relay Post. JEANCOURT.

4. O's.C. 13th. & 14 th. M.G.Squadrons(Right sub-section of Brig ade Frontage) will arrange direct with O.C. 177th. M.G.Coy. the relief of guns by day 15th. & night 15/16th. May.

5. Completion of reliefs will be reported by the code word "TREFCON"

(signed) A. Campbell Ross. Major.
Bde. Major, Secunderabad Cav. Bde.

Disposition of Troops. 5th. Cav. Division. No.G.530/1/15/5/17

Nomenclature.

(a) The Front commanded by the Major General will be known as SECTOR"A".
(b) The front of Canadian Cav. Bde. will be called **SUB-SECTOR** "A"1.
That of Sec.Cav.Bde. SUB-SECTOR "A"2.
That of 176th. Infantry Bde. SUB-SECTOR "A"3.

SECTOR "A"
Major General H.J.M.MACANDREW, D.S.O.

Left — Right

Sub-Sector "A"3.	Sub-Sector "A"2.	Sub-Sector "A"1.
176th.Infantry Bde.	Brig.Genl.Gregory. Secunderabad Cav.Bde. 9th.Hodsons Horse. 18th.Lancers. 14th.M.G.Squadron. 1 Field Troop. Frontage. G.32.d.1.9. - L.24.a.2.9.	Brig.Genl.Seely. Canadian Cav.Bde. 8th. Hussars. No.9 L.A.C.Batty. 1 Field Troop. Frontage. M.8.c.- -G.32.d.1.9.

Instructions regarding War Diaries and Intelligence Summaries are contained in F. S. Regs., Part II. and the Staff Manual respectively. Title pages will be prepared in manuscript.

WAR DIARY
or
INTELLIGENCE SUMMARY.
(Erase heading not required.)

Army Form C. 2118.

Place	Date	Hour	Summary of Events and Information	Remarks and references to Appendices
	JUNE. 1917.			
	1		Capt. W.F.Martin returned to Back Area (CAULAINCOURT)	
	2		Major A.H.Brooke returned to Back Area (CAULAINCOURT), command of Squadron being taken over by Capt. E.W.McArthur. 2nd.Lt. C.V.M.Chase "gassed" and taken to hos--pital.(gas shell). Lieut. B.S.Robinson arrived in the Forward Area as "Intell--igence Officer."	
	3		The reconnaisance of emplacements in the intermediate line, in this sector, was carried out.	
	4		Angles of fire & elevation taken from the emplacements in intermediate line. 1 sergt. & 12 men of "B" Section relieved by a similar number from Back Area (CAULAINCOURT). "A" Section were attached to the Canadian M.G.Squadron.	
	5		Tripods set in the emplacements in the intermediate line.	
	6		Corps Machine Gun Officer inspected the tunnel emplacements by night. "B" Section relieved "C" Section in the line.	
	7		1 N.C.O. & 12 men of "C" Section relieved by similar number from Back Area (CAULAINCOURT).	
	8		No.3 & 4 guns shelled at 10 a.m. with 5.9 & 4.5 shells. Position at L.35.a.3.5. reconnoitred to cover old No.8 emplacement(new No11)This position renamed No.8. Working party worked all night cutting a trench for protection of gun teams of No.3 & 4 positions during shelling.	
	9		Trench dug at L.35.a.3.5. for protection of gun team during shelling. This was a temporary measure until tunnel emplacements were completed	
	10		"C" Section relieved "B" Section in the line.	
	11		Squadron Head Quarter's shelled.	
	12		"B" Section exchanged with a reserve section of the Canadian M.G.Squadron and marched to H.Q's. at the GROTTO", VADENCOURT. Trench stores handed over.	
	13		"C" Section relieved by a section of the Canadian M.G.Squadron and marched into reserve at the GROTTO, VADENCOURT. One sub-section of "B" Section relieved 1 sub-section of "A" Section in forward posts. This completed the relief of the Canadian M.G.Squadron by No.14 Squadron, M.G.C.(Cavalry). 4 L.A.C. Battery guns were attached. Only 2 gun teams being found by this unit.	
	14		"C" Section relieved 3 L.A.C. sections in 2, 3, & 4 positions & 1 gun of "A" Section in MOREVAL COPSE . 1 sub-section of "B" Section relieved remaining gun of 1 sub-section of "A" Section. 4 L.A.C. guns to Divisional Reserve at BIHECOURT "A" Section to Brigade Reserve at the GROTTO, VADENCOURT.	

(A7092). Wt. W12839/M1293. 750,000. 1/17. D. D. & L., Ltd. Forms/C.2118/14.

Instructions regarding War Diaries and Intelligence Summaries are contained in F. S. Regs., Part II. and the Staff Manual respectively. Title pages will be prepared in manuscript.

WAR DIARY
or
INTELLIGENCE SUMMARY.
(Erase heading not required.)

Army Form C. 2118.

Place	Date	Hour	Summary of Events and Information	Remarks and references to Appendices
	JUNE. 1917.			
	15		3 guns of "C" Section relieved 3 guns of L.A.C.Battery. 1 gun of "C" Section relieved 1 gun of "A" Section at MOREVAL COPSE.	
	16		Work on 7 emplacements began in BROWN LINE . Excavation necessary for shelter in SALT Trench made by party of 6 men.	
	17		Work on emplacements continued in BROWN LINE ; also on concrete emplacements at PONTRU.	
	18		The Squadron took part in a raid by 9th. Hodson's Horse on ST. HELENE TRENCH & ST. HELENE VILLIAGE. Dispositions of guns as shown in attached orders and M.G. tables. 3 guns on the left were shelled. The 6 guns in the French Area between BERTHAUCOURT and PONTRUET were slightly shelled. Arrangements were made with the French Medical Service for the evacuation of casualties of guns in the French Area through the BROWN LINE. Casualties - Nil, chiefly owing to a number of enemy shells failing to explode.	
	19		Major A.H.Brooke relieved Capt. E.W.McArthur in the line. Capt. E.W.McArthur & Lieut. T.N.Jones returned to Back Area (CAULAINCOURT).	
	20		Work on emplacements and dug outs continued.	
	21		do do do	
	22		"C" Section relieved "A" Section. "B" Section returned to Back Area(CAULAINCOURT) 1 Section of the 13th. M.G.Squadron attached vice "B" Section. Work on emplacements and dug outs continued.	
	23		1 Section of the 13th. M.G.Squadron relieved the L.A.C. Battery. L.A.C. Batty. to reserve at BIHECOURT. Work on emplacements and dug outs continued.	
	24		Work on emplacements and dug outs continued.	
	25		do do do do	
	26		do do do do	
	27		do do do do "A" Section relieved "C" Section. 2 L.A.C. guns manned by 14th. M.G.Squadron relieved 1 sub-section of the 13th. M.G.Squadron. 2 L.A.C. guns (in reserve) withdrawn from Squadron.	
	28		Work on dug outs and emplacements.	
	29		do do do	
	30		do do do Remaining 2 L.A.C. guns relieved by "C" Sub-Section guns and withdrawn from the Squadron.	

E.W. McArthur Captain. for Major
Comdg No.14 Squadron, M.G.C.(Cavalry).

(A7092). Wt. W12839/M1295. 750,000. 1/17. D. D. & L., Ltd. Forms/C.2118/14.

COPY.

SECRET.

AMBALA BRIGADE OPERATION ORDER No.12.

Ref: Map 62-C. 3rd. June 1917.
1/40.000

1. The Ambala Cavalry Brigade will take over the line from the Canadian Cavalry Brigade in Sub Sector A.1, on the 5th. inst. and night of 5th./6th. in accordance with the attached table. Relief to be completed by 3-0 a.m. 6th. inst.

2. 8th. Hussars and 18th. Lancers will relieve L.S.H. and F.G.Horse respectively, after dusk, dividing line between the regiments being the VADENCOURT-SOMERVILLE WOOD Road to where the road crosses SALT TRENCH, and thence to H.2.b.10.10.

Dispositions as follows :-

Right Sector.	H.Q's.	VADENCOURT Chateau.
	1 Sqdn.	CRESSY TRENCH.
	1 "	SALT TRENCH.
	1 "	PONTRU-Twin Crater Road.
	1 "	INTERMEDIATE LINE.
Left Sector.	H.Q.'s.	COOKER QUARRY.
	1 Sqdn.	(2 Troops SOMERVILLE WOOD. (2 " BONE TREE POST.
	1 "	(1 Troop DRAGOON POST. (2 Troops FORT GARRY. (1 Troop RED WOOD POST.
	1 "	HODSONS POST.
	1 "	INTERMEDIATE LINE.

9th. H.H. will relieve R.C.D. at 3 p.m. in Brigade Reserve VADENCOURT CHATEAU.
1 Section 14th. M.G.Squadron will relieve 1 Section Canadian Bde. M.G. Squadron before the 5th. under arrangements to be made between Officers Commanding Canadian and 14th. M.G.Squadrons.

3. All details of relief and guides will be arranged directly between C.O's concerned.

4. Horses will not be taken East of VERMAND in daylight or East of VADENCOURT by night.

5. (a) All Maps, Air Photographs, Trench Stores, Ammunition and shelters will be taken over and receipts given.
(b) All B.A.B. Trench Code Books will be taken over.

6. Commands pass on completion of reliefs which will be reported by the Code Word "DELHI".

7. ADMINISTRATIVE Instructions attached.

8. Brigade Report Centre will close at CAULAINCOURT at 9.0 p.m. and will open at Chateau De VADENCOURT at 10.0 p.m.

9. ACKNOWLEDGE.

(signed) A. GRAHAM. CAPTAIN.
BRIGADE MAJOR, AMBALA BRIGADE.

Issued at 10.0 p.m.

COPY.

SECRET.

AMBALA BRIGADE OPERATION ORDER No.24.

Ref. Map. 1/20.000
BELLENGLISE. 14th. June 1917.

1. At Zero hour, on the night 18th./19th. June 1917, a raid will be carried out against the enemy's front line trench and roads, in the vicinity of ST. HELENE, with the object of cleaning out that Sector, and securing identifications.

2. Zero hour will be signalled by the explosion of 2 Bangalore Torpedoes in M.3.a.8.6.; the firing of a red and a green Very Light at the same point, and by the appearance of a rocket at the TUMULUS.

3. The raid will be carried out by 2 Squadrons of the 9th. H.Horse, strength each, 2 B.O's, 2 I.O's, 60 other ranks.

4. The raiding parties will leave the hostile trenches at Zero hour plus 45 minutes.

At Zero hour plus 40 minutes a rocket will be fired from the TUMULUS to warn the raiding party that the barrage will cease in 5 minutes time.

5. Machine Gun shoots will be carried out as per attached table.

6. Artillery co-operation will be given for 45 minutes as per attached Barrage Table. (not attached)

7. Watches will be synchronised at B.H.Q. at 6 pm. 18th. inst. by the following :-

Representatives of 9th. H.Horse.
18th. Lancers.
8th. Hussars.
14th.M.G.Sqdn.
17th. Bde. R.H.A.
Can. Cavalry Bde.
French Artillery Co-operating.

8. Acknowledge.

(signed) A. GRAHAM. Captain.
Brigade Major, Ambala Cavalry Brigade.

Table of Details, Issued with Ambala Cavalry Brigade Operation Order No. 24.

1. Times and dispositions of Raiding Parties.

TIME.	UNIT.	PLACE.	REMARKS.
10.10 p.m.	"A" Col. "B" Col.	W. of TUMULUS.	
11.10 p.m.	"A" Col.	Sunken Road in M.3.a.0.5.	
11.30 p.m.	"A" Col.	100 yards West of Wire in M.3.a.8.6.	"Jumping off" Point Torpedo-carring parties work forward to place and fire torpedoes.
12.00 m.n.	"A" Col.	About to pass through hostile wire.	Zero hour will be taken from explosion of torpedoes and firing flares and rocket, as per Operation Order. It should be any time after 11.50 p.m.
Between Zero hour and Zero plus 45 mins.	"A" Col.	Crosses hostile trench in M.3.a.9.6. and works down BUISSON GAULAINE FM. PONTRUET Road, to junction of road and trench in M.3.d.7.6. Thence West along trench in M.3.d.2.5. to prepare exit gap in wire, if not already done by x Patrol. Thence cleans up trench to FISHER CRATER- BELLENGLISE Road.	
	"B" Col.	Enters hostile trench in M.3.a.9.6. and works down South to FISHER CRATER where it prepares a gap.	

2. X Patrol, strength 1 I.O. 5 O.R. will proceed with the third torpedo from Robinson's REDOUBT to cut an exit for the raiding party in the hostile wire at about M.3.d2.5. It will be within 200 yards of above point at 11.50 p.m. and will place and fire torpedo, as soon as possible after Zero hour. It will await the raiding party at the gap, and will attract its attention by blowing whistle.

3. From 10.30 p.m. till Zero plus 60 minutes,

(a) MAX WOOD ANGLE BANK will be occupied by half Sqdn. 18th. Lancers.

(b) FISHERS CRATER " " " " " " 8th.Hrs.

Machine Gun Barrage and Fire Table.

No. of Gun.	Position.	Time of Firing.	Point of Aim.	Length of time of firing.	Method of Fire.	Remarks.
1.	M.9.c.9½.3½.	Z E R O.	G.34.c.5.2. to G.34.a.5.0.	Z E R O + 45 mins.	Bursts of 30 rounds Aim checked between bursts.	Direction obtained by compass bearings. Elevation by elevation dial and clynometer. Direction maintained by A.A. Posts. Elevation do by A.A.M. Depression by sandbags. Traverse determined by pegs) on either sandbags) side of gun.
2.	M.9.c.8½.3½.		M.4.a.5.7. to G.34.c.5.2.			
3.	M.9.c.7.7.		M.4.a.5.0. to M.4.a.5.7.			
4.	M.9.c.6.8.		M.4.c.Cent. to M.4.a.5.0.			
5) 1st. 6) Phase.	M.8.d.6.7. M.8.d.5.6.		M.3.d.8.5.	Zero + 10 mins.	Rapid.	
5) 2nd. 6) Phase.	do	Zero + 10 mins.	M.4.a.0.4. M.4.a.9.9.	Zero + 45 mins.	Bursts of 30 Check as above.	
7. 1st. Phase.	G.32.d.5.4.	Zero - 10mins.	Square Copse. ~~G.33.c.7.8. G.33.d.0.8.~~	Zero.	Intermittent.	
9.	do	Zero.	G.33.d.5.0. G.33.d.9½.2.	Zero + 45 mins.	Rapid.	
8.	G.32.d.2.6.		G.33.d.5.0. to G.33.d.9½.2.	Zero + 45 mins.	Bursts of 30 Check as above.	
7. 2nd. Phase.	G.32.c.4.2.			Zero + 45 mins.	do	

Instructions regarding War Diaries and Intelligence Summaries are contained in F. S. Regs., Part II. and the Staff Manual respectively. Title pages will be prepared in manuscript.

WAR DIARY
or
INTELLIGENCE SUMMARY.
(*Erase heading not required.*)

Army Form C. 2118.

for July 1917

14th Machine Gun Squadron
Ambala Brigade

Place	Date	Hour	Summary of Events and Information	Remarks and references to Appendices
Forward Party at VADENCOURT and Back Party at CAULINCOURT on OMIGNON RIVER	July		From 1st July to 9th July inclusive Two Sections (8 guns) of the 14th M.G. Squadron and one Section (4 guns) of 13th M.G. Squadron under Major Brooke (14th M.G. Squadron) were posted at the Grotto, VADENCOURT - Also 2 guns I.A.C. Battery the 5th inst - Operations on this front under the direction of the Secunderabad Brigade -	
	1st		C Section relieved A Section - work carried out on gun emplacements etc.	
	2nd to 6th		Sections remained in the trenches & do —— do.	
	7th		A night raid carried out by a small party of the 7th D.G's. Two Sub Sections of 14th M.G. Squadron in conjunction with the Artillery formed a barrage fire for 30 minutes on NATLINS STREET and SWAN REDOUBT - 14,500 rounds fired - Raid a failure owing to advance party coming across a German patrol - Torpedoes for destroying wire in consequence could not be fired -	

(A7092). Wt. W12839/M1293. 750,000. 1/17. D. D. & L., Ltd. Forms/C.2118/14.

Army Form C. 2118.

Instructions regarding War Diaries and Intelligence Summaries are contained in F. S. Regs., Part II. and the Staff Manual respectively. Title pages will be prepared in manuscript.

WAR DIARY
or
INTELLIGENCE SUMMARY.
(Erase heading not required.)

July Continued — 14th M.G. Squadron.

Place	Date	Hour	Summary of Events and Information	Remarks and references to Appendices
VADENCOURT forward Party	8th	11pm	Three subsections (6 guns) supported a night raid organised by the Canadians, and in conjunction with 28 machine guns operating on our left (Canadian Brigade), put up a barrage fire for 1½ hours before and 1½ hours after zero hour — Raid a complete success — 1 Officer and 35 Germans captured, also 1 German machine gun — 6000 rounds fired by our 6 guns —	WMcL
			Pte Wisson no 47343, 14th M.G. Squadron severely wounded by shell fire in a dug out — he subsequently died —	
Back Party	"	5pm	Back Party of 14th M.G. Squadron owing to the shelling of CAUIINCOURT WOOD by a German long range 5.9 gun were moved to a valley N.E. of village TERTRY —	WM
TERTRY	9th	midnight	Forward party returned to Back Area TERTRY —	WM
	10th		Exercise, Grazing, fatigues	
	11th		Do — Captn R.G.R DAVIES (3rd M.G. Sqdn) assumed command of the 14th M.G. Squadn vice Major Brooke reverted to Regimental Duty (18th Lancers).	WM

(A7092). Wt. W12839/M1293 750,000. 1/17. D. D. & L., Ltd. Forms/C.2118/14.

Instructions regarding War Diaries and Intelligence Summaries are contained in F. S. Regs., Part II. and the Staff Manual respectively. Title pages will be prepared in manuscript.

Army Form C. 2118.

~~WAR DIARY~~ or INTELLIGENCE SUMMARY.

(Erase heading not required.)

July — 14th M.G. Squadron.

Place	Date (July)	Hour	Summary of Events and Information	Remarks and references to Appendices
	13th	2.30 pm	The 14th M.G. Squadron with other Units of the Ambala Brigade marched to BUIRE, across COLOGNE RIVER - 6½ miles	WFM
	14th	6. am	The Squadron marched to SUZANNE via PERONNE and MARICOURT - Captn W.F. Martin appointed 2nd in command of the Squadron -	WFM
	15th	7.15 am	The Squadron marched via Bray to MORLANCOURT - and Officers & men were billeted in the village	WFM
	16th	5. am	The Squadron marched to SARTON - In billets	WFM
	17th	5.15 am	Do to billets allotted in ROELLECOURT	WFM
	18th to 31st July		The Squadron remained in billets at ROELLECOURT - Training in dismounted work continued till the end of the month -	WFM

W.F. Martin
Captn 14th M.G. Squadron
for OC Captn R.G. Davies

(A7092). Wt. W12839/M1293. 750,000. 1/17. D. D. & L., Ltd. Forms/C.2118/14.

Instructions regarding War Diaries and Intelligence Summaries are contained in F. S. Regs., Part II. and the Staff Manual respectively. Title pages will be prepared in manuscript.

WAR DIARY
or
INTELLIGENCE SUMMARY.

(*Erase heading not required.*)

Army Form C. 2118.

Place	Date 1917.	Hour	Summary of Events and Information	Remarks and references to Appendices
ROELLECOURT.	1st. August. to 31st. August.		Squadron billeted at ROELLECOURT from 1st. to 31st. Aug. During the month mounted & foot training carried on under Section arrangements. Also range firing (short range)	
	10th.		Squadron took part in Brigade Tactical Exercise.	
	12th.		Brigade Horse Show.	
	15th.		Divisional Horse Show. The Squadron winning (1) 1st. in Best L.G.S. Wagon and (2) Best turned out sub-section.	
	21st.		Inspection by G. O. C. Full marching order.	
31/8/17.			[signature] Captain. Commanding 14th. Machine Gun Squadron.	

(A7092). Wt. W12839/M1293. 750,000. 1/17. D. D. & L., Ltd. Forms/C.2118/14.

Serial No: 325 Army Form C. 2118.

Instructions regarding War Diaries and Intelligence Summaries are contained in F. S. Regs., Part II. and the Staff Manual respectively. Title pages will be prepared in manuscript.

14TH. MACHINE GUN SQUADRON.

WAR DIARY

~~or~~

~~INTELLIGENCE SUMMARY.~~

(Erase heading not required.)

Place	Date	Hour	Summary of Events and Information	Remarks and references to Appendices
ROELLECOURT.	Sept. 1917.		The Squadron remained in billets at ROELLECOURT during the month.	RCD
			Training comprising mounted and dismounted drill, firing etc. continued during the whole period.	RCD
	2nd.		Captain W.F. MARTIN and 47410 Sergt. WAUGH proceeded to CAMIERS - - Small Arms School - for an advanced course in machine gunnery.	RCD
	4th.		Lieut. B.C. KING evacuated to Base Hospital.	RCD
	14th.		2nd. Lieut. M. GREENWAY joined the Squadron from Base Depot.	RCD
	28th.		Lieut. B.S. ROBINSON detailed to undergo a course of signalling at Divisional Headquarters.	RCD
1/10/17.			R C Davies Captain. Commanding 14th. Machine Gun Squadron.	

(A7092). Wt. W12839/M1293. 750,000. 1/17. D. D. & L., Ltd. Forms/C.2118/14

Instructions regarding War Diaries and Intelligence Summaries are contained in F. S. Regs., Part II, and the Staff Manual respectively. Title pages will be prepared in manuscript.

WAR DIARY 14th. MACHINE GUN SQUADRON.

~~INTELLIGENCE SUMMARY.~~

(Erase heading not required.)

Army Form C. 2118.

325

Place	Date 1917.	Hour	Summary of Events and Information	Remarks and references to Appendices
	OCTOBER.			
ROELLECOURT.	1/6th.		The Squadron remained in billets at ROELLECOURT. The usual Squadron training was carried on.	[illegible]
	2nd.		Lieut. B.C. KING having been evacuated to ENGLAND is struck off the strength from 2nd. October.	[illegible]
	7th.		The Squadrom marched with the Brigade and billeted at THIENNES.	[illegible]
	10th.		" " " " " " " " " WATOU. Owing to the state of the ground and the bad weather all idea of cavalry operations had to be abandoned.	[illegible]
	14th.		The Squadron marched with the Brigade and billeted at CAMPAGNE	[illegible]
	15th.		" " " " " " " " " LE LOQUIN.(THIEMBRONNE)	[illegible]
	16th.		" " " " " " " " " WAMBERCOURT where it remained until the end of the month. Training carried on as usual.	[illegible]
WAMBERCOURT.	29th.		Sergt. FROST returned from a months course at G.H.Q. Small Arms School.	[illegible]

R. C. Davies
Captain.
Commanding 14th. Machine Gun Squadron.

31/10/17.

(A7092). Wt. W12839/M1293. 750,000. 1/17. D. D. & L., Ltd. Forms/C.2118/14.

Army Form C. 2118.

325

Instructions regarding War Diaries and Intelligence Summaries are contained in F. S. Regs., Part II. and the Staff Manual respectively. Title Pages will be prepared in manuscript.

WAR DIARY or ~~INTELLIGENCE SUMMARY~~

(Erase heading not required.)

14TH. MACHINE GUN SQUADRON.

Place	Date	Hour	Summary of Events and Information	Remarks and references to Appendices
	NOVEMBER 1917.			
WAMBERCOURT.	1st.	to 8th.	The Squadron remained in billets at WAMBERCOURT till the 8th. inst.	
	7th.		Captain R.G.R. Davies proceeded to CAMIERS to attend an advanced course in machine gunnery. Captain W.F. Martin remained in temporary command of the Squadron.	
	9th.	9.0am.	The Squadron marched with the Brigade and billeted at MEZEROLLES.	
	10th.	"	" " " " " " " " " LA HOUSSOYE.	
	11th.	4.0pm.	" " " " " " by night and billeted at SUZANNE.	
	12th.	"	" " " " " " " " " " " BRUSLE.	
	"	to 19th.	" " halted at BRUSLE.	
	19th.		Captain R.G.R. Davies ordered by wire to rejoin the Squadron in view of subsequent operations.	
	20th.	1.0am.	The Squadron marched with the Brigade to take part in the operations against CAMBRAI arriving at DESSART Wood, N.E. of FINS at Zero hour 6.20 a.m. when the attack was launched by the Tanks and Infantry. At 2.0 p.m. the Squadron moved up with the Brigade to a position about 1,000 yards from VILLERS-PLUICH on the right of the VILLERS-PLUICH - MARCOING Road and remained there for the night, the advance being held up owing to the fact that the MASNIERES-BEAUREVOIR line had not been captured	
	21st.	2.0pm.	The Ambala Brigade was ordered up to support the 1st. Cavalry Division who were in dismounted action at CANTAING. The Squadron marched via MARCOING and bivouaced for the night in the village of RIBECOURT.	
	22nd.	7.0am.	The Squadron marched back with the Brigade to EQUANCOURT and bivouaced.	

2449 Wt. W14957/M90 750,000 1/16 J.B.C. & A. Forms/C.2118/12.

Army Form C. 2118.

Instructions regarding War Diaries and Intelligence Summaries are contained in F. S. Regs., Part II. and the Staff Manual respectively. Title Pages will be prepared in manuscript.

WAR DIARY
or
INTELLIGENCE SUMMARY
(Erase heading not required.)

Place	Date	Hour	Summary of Events and Information	Remarks and references to Appendices
	NOVEMBER 1917.			
	23rd.	9.0am.	The Squadron marched with the Brigade to billets at BRAY.	
	27th.	"	" " " " " " " " " TERTRY preparatory to taking over the same sector of the line which the Brigade occupied the previous summer (April to June) viz. VADENCOURT - LE VERGUIER.	RCD
	30th.	"	The Squadron received sudden orders to turn out at once mounted and with the Brigade proceeded at a trot to VILLERS FAUCON owing to a heavy unexpected attack by the enemy who succeeded in temporarily breaking the line and capturing the villages of VILLERS GUISLAIN - GOUZEAUCOURT - GONNELIEU. 1 sub-section under Lieut. B.S. Robinson at this point was attached to the 8th. Hussars. The Brigade then moved in open order to a valley about a 1,000 yards East of HEUDICOURT from where the 8th. Hussars were sent forward mounted with the intention of occupying GAUCHE Wood but came under heavy shell fire while passing through our rear lines of defence and eventually took up a position in the sunken road 800 yards West of GAUCHE Wood. The remainder of the Brigade remained in their position in the valley near HEUDICOURT. At 7.30 p.m. the 18th. Lancers with "C" Section (4 guns) of the 14th. M.G. Squadron under Lieut. M.S.H. Jones & Lieut. C.S. Kernick proceeded to relieve the 8th. Hussars in the sunken road.	RCD

[signature]
Captain.
Commanding 14th. Machine Gun Squadron.

2449 Wt. W14957/M90 750,000 1/16 J.B.C. & A. Forms/C.2118/12.

Army Form C. 2118.

325

*Instructions regarding War Diaries and Intelligence Summaries are contained in F. S. Regs., Part II. and the Staff Manual respectively. Title pages will be prepared in manuscript.

14th. MACHINE GUN SQUADRON.

WAR DIARY or ~~INTELLIGENCE SUMMARY.~~

(Erase heading not required.)

Place	Date	Hour	Summary of Events and Information	Remarks and references to Appendices
	DECEMBER 1917.			
	1st.		The 18th. Lancers attacked the wood at 7.45 p.m. 2 guns under Lieut. C.S.Kernick assisting from their right flank in the sunken road. This ~~XXX~~.Officer was severely wounded just prior to the attack and subsequently died. 1 sub-section went forward in rear of the dismounted attack for consolidation. The 2nd. Grenadier Guards, who had attacked the wood at the same time, were holding a position on the right of the 18th. Lancers, South of the Wood. The 2 guns took up a position covering the right flank of the Guards which was in the at the time. 2 more guns were subsequently pushed up from the sunken road to a position of readiness in the Wood being replaced by 2 ~~xxxxxxx~~ of the guns further back. No. counter attack was made. At 9.0 p.m. the 4 guns in GAUCHE Wood were relieved by the 13th. Machine Gun Squadron. 2 more guns were brought up to the sunken road to assist in the barrage.	R.C.I.
	2nd.		The remaining guns were finally relieved by the 2nd. Machine Gun Sqdn., the following evening. Casualties :- 1 Officer (died of wounds), 1 O.R. killed, 1 O.R. wounded	R.C.I.
	3rd.		The Squadron marched and bivouaced S.E. of VILLERS FAUCON.	R.C.I.
	4th. - 7th.		The Squadron remained in bivouacs at VILLERS FAUCON.	R.C.I.
	8th.		The Squadron marched to and billeted at BRUSLE.	R.C.I.
	9th. - 10th.		The Squadron halted at BRUSLE.	R.C.I.
	11th.		The 14th. Squadron with the 13th. M.G.Squadron & Canadian M.G. Squadron under Major Walker in command were ordered to proceed to the VIth. Corps Area and marched to and bivouaced at BEAULENCOURT	R.C.I.
	12th.		The Squadron marched North and bivouaced N.E. of ERVILLERS near the ST.LEGER Road being attached to the 40th. Infantry Division, VIth. Corps.	R.C.I.

(A7092). Wt. W12839/M1293 750,000. 1/17. D. D. & L., Ltd. Forms/C.2118/14.

Instructions regarding War Diaries and Intelligence Summaries are contained in F. S. Regs., Part II. and the Staff Manual respectively. Title pages will be prepared in manuscript.

WAR DIARY

or

~~INTELLIGENCE SUMMARY~~.

(Erase heading not required.)

Army Form C. 2118.

Place	Date	Hour	Summary of Events and Information	Remarks and references to Appendices
	DECEMBER 1917.			
	13th.		Reconnaissance of 40th. Division rear defence lines was made and 3 battery positions selected for the purpose of barrage fire.	R c-)
	14th. - 15th.		The Squadron was ordered to "Satnd To" from 6.30 a.m. to 9.30 a.m.	R c-)
	16th. - 19th.		The Squadron remained in bivouacs at ERVILLERS.	R c-)
	20th.		The Squadron marched to and bivouaced at BEAULENCOURT.	R c-)
	21st.		" " " " BRUSLE.	R c-)
	22nd.		" " " billeted in huts at CAUVIGNY Farm, near TERTRY.	R c-)
	23rd. - 31st.		The Squadron remained at XXXXXX CAUVIGNY FARM.	R c-)

R. G. Davies

Captain.

Commanding 14th. Machine Gun Squadron.

31/12/17.

(A7092). Wt. W12839/M1293. 750,000. 1/17. D. D. & L., Ltd. Forms/C.2118/14.

1/31 January 1918

Instructions regarding War Diaries and Intelligence Summaries are contained in F. S. Regs., Part II. and the Staff Manual respectively. Title pages will be prepared in manuscript.

WAR DIARY
or
~~INTELLIGENCE~~ SUMMARY.
(Erase heading not required.)

1st Squadron M.G. Cavalry
5th Cavalry Division

Army Form C. 2118.

325

Place	Date	Hour	Summary of Events and Information	Remarks and references to Appendices
TERTRY	1/1/18 to 25/1/18		Squadron was employed on completion of construction of Camp i.e. building huts & brick standings for horses etc	
"		AM 7 to	Horses exercised daily	
"	"	10.30		
"	1/1/18 to 28/1/18		Two machine guns mounted for anti aircraft purposes	
"	1-1-18 to 14-1-18		Barrage drill	
"	23		Capt K.R. Davies & section officers reconnoitred Brigade sector of line prior to taking over	
"	25/26	night	Eight guns relieved eight guns of 1st M.G. Squadron in the line between LE VERGUIER and PONTRU.	
"	28/29	night	The remaining four guns of the Squadron were sent up to the line to form a Barrage Battery	
"	29	9 PM to 10.30 PM	Enemy aeroplanes visited vicinity of camp & dropped bombs. There were no casualties.	
	30	9 AM	Back party of Squadron marched from area with Brigade	

(A7092). Wt. W12839/M1293. 750,000. 1/17. D. D. & L., Ltd. Forms/C.2118/14.

II

1/31st January 1918

Instructions regarding War Diaries and Intelligence Summaries are contained in F. S. Regs., Part II. and the Staff Manual respectively. Title pages will be prepared in manuscript.

WAR DIARY of 14th Squadron MGC Cavalry 5th Cavalry Division ~~INTELLIGENCE SUMMARY.~~

(Erase heading not required.)

Army Form C. 2118.

Place	Date	Hour	Summary of Events and Information	Remarks and references to Appendices
LAMOTTE en SANTERRE	30-1-18	3 P.M.	Days march completed & squadron billeted.	
"	31-1-18	6 AM	March with Brigade continued	
NAOURS	31-1-18	4.30 PM.	Days march completed & squadron billeted	
			No action took place during the month.	
			B. S. Robinson Lt for Capt Commanding 14th M.G. Squadron	

No. 14 SQUADRON, M.G.C. (CAVALRY), AMBALA CAV. BDE.
No. ....
Date 4-2-18

(A7092). Wt. W12839/M1293 750,000. 1/17. D. D. & L., Ltd. Forms/C.2118/14.

Instructions regarding War Diaries and Intelligence Summaries are contained in F. S. Regs., Part II. and the Staff Manual respectively. Title pages will be prepared in manuscript.

14th M.G. Sqdn.

WAR DIARY
or
~~INTELLIGENCE SUMMARY.~~
(Erase heading not required.)

February 1918

Army Form C. 2118.

325.

Place	Date	Hour	Summary of Events and Information	Remarks and references to Appendices
CAUVIGNY FARM	1st		Back Party with horses marched into permanent billets at EPAGNE and EPAGNETTE.	RCD
	10th		2 gun positions in PARKER COPSE heavily shelled during morning.	RCD
			51360 Pte. F. Collins slightly wounded.	RCD
	12th		12 guns of the Squadron cooperated in a raid by 18th Lancers on the Southern portion of ST. HELENE TRENCH (NAUROY Special Sheet). 2 Batteries of 6 guns each, under Lt T.W. Jones and 2nd Lt. W. Scamell respectively, were placed in Quarry and Sunken Road leading to Quarry SOUTH of BERTHAUCOURT to create a right flank barrage. About 40,000 rounds were fired during the raid which, however, was unproductive owing to the fact that the trench was unheld. — Armr. Staff Sergt. Parfrey J. wounded in foot.	RCD
	13th/14th		The Squadron was relieved by the 1st M.G. Squadron. Dismounted Party moved to VERMAND.	RCD
	14th		The Squadron was notified to be ready to proceed to EGYPT at short notice.	RCD
	15th		Dismounted Party moved to ROISEL.	RCD
	16th		Dismounted Party joined Back Party in billets.	RCD
EPAGNE	21st		2nd Lt. M. Greenway and 9 O.R.s entrained at SALEUX as advance party to the Squadron.	RCD

(A7092) Wt. W12839/M1293. 750,000. 1/17. D. D. & L., Ltd. Forms/C.2118/14.

Instructions regarding War Diaries and Intelligence Summaries are contained in F. S. Regs., Part II. and the Staff Manual respectively. Title pages will be prepared in manuscript.

14th M.G. Sqdn. WAR DIARY (Continued) ~~or INTELLIGENCE SUMMARY.~~ February 1918.

(Erase heading not required.)

Army Form C. 2118.

Place	Date	Hour	Summary of Events and Information	Remarks and references to Appendices
EPAGNE	24th		The Squadron marched independently to RUMIGNY.	RCD

R. Edwards Capt.
Commdg. 14th M.G. Squadron.

NO. 14 SQUADRON, M.G.C. (CAVALRY), AMBALA CAV. BDE. No. ... Date 1/3/18

www.ingramcontent.com/pod-product-compliance
Lightning Source LLC
Chambersburg PA
CBHW080920230426
43668CB00014B/2160